MENZIES
Last of the Queen's Men

MENZIES
Last of the Queen's Men

KEVIN PERKINS

ANGUS & ROBERTSON (U.K.) LTD—LONDON
RIGBY LIMITED—ADELAIDE

First published in Great Britain 1968 by
Angus & Robertson (U.K.) Ltd,
54-58 Bartholomew Close, London, E.C.1
in association with
Rigby Limited
Adelaide, South Australia
Copyright 1968 by Kevin Perkins
Library of Congress Catalog Card 68-16578
S.B.N 207 95016 A
Printed in Australia

Speak the speech, I pray you, as I pronounc'd it to you, trippingly on the tongue; but if you mouth it, as many of your players do, I had as lief the town-crier spoke my lines. Nor do not saw the air too much with your hand, thus; but use all gently: for in the very torrent, tempest, and, as I may say, whirlwind of your passion, you must acquire and beget a temperance, that may give it smoothness. O! it offends me to the soul to hear a robustious periwig-pated fellow tear a passion to tatters, to very rags, to split the ears of the groundlings, who, for the most part are capable of nothing but inexplicable dumb shows and noise: I would have such a fellow whipp'd for o'erdoing Termagant; it out-herods Herod: pray you, avoid it.

Hamlet

Author's Note

This is not a political book. It is the story of a man who made politics his life and who succeeded—and failed—in this world like no other Australian before him.

To know a man it is said you must talk to his enemies as well as his friends; from what they say you may arrive at something near the truth. In compiling this story I have spoken not only to members of Sir Robert Menzies' own family, and some other intimates, but also to many men who were his supporters and others who were his political enemies while he led the Australian Government or sat in Opposition; men who constantly observed him in action as they walked with him down the "corridors of power," sometimes abreast, sometimes ahead, sometimes at a tangent, and sometimes a long way behind.

Almost two years of intensive research went into this book. My aim was not to produce a narrative setting out in more or less chronological order the essential details of Sir Robert's career, but a personal and lively human account of the man and his times. One of the enigmas of Sir Robert Menzies has always been that few who came into contact with him in public life ever knew him as a man. Here was a fascinating challenge to seek out the man behind the mask.

Naturally I have drawn upon such raw material as newspaper files, parliamentary and public library records to form a skeletal basis, but mostly I have concentrated on the freshness of personal experience as felt or witnessed through the eyes of other people. Thus, in creating this picture of the most remarkable politician in Australia's history, I have tried as far as possible to obtain the "living stuff" from direct sources.

These sources, among them men who sat in the conclave of Cabinet meetings, each had vivid glimpses that you could liken to a series of spotlights, all focussed on the same subject but coming from different directions. The unenviable task of the biographer then was to capture this kaleidoscope of fact and considered opinion and, in the light of his own interpretation and understanding, mould it into one consistent pattern.

Most especial thanks are hereby given to the Earl of Avon, the former British Prime Minister Sir Anthony Eden, for his generous contribution; to Mrs Isabel Green (Sir Robert's sister) and Mr Frank Menzies, the unofficial family historian, for their splendid and gracious spirit of co-operation; to Sir Arthur Coles, Dr J. F. Cairns, M.P., Messrs Ted Roach, W. V. McCall, and Michele Dearing; and to my personal friends, including Bill Williams, who have some knowledge of the subject matter and to many eminent Australians who should remain anonymous for various reasons, one principal reason being that some of them are still engaged in active politics. In a majority of cases those who helped me gave not one or even two, but numerous interviews to ensure that everything of significance might be brought out. To every one of them, I shall be grateful always.

I can only add that in the time devoted to this biography, no effort has been spared in an attempt to make it the fullest possible picture of the man.

23 November 1967   Sydney

Contents

Illustrations

The illustrations have been grouped between pages 116 and 117.
Their sequence is as follows:—

I

When the wind blew in the Mallee, sand whirled high and piled up against fences and the huts of sheepherders and wheatfarmers, and the whole place was a dustbowl.

Few people in Australia in the pioneering days of the late nineteenth century knew much about the Mallee, in north-west Victoria. It was a country that nobody had done much good with, that had broken the backs of many men, the hearts of quite a few; a country containing the skeletons and the ugly ghosts of many a bright dream.

Haunted by the spirit of Australia's heritage of desolation the Mallee, even well into the turn of the century, was endurable only to those who loved the wilderness or who gamely laboured for its redemption.

For many years after the first settlers straggled in, it was still an absolute unknown; a wilderness of dull green leaves, of ragged brown stalks seeming to afford nothing more useful or nutritious than the arid soil which produced them. They were too stiff to move wavelike to any wind that might pass over and through them, nor did they yield any music for pleasant bushland sounds.

You heard only a dry sort of rustle like the inarticulate murmur of many parched tongues from the leaves and the innumerable strips and shreds of dead bark beating on stems, like wasting garments against the bones of a gallows.

The broad wing of an eagle often showed against the dismal earth or the bright blue of the sky. And black crows were always cautiously present, their harsh cries mingling staccato-like with the eerie rustle of bark and shreds.

Aborigines roamed the Mallee undisturbed up to the late 1850s. But mostly they moved further inland when settlers began pushing into the Mallee as the gold rush days came to an end. In bullock drays and carts or on horseback and carrying all their worldly possessions, these hardy hopefuls jolted their way along the tracks and climbed over sandhills to take up their modest holdings in the midst of the scrub.

Robert Gordon Menzies was born in the Mallee, in 1894.

His roots went deeply into Australian soil. His father, James Menzies, was the son of Scottish crofters who emigrated to Australia in the mid-1850s in the wake of the gold rush.

James Menzies' father, a Calvinist, was born in Dumfries, and both parents were dour, hardy, strictly religious, and poor. They followed the ancient Scottish custom of pronouncing the name of the Clan Menzies, Meeng-us.

The Menzies Clan was one of Scotland's oldest, going back to 1224, but it was never large in numbers. Though the clan descended from a Gaelic-speaking race, its chiefs were of Lowland origin. The once-imposing Castle Menzies is today a crumbling Scots baronial pile standing vacant at Aberfeldy.

The Menzies parents settled in the bustling Victorian town of Ballarat where the gold fever had reached its peak. The Menzies' breadwinner went into partnership with a man named Pawsey as a mining machinery merchant and their names appeared on the top of modest premises in subdued letters.

James Menzies was born in Ballarat on 9 August 1862. As a young man he had definite artistic ability. Some of his drawings were considered in the district to be outstanding. He won a scholarship at the School of Mines in Ballarat which would have enabled him to continue his artistic work, but at this time his father died while only in his early forties, leaving a widow and ten children.

This altered the course of James Menzies' personal history, compelling him while still only a boy to go out to work and take on heavy responsibilities to support his younger brothers and sisters. This he did with characteristic courage and fidelity. He went to work in the Phoenix foundry in Ballarat as an apprentice coach painter.

This enthusiastic, serious young man, working hard to help support his closely-knit British family, eventually set up his own coach-painting business. Work came his way when Hugh Victor McKay in 1884 invented and constructed the Sunshine stripper-harvester, the first commercially successful machine which could strip, thrash, winnow, and bag the wheat in one continuous operation.

Young McKay built his new-fangled machine with crude equipment in a log and bark smithy on his father's farm at Drummartin, Victoria, using wooden and iron parts he fashioned and worn out bits from other farm machines. The machine, made in Ballarat, revolutionized wheat harvesting methods, and James Menzies painted the first harvester produced and many more afterwards. He was usually paid £2 10 0 for each one he painted.

Among the hordes of other British families to flock to Victoria to cash in on the gold rush were the Sampsons. John Sampson was a Cornish miner, born in Penzance, and his wife was English. They landed some time before the Menzies and went to Ballarat where Sampson became a miner on the goldfields.

At this time frenzied interest in Australia had been created by a report in *The Times* on 2 September 1851, reprinted from the *Sydney Morning Herald* telling of the gold strike in Victoria. Other reports described fortunes being won on the Victorian fields, thousands of pounds for a few days' work. The wealth seemed limitless, with creekbeds paved with gold. And some of the nuggets found were so big a man could hardly lift them: The Welcome Nugget weighed 2,217 ounces, the Welcome Stranger 2,284 ounces.

John Sampson was not among the early arrivals on the goldfields and he certainly did not find his El Dorado there. He took a mining job with one of the companies and was far from happy about wages and conditions paid to miners. At one stage while living and mining at Creswick, a little hamlet about 11 miles from Ballarat, he led a strike for an increase in wages from £2 to £2 2 0 a week. Later he helped the Australian Labor leader W. G. Spence form a miners' union, the first in Victoria. This was the forerunner of the Australian Workers' Union. Sampson became the first president of the Miners' Federation.

For these activities he was sacked, blacklisted, and never allowed to work in a mine again.

While living at Creswick, Sampson had two sons named Syd and John and a daughter named Kate.

The paths of the Sampson and Menzies families crossed in 1889 when James Menzies met Kate in Ballarat. Kate was then a tall, slim, shy, good-looking girl who played parts in small plays as a hobby.

A dodger advertising one of the plays was delivered to the Menzies' home and James went to see it one evening. There he saw

Kate for the first time, fell in love with her and went home to his mother and announced: "I've met the future Mrs James Menzies," and married her soon afterwards. They honeymooned in the district, travelling by horse and coach.

Both were strong characters in different ways. He was vigorous, impatient, serious, inclined to be explosive. She was shy but calm, with a ready sense of humour, and with emotions which ran deep.

An incident after the honeymoon draws a realistic distinction between the couple. Proud of his new bride James Menzies took her and introduced her to his grocer in Ballarat. Then he said to her, "Now you want to give an order, Kitty."

"Oh, I don't know that we want very much," she said.

"Oh, yes, we must have an order." Mrs Menzies ordered a few things and her husband said, "Now, you haven't ordered any rice, sago, or tapioca."

"Well, I don't eat any of them," she said.

"I do," he replied and ordered a dozen pounds of each. Mrs Menzies spent the next few months giving the stuff away.

A family was soon on the way and by 1893 there were two boys, James Lesley and Frank Gladstone, and a girl, Isabel. Fervently patriotic to the Old Country, a feeling which Mrs Menzies fully shared, James Menzies named his second child after W. E. Gladstone, the then Prime Minister of Great Britain, as an example to live up to.

James Menzies worked himself into the ground to provide for his young family, but his health troubled him. This caused him and his wife to look for opportunities in a better climate. Syd Sampson, Kate's brother, had gone to Warracknabeal, a town in the northern Wimmera Plains, with a view to settling on wheat land. But he went further afield to the township of Jeparit, and sensing it was a good spot for a district newspaper, established the *Jeparit Leader* there with an Albion press in one room. The town was not linked to the outside world by rail, but land was being opened up and it seemed the district would go ahead.

Syd Sampson showed signs of being a businessman and bought a struggling general store in Jeparit from Mr John Rae for a small amount. It had been established originally by Mr J. Hastwell, but with slow trade and limited finances he found himself in trouble. Syd proposed to Jim that he and his wife take over the store. Jim Menzies was not only game enough to give it a go but felt sure he'd make a fortune.

Menzies went on ahead in December 1893 and an advertisement soon appeared in a column of the newly-launched *Leader* inviting tenders to put up living accommodation at the back of the shop, a board structure at the corner of Roy and Charles Streets. Mrs Menzies followed soon afterwards from Ballarat with the three children.

And so the Menzies couple, neither of them with any store experience, and both too generous to succeed in such a venture, set up shop in this outpost of the Mallee wilderness.

The banks of the Wimmera River at the back of the town were in flood when Mrs Menzies arrived there. With its muddy streets, its few scattered buildings, its isolation, Jeparit was a bleak place.

The Mallee Country is not more than 500 feet above sea level and appears to have been formed mostly by the wearing down of a continental plateau overlaid by sandy material or partial soil covering. Today large portions are still clothed in scrub, with the Mallee gum predominant among the small trees, but some areas carry bulky trees in their swamps. Other areas are of loam sand plains with many rocky and barren patches.

The term Mallee grew up because that was the Aboriginal name for the chief small tree of the area.

The Wimmera district, immediately south of the Mallee Country but originally part of the Mallee, is about 9,200 square miles of mainly undulating plains with soils alternating from loams to sand. Today it is a highly-developed wheat growing area also producing fine sheep, wool, and fat lambs. The Wimmera was so named because that was the name the Aborigines gave their throwing sticks or boomerangs used for hunting.

About 1870 a small settlement appeared in the Wimmera at a place named Jeparit by the Aborigines. Jeparit meant "home of small birds."

It lay in a hot, dusty, newly-settled area between the Mallee Plains and the Wimmera Plains on the fringe of the developing Wimmera wheat land.

Tough German emigrant pioneers who came across from Adelaide in covered waggons are said to have started the tiny township. The first settlement in the district was at Antwerp, a few miles south, where Moravian missionaries trained in Germany founded a church and mission station to Christianize and civilize the Aborigines. They built their church from local limestone and hand-hewn timber.

A great drought beginning in 1878 and lasting until the early '80s focused public attention on the need for water supplies for the Mallee plains. A Royal Commission was held in 1884 leading to the Irrigation Act two years later. This resulted in irrigation only to the north along the Murray River but it did mean the building of weirs on the Wimmera River with channels to supply a substantial area of the Wimmera Plains. An extension of the Wimmera reticulation system was generally believed to be the answer to future development and problems.

Jeparit, beginning to flourish in the general atmosphere of slow-moving progress, in 1891 had twelve buildings with fifty-five inhabitants. It could have passed as any small town of the American Middle West from a slightly earlier period.

When the Menzies family arrived there it boasted about thirty buildings and almost 200 people.

The town had no railroad. The only excuse for its existence was that it lay on a stock run because of its precious near-by water—the Wimmera River and Lake Hindmarsh—and its rough stores provided for the needs of stockmen and the scattered settlers.

The dozen or so rude wooden houses along the wide dirt main street all had big verandas supported by posts to provide shade from the hot Australian sun. The other main features were two blacksmiths' shops, a pub named "The Hopetoun," two general stores, a tiny one-roomed school, and a brand new newspaper office.

Two modest church buildings adorned the street, one a Methodist church where a poorly-paid clergyman each week dispensed hellfire and brimstone, and a Lutheran chapel where the men sat on one side, the women on the other.

2

Business was poor and there was little money about. To try to keep the wolf from the door Jim Menzies started a few agencies. He became the first selling agent in Jeparit for H. V. McKay and the representative of Wilson Bolton and Company, a Wimmera stock and station business. Often in the daytime Jim Menzies would be away making tedious journeys in a horse and waggon taking supplies to outlying farmers, leaving Mrs Menzies to look after the shop and mind the children.

Clearly it was to be a struggle for existence.

Within a couple of months of coming to Jeparit Mrs Menzies discovered she was to have another baby. The prospect was frightening. Things were so tough she could hardly endure life already and a fourth child at this difficult time was a crisis. It seemed as though the end of the world had come.

But she struggled on trying to make the best of her life of drudgery and hardship. And inside the confined cabined walls of a room at the rear of the store, on 20 December 1894, the baby was born.

A doctor delivered the boy, whom they named Robert Gordon —the Gordon being inspired by the contemporary figure of General Gordon, again as an example to live up to. The modest means of the Menzies did not permit a cot or crib and the cherubic Robert Gordon was popped into the household linen basket.

His entrance to the world was, therefore, not much different from Abraham Lincoln's log cabin.

In the next few months Mrs Menzies often felt she wanted to

bundle all her children into the pram and wheel them back to her mother near Ballarat, where life must surely have been easier.

The Menzies parents were humble but not too much so: humble as far as worldly possessions went, but with all the Christian virtues.

Far from "making a fortune" they toiled to eke out a living, but did everything possible for the children. Kate Menzies leavened her hardships with a lively if sometimes quirky sense of humour. Although often on the point of despair she remained firm and dependable, always putting on a cheerful face.

Jim Menzies was very much the head of the house. He lived by the simple rule: "Fear God and honour the Queen, and whatever you do, do it with all your might."

Generous to a fault, he worked tirelessly to provide for his own, but always found time to help others in need. Although a Presbyterian he conscientiously took his family to the Methodist church because, along with the Lutheran, it was the only church in Jeparit. He was devoted to the interest of his chapel where he became a steward, and occasionally he preached at the Lutheran church as well. He was always keen to see what could be done to improve the town generally.

These were pioneering times. Electric light and a water supply did not exist. The only water in the town was rain water caught in galvanized tanks, and light came from lanterns or candles. Often they carried water from the river in very dry periods.

About the time Robert was born the railway line reached Jeparit from Ballarat, going on to Hopetoun and Quambatook. This was a big thing for the district, resulting in virgin scrub being cleared for wheat growing on both sides of the line. The greater part of the Mallee taking in the Wimmera district was still remote from railways and a good deal remained unsettled.

Many farmers had reason to be grateful to the Menzies for giving them food on credit until their next harvest came in. The gesture caused Jim Menzies to get into debt with the merchants of Ballarat and Melbourne because without the farmers' payments he could not meet his bills; he battled on under the burden of having to pay 10 per cent interest on unpaid bills.

As a child Robert Menzies was fat and good tempered. Nothing troubled him. His mother gave him the same affection and care as the other children, and being a bright and chirpy little fellow he gradually became her favourite—perhaps because he was the youngest, perhaps because of some maternal bond resulting from the difficult circumstances of his entrance to the world.

The first thing of significance in young Bob's life was at the age of four and a half when he went to school. That was in June 1899. He went to the Jeparit State School where his two brothers and sister attended. A one-roomed affair on an allotment adjoining the old Mechanics' Institute, it was attended by about thirty pupils in six grades, all taught by the one teacher, Mr J. L. Livingston, whom they all called Dad among themselves because they thought him so old.

Bob, as he was called, soon showed brightness at his lessons and in the next few years more than one pupil, among them Geoff Shiells, who sat next to him, was glad of some of Bob's assistance "under the lap" during examinations to help him get a better pass.

Queen Victoria died on 22 January 1901, when Bob was six. This Empire-shaking event was of momentous importance in the Menzies household, and greatly talked about. Robert Menzies was to remember it and refer to it more than sixty years later when he returned to his native Jeparit after making his way in life. And knockabout Australians, discussing the links this boy established with British royalty when he grew up, were to remark with penetrating humour that he never really recovered from the emotional shock of Queen Victoria's death!

As a boy Bob enjoyed with his brothers and sister the typically normal happy life of youngsters in a bush town of the time. The family had a horse and buggy and often trotted around the district in it. The children went cray fishing and sometimes dropped a makeshift line attached to a stick into Lake Hindmarsh hoping to catch redfin. They also fished in the Wimmera River and went boating. As a diversion they walked through the bush around Jeparit.

On one occasion the four children, against their parents' wishes, ran away to see the circus when it came to town. And the boys received a merciless thrashing from their father.

In those days Jeparit was uniquely Australian with an abundance of kangaroos, emus, small birds, and wild flowers. The Menzies children, including Bob, played on the river bank among the "canoe trees"—trees bearing scars where Aborigines had chopped bark to make canoes or food containers.

But of all the children, including another son Sydney, who was to be born later, Bob was the most studious—and right from the time he went to school. He learnt to read quickly and furnished his mind from books.

The clannish Menzies family preserved the Scottish custom of

9

one member reading to the rest while some practical chore was being done. The women sewed and the men perhaps prepared for the next day. Jim Menzies' father had brought the custom to Australia with him and the son retained it, believing it to be a good way of keeping the family united through discussion and communication and to remind them while all together of the moral and spiritual standard they should uphold. It was also a good way of "improving the mind."

In a place like Jeparit, cut off as it was from the world and without even a minimum of social life, this was a useful exercise.

It was really Kate Menzies who developed in the children a love of reading, although Jim Menzies, who had little formal education, was fond of books and set the pattern by often reading aloud. "You must have a love of reading," he told them repeatedly.

Because Mrs Menzies loved Dickens and could quote extensively from his works, Jim usually chose Dickens to read from. Bob and the other children were obliged to sit for hours while their father read from *Bleak House, The Cotters Saturday Night,* and other works. Young Bob submitted, but Isabel developed a hatred of Dickens—she felt bored and wanted to be doing something else.

When it came to Kate Menzies' turn to make a selection for the evening, she usually chose something on the lighter side. A favourite with her were the witty novels of Jerome K. Jerome—*Three Men In A Boat, Tommy and Co.,* and *Idle Thoughts of an Idle Fellow.* Bob was the only one of the children who could read *Three Men In A Boat* with a straight face, and was usually complimented for his good work.

Robert Menzies developed a passion for reading. Often he incurred the wrath of his father and brothers because while work was to be done around the house or an errand run he had his nose stuck in a book. Once, when a small children's party was given at the Menzies' home, Robert was found to be missing just when the tea was about to be served. They all went looking for him and found him at the back of the shed with his face buried in a book of Shakespeare.

For one so young Bob read widely. History books, which might have been as dry as dust to most other people, were a favourite with him. And the fatter the book the better. *Deeds That Won The Empire* and *Scottish Chiefs* were some of the titles that came his way. If there was a word he didn't understand he went to the dictionary.

When still only a small boy he found in the Mechanics' Library a long-winded account of the Peninsula War, setting out the Duke of Wellington's campaigns against Napoleon's army in Spain. These campaigns included the siege of Badajoz, an important fortress town on the borders of Spain and Portugal surrendered by Spanish soldiers to the French in 1811. The British captured it only after losing 5,000 men.

Not long after reading that, a fierce wind storm hit Jeparit at night while Mrs Menzies was alone with the children, and fearing it would blow the walls down, she threw herself against the threatened side of the house and called on the children to lend their weight. Young Robert, remaining in bed at first, told his mother it was "nothing to the siege of Badajoz."

He often declaimed from the *Scottish Chiefs* and when reading Dickens' *Children's History of England,* at the point where the Scots had been routed and demoralized he discovered what he believed to be an historical inaccuracy. "This is all wrong," he told everybody. "Dickens might be a good novelist but he's no historian."

Bob even argued on that point with a school inspector who was a guest at his father's house. And from memory he recited passages from *Scottish Chiefs* (which ran to about 600 pages), to prove his point.

Apart from Shakespeare, which was to become an absorbing study for him, Bob studied the Bible at length, showing an unusual capacity to remember anything he had read.

When eight he came home one day and climbed dreamily up on to the dinner table, looking vaguely into the distance.

"Wake up, Bob," Mrs Menzies said. "Dreamers never get anywhere."

"What about Joseph in the Bible?" he answered quickly.

The arrival of the mail train in Jeparit was always an important event and young Bob, along with some other youngsters and a number of the townspeople, were usually on hand when the train hissed to a halt. When the Melbourne papers were produced Bob was often handed a copy. He would then get up on a barrel and read the main items of news to the assembled residents; some, being characters, often sought his comments and argued with him.

Near this time, when Bob was eight or nine, he used to help get the *Jeparit Leader* ready for publication. His uncle, Syd Sampson, had sold out the *Leader* to Albert Williams but the youngster continued to drop in after school; he normally cut through the yard at the back of the newspaper office on his way home.

The *Leader* was almost entirely a one-man show, and Bob was fascinated watching the printer at work setting each letter by hand.

The naturally inquisitive young fellow would give his services free on the day Mr Williams went to press, acting as ink slogger and delivery boy. His job was to "fly the paper"—fling the pages quickly from the clacking press onto the table. Then he folded the four-page *Leader* and delivered the 250 or so copies around town on his bike, usually chewing a piece of the roller composition of the *Leader*'s press for gum.

By being curious, by reading well, and showing that he remembered things, young Bob Menzies learnt that he was recognized more than some other boys in the tiny town.

Grandfather John Sampson, who had lost his job because of his radical views on unionism, sometimes came to Jeparit and chatted to the Menzies boys but particularly to Bob. The old man was a socialist. He always professed to be an agnostic but used to talk of the "lowly carpenter of Nazareth."

He was a humanitarian, a man who hated dishonesty or dirty dealings, a man of strong moral character. Whether he earned enough money to keep his family adequately was another matter, but times were hard and there were no public means of assistance such as social services then, and people had to scratch along as best they could.

John Sampson at times would read long passages from the Labor paper, *The Worker*, to his favourite grandson and then demand brusquely, "Well, what do you think of that?"

Young Bob would say he didn't think much of it and the old man would then demand to know why. If there was one thing John Sampson appreciated it was independence of thought and in this way he taught his grandson to think for himself. Bob Menzies was to grow up with a proper indignation over the victimization of his grandfather.

John Sampson's son Sydney also influenced the small boy. After selling the *Jeparit Leader,* Sydney ran a small newspaper in a town 20-odd miles away and regularly called to see his sister. He would get into deep discussions with the children and one day asked Bob out of the blue what he thought of the American Constitution.

Bob had never heard of it. But he borrowed a book touching on it from the Mechanics' Institute Library and found it interesting. He began borrowing every book possible on constitutional law, although the subject was years beyond his knowledge.

Life did not come any easier to the Menzies parents even after eight years in Jeparit. It continued to be a struggle for existence.

In 1902 a great drought struck the area and it was to last with virulence for three years. Only two inches of rain had fallen that season, and all at the wrong time for the wheat sowing.

Not a blade of grass, even dead, was to be seen. In that stark area erosion became a real problem and the wind piled sand up against fences and buildings. The Wimmera River stopped flowing: it became nothing more than a few stagnant pools. Lake Hindmarsh, normally up to 12 feet deep, 13 miles long and 6 miles wide, was bone dry. Sheep and cattle died and wheat stalks withered.

Then, by what was regarded as an act of Providence, a bulbous growth like a small rush came out on the bed of the lake. It was a nutritive, and starving stock were brought in from miles around.

Jim Menzies was the instigator of the scheme to save the cattle. As chairman and driving force of the Starving Stock Relief Committee, he saved untold numbers of cattle through his organizing ability.

Cattle would be brought in along the Dimboola Road and young Bob and everyone else in the town could hear the trample of hooves up the road and see the dust cloud as they approached.

A kind of zinc badge or symbol was hung around the neck of the cattle so they could be taken to the lake for a certain time and then removed, and others take their place. Mrs Menzies was in charge of the symbols and kept a record of them in the shop.

At this time Jim Menzies was president of the Dimboola Shire Council. He used to travel 24 miles to council meetings at Dimboola in a horse and buggy, a journey of several hours each way. Menzies was the most public-spirited man in the district and it was he who provided the stimulus for Jeparit's first civic pride. He helped formulate the early municipal laws and fought for all the early worthwhile local institutions; a Justice of the Peace, he took a keen interest in the country's laws.

When the big drought began Jim Menzies was leading a fight to get a branch line of the railway built from Jeparit to Lorquon, and he bombarded the Railway Standing Committee with reasons why it should run from Jeparit and not from Nhill, a town to the south-west.

Success would have meant the opening up of more Mallee land west of Jeparit. The committee recommended the line from Jeparit but the Victorian Government decided to take no action. Jeparit didn't win, but mainly through the passion and doggedness of Jim Menzies, the Nhill interests didn't succeed either.

Kate Menzies, too, took an interest in the town's affairs and many people came to her with their problems. Through all her tribulations she could produce humour, and many a gloomy burden of other people was lightened by her sense of fun.

An example of Mrs Menzies' sometimes odd but always effective humour was when a little girl belonging to a Jeparit family died, and her mother came to the store with a problem. She had worked out what was to be painted on the simple tin headstone: "We've laid her little clothes away, and there she is an angel gay."

The mother said, "I can't think of another line."

"What about ta-ra-ra-boom-de-ay?" Mrs Menzies suggested quickly.

One day at school in 1904 when Robert was nine, "Dad" Livingston told the children that a phrenologist was coming to the school next day. He explained that a phrenologist was a person who read your character, and perhaps foretold the future by "reading the bumps" of your head. He suggested that anyone who wanted to have their bumps read should bring sixpence along to pay the man.

Young Bob was among those who took their coins next day and waited excitedly for the stranger to appear. A tall and distinguished man with mutton-chop whiskers and a beard, the phrenologist, went about his work very seriously as he ran his hands over the children's heads.

When it came to Robert's turn the bump reader, with solemn mien, felt his head for several minutes then wrote on the aptitude chart: "This boy will make a successful barrister and public speaker." He handed the form to Robert, telling him to take it home to his parents.

After school the boy burst in on his mother and asked her what was a barrister. When she asked why, he said, "Because that's what I'm going to be."

Mrs Menzies explained that a barrister was a man who knew all about the law, who went to courts and spoke to judges and magistrates on behalf of people who needed help.

She went to some pains to explain to Robert that it took a lot of money and hard work to become a barrister, that you had to go to university and study a great deal. Robert persisted in saying he would become a barrister, and Mrs Menzies, not wishing to discourage him completely, told him there just might be a faint chance if he worked very hard at his studies and won scholarships to pay his own way.

Knowing that his family did not have much money, Bob Menzies wondered if he could succeed on his own as his mother had suggested.

14

3

After the phrenologist's visit he worked even harder. Each day he came home and told his mother what he had learnt.

He showed ambitions of wanting to get somewhere, to be somebody. It wasn't long before he was telling people he would become Chief Justice of Victoria, or even Australia. He knew that if he wanted to be a barrister he would have to go to Melbourne University, and the only way he could do that was entirely by his own efforts.

When he was eleven and sitting for his first big examination at Jeparit State School, Bob's father gave him his first fountain pen. He was to win with it £600 in scholarships and essays during his student career.

By the time he was twelve the tiny Jeparit School had taught him all it could and, in line with the Menzies' parents belief in giving their children the best education possible, they decided to send him to the Humffray Street State School in Ballarat. But they could not afford to place him in a boarding school and it was achieved only by the fact that Jim Menzies' mother, a rather narrow minded, Calvinistic old lady, agreed to take Robert in.

Isabel Menzies, through skimping and saving by her parents, was already staying with the old lady and attending private school at Queen's College in Ballarat. And Frank Menzies, two years Robert's senior, was already at the Humffray Street School but staying with another relative in Ballarat. The eldest son, James, had gone straight from the Jeparit School to Melbourne where he did a commercial course and entered the public service. The three children in Ballarat sometimes returned to Jeparit at week-ends and always on holidays.

Jim and Kate Menzies paid Grandmother Menzies ten shillings a week each to keep Isabel and Bob.

From the earliest days in Australia education has been provided free by State schools. But free education in those days did not go as far as the secondary or grammar school stage. Higher learning was available in the various church and other private schools, but it had to be paid for. However, the State provided a number of scholarships to enable the cleverest State school pupils to attend a private school. Young Bob had his sights set on one of these.

It was a wrench for the boy to be parted from his mother, to whom he was deeply attached, but everyone knew it was inevitable if he were to get on and make something of his life. Besides, there were many relatives in Ballarat and the *Worker*-reading Grandfather Sampson was one of them.

In this period the ambitious boy often worked by candlelight until midnight, either at his schoolwork or reading from a stack of books. Grandmother Menzies didn't always see the point of this; her idea of reading was the Bible and *Pilgrim's Progress*. She could not understand why Robert always wanted to sit at a table with a pile of books.

The kindly old lady caused a family dispute at one stage. Isabel and Bob each received threepence a week pocket money and once a week they bought a penny's worth of toffee, and if there was a football match on, paid a penny to see the game. This way they saved a penny a week.

When Grandmother Menzies discovered this she obtained a denial box for the missions and told them to put their spare pennies in it. She felt that as they hadn't spent the pennies they didn't need them and they should go to someone more deserving. Isabel wrote to her father and complained, and he hurried to Ballarat to straighten out the problem.

Teachers at the Humffray Street School soon realized that Bob was an exceptional student. They felt he would reach the scholarship standard at the end of the first year. Bob would then be thirteen, whereas the average age for a scholarship was fourteen and a half. Bob had one main rival for the goal, a boy named Alastair Sutherland, also of Scottish origin; it was usually a toss-up between them for first place in class.

Bob sat for the examination at the end of the term and grew nervous and anxious as the time approached for the results to be published. He feared he wouldn't pass. Frank and Isabel and Bob were home on holidays and James also happened to be there, with the whole family involved in the scholarship drama. They waited day after day for the results to come out and each time the mail train steamed in, Frank dashed to the station to buy a copy of *The Age*.

Finally, one day while Frank and his father were painting the shop (Bob was merely lending moral support by his presence), the train came in and Frank as usual ran to the station. He opened *The Age* and glanced through until he saw the headline, State Scholarship Examination Results. Looking down the list, his eye hit the first name—Menzies, Robert Gordon. Alastair Sutherland was second, thirty-six marks behind.

Not only had Bob won his first scholarship by a good margin while a year younger than the other candidates, but he was first for the State of Victoria.

Frank ran home with the news and there was joy and slaps on the back all round for Bob. Unable to contain his pleasure Frank leapt aboard a rattling old bicycle and on a hot day rode 24 miles along dirt tracks to tell his Uncle Syd.

A couple of days later Kate Menzies received a letter from the education authorities saying Robert's English paper was perfect.

Bob Menzies had learnt that by applying his mind he could beat his fellows. This was the way to succeed, the way to be recognized.

The scholarship entitled Bob to go to Grenville College in Ballarat without paying fees. He was to attend there for the next two years; a tough two years in which great demands were made on his stamina.

At the time the privately-run college was in decline and poorly patronized. A State school backed by Government money does not have to worry about financial problems, but when they occur in a private school the standard of education usually suffers because the school officials cannot afford to engage the best teachers. The headmaster at Grenville was desperately trying to lift the standard of examination results to put the school back on its former footing. And any boy who showed ability was crammed.

Bob Menzies, already having shown brilliance, was now pushed to the limit. One result of the Grenville College situation was that he was taught mathematics badly by a teacher whose subjects were Latin and Greek, and from that time onwards was never very proficient at the subject, although he had been previously.

Anxious to achieve the best results for the school, the headmaster entered Bob for the Junior Public Examination at the end of his first year. Among the eight subjects required were Latin and Greek, at which he was a beginner; this programme for a boy of just fourteen was a big strain. But he proved his exceptional capacity for work by getting up from the tea table at precisely six-fifteen every evening, going straight to his bedroom and studying until twenty minutes past midnight. He did that six nights a week for the first year.

At an earlier age than all the other boys in Victoria he sat for the Junior Public and passed brilliantly in all subjects. The headmaster entered him for the Senior Public Examination at the end of his next year. The same number of subjects were required at a higher standard and Bob continued to study just as hard. But he overdid it, went stale, and failed, the only time in his life he did not pass first time.

Cramming of this nature has spoiled many a brilliant boy but it proved only a temporary setback in this case. Bob continued to absorb knowledge, and his ambition ran on unabated. In fact, if anything, the failure increased his ambition.

Around this time he was nicknamed Judkins Junior because of his penchant for an argument. Judkins, a Melbourne preacher, was in those days the arch wowser. Although Bob was not wowserish he would take up an argument in any direction, for or against anything.

Contemporaries of the Ballarat schoolboy of those days cannot remember him ever being involved in a fist fight but they say he was no milksop. He played Australian Rules football in a Jeparit team, and cricket, but preferred study to sport.

When he was fourteen an important event occurred. He was in Jeparit, in 1909, when the decision was finally made to extend the railway line from Jeparit to Lorquon instead of from Nhill to Lorquon. This had been argued about for years and his father had often worked himself into a frenzy as he fought for Jeparit. It was a great victory for Jeparit, because the Lands Department had already sub-divided scrub land near several other towns confidently expecting that the old line to Nhill would be extended.

With the Jeparit extension the boom in Mallee land reached its zenith. But a newly-opened railway line further north to Ouyen and Murrayville and the bumper wheat crops of the next year or so were to cause a further rush for Mallee land, with applications outnumbering blocks by ten to one. In the rush near Murrayville, 140 applicants in one instance competed for a single block of no special value or possibilities. Such was the importance of a railway line to a new country.

18

Bob Menzies looked on when the members of the Railways Standing Committee and several members of the Victorian Parliament came to Jeparit to finally examine the railway proposal and hear evidence. These politicians would shape the great decision on the issue which had been the main talking point in Jeparit for years. They were influential men.

Young Menzies was impressed with their power and stature. He marvelled at how wonderful it must be to present yourself to the world as a Member of Parliament. It must have made a big impression, for he began telling some of his school pals he was going to be Prime Minister of Australia.

Perhaps the thought that it was his ordained role to be Prime Minister was not news to him—it had probably stirred within him in a child-like way for some time. For him to dwell on politics was not really so remarkable, because from an early age he had been brought up on such a diet. Jim Menzies' brother, Hugh Menzies, had represented the electorate of Stawell in the Victorian Parliament from October 1902 to May 1904. And Uncle Syd Sampson, a man who had hardly ever gone to school, became a member of the Federal Parliament and remained there for about ten years.

Jim Menzies was always talking politics in Jeparit, as many of the improvements he sought for the district were bound up in political decisions. Young Bob had often looked on wide-eyed while his father jabbed the air with a carving knife over the Sunday roast, expounding some point or criticizing some new Bill before Parliament. And Jim Menzies, in the same year his young son saw a practical demonstration of the politician's power, was rewarded for his community work by being elected to the Victorian Parliament as the Member for Lowan, a local seat he was to hold for ten years.

About five years before, as a land reform movement member, James Menzies helped to fight a furious campaign against Sir William Irvine, then the Member for Lowan and Premier of Victoria, known as Iceberg Irvine because of his aloofness. Menzies went to a neighbouring town and made such a fiery speech directed at Irvine on the land question that he was asked to stand against him. However, Irvine backed down on the issue, gave way to a colleague, Thomas Bent, as Premier, and stood as a private member. Menzies did not stand but it put him in the running for the seat in future. He was beaten on redistribution the first time he stood, but went in a year or so later.

James Menzies always led an exemplary and dedicated life in

the interests of other people. He found jobs for hundreds of unemployed, and anyone who went to him with a hard luck story could be assured of help. Frank Menzies was to develop a good many of these characteristics of his father as he grew up.

Jim Menzies gave his energies to the local agricultural society and other public and local bodies without thought of profit for himself. In addition, he was responsible for alienating Crown land for use as Jeparit's showground and sports reserve, although he had no time or inclination to play sport himself; the grant of a site for a memorial hall and the right to finance on the old Mechanics' Institute site; improved postal and telephone services including eventually a new post office; the establishment of a game sanctuary along the Wimmera River south of Jeparit, and many other developments.

He called everyone by their first name and interviewed all his constituents on the footpath outside the odd little office he occupied adjoining the Hopetoun House Hotel. Few people saw inside the office where in peace and quiet he fashioned the eloquent phrases, colourful if somewhat flowery, that he let loose in his speeches. And he always spoke without notes.

As an orator he was a marvel to behold. When in full flight he appeared to be inspired by some occult or inner being, as though bent on exorcizing evil spirits. It was a popular style of the times.

Although deeply religious he could be fiery and quick-tempered with anyone who did not agree with his point of view; but for all that he was generous, warm-hearted, kindly, and completely genuine.

When he first got into Parliament at a salary of £300 a year he was also appointed chairman of the Railways Standing Committee, which brought in another £200 a year. Although he could have continued in office he went to a friend, Dick Toucher, a member of the committee, and said, "It's your turn, old man." That was his make-up.

Such was his strict code of living in Jeparit days that he did not allow Isabel to go to the theatre until she was eighteen. To him the theatre was the house of the devil, although he changed in later life. He never touched a drop of liquor and if he could have seen his daughter, at the age of seventy, smoking a cigarette, he surely would have turned in his grave.

Jim Menzies' interest was the shop; his love was his wife and children. And most of what the Menzies children were to achieve was due to the guidance and self-sacrifice of Jim and Kate Menzies. Although they had to economize to the point where every penny

20

counted, there was never any shortage of food and the children received every educational opportunity.

Frank Menzies was to write later of life in Jeparit: "I will always think of mother and father as striving to free themselves from a burden of debt induced on the one hand by almost unlimited credit to the struggling farmers of the district, and on the other hand by heavy interest charges on overdraft accounts to city merchants.

"No one will ever know the anguish of mind through which they went in those early days when they both steadfastly refused to accept the advice of friends to file their schedule and make a fresh start in easier surroundings.

"I prefer to think that the enrichment of character which came from the fight they successfully waged (not from a financial point of view) found its reward in much greater satisfaction of family life which, I venture to say, was their greatest asset."

Kate Menzies would have been the last person to admit she suffered any privation on behalf of the children. A capable and energetic woman, she met and overcame every hardship but usually kept her inner feelings to herself. She could be described as a retiring type, but a tower of strength behind the scenes, whereas her husband was dynamic.

Kate's calmness was a strong balancing agent against Jim Menzies' pronounced emotionalism.

His excitability showed in many ways. For instance, when Kate Menzies whacked Bob for small misdemeanours, he always told her it didn't hurt. But when father handed out the punishment it was different: he would work himself into a high pitch of anger, dispense a thorough hiding and Bob would have to sit on a tin trunk after the ordeal until his sobbing ended.

If Bob or any of the other children got on to a tramcar in Ballarat with their father there was often a lively scene if he had to stand up while juveniles sat down.

"Here," Menzies would say to the youngster, "shift your stone feet."

"Oh, father, please," Bob or one of the other Menzies children would plead.

Jim Menzies would explode. "I'll never pass injustice," he would say, almost shouting. "I'll never stand up while children sit down."

And the Menzies adolescents would be embarrassed.

Another example of his impetuosity can be seen in an incident

21

a few years later when he had improved his lot, and Kate Menzies each morning fixed a rosebud in his buttonhole as he left home.

One morning he wanted a letter. "Now, Kitty," he said to his wife, "I put that letter there," indicating a spot in the living room.

"I don't think you did," she said.

"But I *know* I put that letter there. Someone has moved it."

And he grew hot under the collar. Then *out* of the house he stalked, *out* the gate banging it shut, up the road to the tram.

When he got to the corner he thought, "I didn't kiss Kitty goodbye." So back he came to the house, kissed Kitty, got his rosebud and went on his way—without the letter.

His anger rose sharply, but passed almost as quickly. And when he made a political speech he got so emotionally worked up about it that at least two of the Menzies children, Isabel and Bob, became uneasy, almost sickened, listening to him.

This made an impression on Bob Menzies that was to affect him for the rest of his life. He felt his father was too emotional; the feeling reacted on him in such a way that he developed a dread of showing emotion. Consciously he set out to suppress his feelings.

Whether this was the reason for his growing up an essentially shy and nervous person, or whether these qualities were inherited, cannot be determined with any certainty. But the fact is that his father's explosiveness was such that nearly sixty years later when publicly reminiscing about his father he recalled his early days vividly, declaring that Jim Menzies had been a little intolerant and a little bit disposed to get his way.

In contrast to his relations with his father, a powerful bond developed at an early stage between Bob and his mother. He adored her and somehow it became more important for him to please her than his father. Her influence on him was immense. Always it was his mother who was there to advise him, encourage him and guide him, and he turned to her for help.

Bob was Kate Menzies' favourite and he never had to worry whether he was doing the right thing or not: mother always told him.

Bob's talent for learning was acknowledged to be unusual by his mother, and from the outset it was to be an unparalleled procession of successes; with Kate Menzies, the main driving force, telling him what The Establishment expected of him. There was no such word in those days, of course, but if a phrase had to be chosen for the time it would be The Administration, the ruling class.

This was the road to success, the way to get on—stay with them. And the right thing in that little town away from the bustle of city life involved high standards of conduct, both morally and spiritually, and something of the spirit of service.

As far as Jim Menzies was concerned, his guidance of Bob was more by example and deed than by personal and intimate conversation.

In these respects a fascinating contemporary parallel existed with the mother of Herbert Vere Evatt, a future Australian Labor leader, United Nations president, and arch rival and enemy of Bob Menzies. A star pupil at Fort Street High School in Sydney, he went home one day and proudly announced he had achieved eight A passes.

Ruthless in her fostering of his ability, but not that of the other Evatt boys, Mrs Evatt demanded: "You sat for nine subjects —what happened to the other one?"

Privately Bob Menzies always considered himself to be a Sampson, as belonging to his mother's side. When attending the funeral of Uncle Syd Sampson in later years he remarked to several intimates: "You know, the emotions of the Sampsons run very deep." That was an expression of his own self.

Bob was so close to his mother that within his own being he probably resented the fact that she was kept in that bush town to struggle. He grew up with his father always having to pay 10 per cent on unpaid bills. And he never really appreciated his father's character—a fact which showed out in later life when he gave details about his father for a publication, and some other members of the family felt that Jim Menzies had been done scant justice.

A reason always exists for phenomena. Bob Menzies is to a large extent a product of the matriarch; and today more than previously, it is a common pattern for the mother to be the dominant parent because of the complexity of urban life. She happens to be on hand more often than the father and children grow up closer to her, taking on her values.

A psychiatrist of international standing has told the writer that if a child doesn't completely trust a person or a group of people, he often doesn't communicate what he feels because he believes if he doesn't show involvement, he cannot be hurt or attacked. Often a child who is cowed or inhibited by an explosive type of father can have difficulty in communicating a sense of anger,

23

shame, despair or other feeling because he believes that if he does, the father will make his normal outward exhibition.

Consequently, you have a child who does not trust the expression of his own feelings. Psychiatrists believe that the child who anticipates physical or psychological injury becomes more cautious about communicating his feelings, and this basic truth is characteristic of all society.

If you do not have the freedom to communicate your feelings you place a check on them, and this gradually becomes a built-in pattern of behaviour. You may not even know the reason why you act this way.

In a psychological analysis of any person it is unwise to suggest that if as a child he had a different father or a different mother things might have worked out differently, for the interaction of forces between the father and mother and the boy in his relationship to his brothers and sisters, are all important factors. Man is a product of many things that go on around him—he does not become the person he is because of one single causative factor.

Certainly in the case of young Menzies the influence his mother had on him seems to demonstrate a kind of exploitation of his intellectual skill. He could not please his mother by trying to gain emancipation from her or by not going to school, so he did so by applying his mind and excelling at his lessons. The intellectual qualities dominated, as it were, the emotional aspects of his life.

Perhaps Kate Menzies in recognizing his brightness pushed him along to achieve something in contrast to her husband, something her husband had wanted to achieve but could not because he left school so early; Jim Menzies frequently stressed to the children that they must "improve the mind." And Bob, whose social identification was more with his mother, perhaps picked up this attitude of Mrs Menzies towards her husband. Thus they would team together unknowingly.

But Jim Menzies, too, was a significant influence in his son's development, although the attitudes and characteristics Bob picked up from his father were to be shown in a different way. As so often happens in any normal family, the father would show his emotion, the son wouldn't.

Other factors that had some significance in the boy's development were the phrenologist's forecast and the visit of the Members of Parliament to Jeparit. The fact that he remembered the politicians' visit long afterwards shows it was important: phrenology, regarded as a pseudo-science, probably succeeded in those days because bump-readers said positive things. That old bump-reader might have told others in the class they would make good barristers, but somehow it got through to Bob Menzies.

However, these factors are only part of the story. In each of our childhoods we can remember experiences that were important to us, but our parents were unaware of these influences. We didn't tell anyone.

A study of top flight intellectuals in various fields by an American University faculty several years ago showed an overwhelming majority of these people to be first-born children. It did not mean their genetic structure was any better than the second or third child, but it did indicate that they looked up to their parents in a different fashion from subsequent children.

Bob Menzies was the second youngest in a family where the other children, too, had pretty good ability. He may have been exposed to some extent to different courses than the others, with his mother's passionate encouragement and older brothers to help shape him. And Grandfather Sampson and Uncle Syd seemed to spend more time with him than the others.

In any case, it is not possible to know all the multiplicity of experiences that framed his personality or to pinpoint the most important single factor involved in giving him the desire to kick out against poverty in a small town environment. Whatever the outside influences, Bob Menzies had it within himself to succeed. Probably the truth lay in a reverse of the observation of Julius Caesar, "The fault, dear Brutus, is not in our stars, but in ourselves, that we are underlings."

The immediate recognition Menzies achieved by applying his mind and beating those around him was the spur that drove him on: he wanted to be better than anyone else.

Psychiatrists believe that a person usually has a sense of deep inadequacy when it becomes important to be better than anyone else. It's nice if he turns out better, but he is forever trying to prove himself. And in so doing he tends to overcompensate.

One of the puzzling features of the human makeup is that a person who seems to have achieved the pinnacle of success is often still striving to go one better. A case in point is the American pianist Rodney Horwitz. Although brilliant he had a terrible sense of inadequacy, believing that people told him he was good only because they wanted to be pleasant. "I'm really no good," he used to say, and his complex eventually resulted in psychiatric illness.

Menzies had always to bear the cross of his own brilliance, and remain an enigma to most people who came in contact with him.

4

The Menzies left Jeparit at the end of 1909.

James and Frank, the two older boys, were in the public service in Melbourne, with Frank studying law at night. Isabel had finished her schooling in Ballarat and Syd, the youngest member of the family, who had been born five years earlier, was at the Jeparit school.

Bob had continued to shine, by winning a scholarship from Grenville College to any one of the first-class colleges in Melbourne. Kate Menzies, with the argument that all the family must go and stay together persuaded her husband that he could continue his political work just as well in Melbourne.

Jim Menzies left the town flat broke after nearly twenty years there. He had improved his status to the extent that his family had moved into a separate house and a better store, but he still owed the merchants a good deal of money. He had bought a 640-acre farm 4 miles from Jeparit for £200 a few years before and paid for it on terms by leasing it out. This he now sold for £2,080 which enabled him to clear his debts and move the family to a house in East Melbourne. All he had was a seat in Parliament and £300 a year.

Bob's father sent him with an introduction to the headmaster of Scotch College, the Presbyterian school. But he finished up going to Wesley College, the school run by the Wesleyan Methodist Church and one of the original public schools that grew up in the middle of the 19th century. Young Bob was influenced by some of his friends who went to Wesley and who talked fondly about the headmaster, Dr L. A. (Dicky) Adamson.

"Never mind about Scotch, come to Dicky Adamson's school," they said. Later he regretted not having gone to Scotch College, although he had no reason to complain about his progress at Wesley.

He followed the Methodist religion at Wesley as he was obliged to, but attended the Presbyterian chapel in the suburb of Camberwell each Sunday with his family. It was said later by some critics he changed his religion, but this was not so—his family followed the Methodist faith in Jeparit because there was no Presbyterian church there, and reverted to the Scottish faith on going to Melbourne.

One of the girls attending that same chapel was a youngster named Pattie Maie Leckie who came from the country and whose mother had died when she was only a few years old. With her two sisters she was a boarder at the Presbyterian Ladies College. At this time her father, Mr J. W. Leckie, was a fellow member of the Victorian Legislative Assembly with Jim Menzies. Bob Menzies and Pattie Leckie often looked at each other in church.

Kate Menzies for the first time was able to devote all her energies to the family. Young Syd also showed aptitude at his studies and was sent to Trinity Grammar School. Bob did not live in at Wesley College and came home each evening. His mother regularly discussed his progress with him, encouraging him to do better.

Jim Menzies, who often returned to Jeparit to meet his constituents, became a fairly successful Parliamentary lobbyist for The Broken Hill Proprietary Limited, the big Australian steel complex, and one or two other organizations. In this respect it could be said that young Bob inherited all the best qualities from his father for his future career.

At Wesley it was the same story for Robert Menzies: if he wanted to go to university he had to earn his way by winning a scholarship. Father still could not afford to put him through university.

Bob set about his studies in the same painstaking way, placing them before everything else. The youth began to consolidate his early promise, proving once and for all he was no flash in the pan, but a genuine scholar.

He did best at English Language and Literature and History, although Latin and French followed closely. He didn't particularly like Mathematics or Science but passed in these subjects, admitting later that he had been a master of the book work through a good memory, but had not known what it was all about.

27

Two teachers made a profound impression on young Menzies; Harold Stewart, the Latin and History teacher, and Frank Shann, the English master. Stewart hated inaccuracy and his criticisms were personal and stinging. If you took him seriously, and you had to, he helped develop a disciplined and orderly mind. He implanted in Bob an appreciation of a sense of history.

Shann was a great stylist, a stickler for simplicity and clarity of thought. He did a great deal for Menzies in shaping a straightforward and unaffected style, both in writing and speaking. He never belittled students, but encouraged them to state exactly what was in their minds.

Bob Menzies enjoyed fun as much as anyone else. He joined enthusiastically in the singing at assembly of a boat song beginning, "When I was a new boy and an addle-headed cub," and in magnificent applause at the most instructive physics lesson of the day whenever one of the braver types at the front pushed a form back as the boys filed into the school hall, causing all the forms right back to the wall to sink backwards.

But he did very little in sport. Although he did play games he was not much good at them and did not make any of the teams. *Besides, you could not get on by spending too much time at sport.*

The only archives material kept on former students at Wesley is the College Chronicle, and Menzies' name appears in that only seldom, chiefly as a member of the school. He was not elected prefect or to any school office. He wrote a few articles for a magazine called *The Lion* that ran for a while.

Menzies used to follow the cricketers around at net practice, usually with a book of Shakespeare under his arm. He would expound his knowledge of the Bard at the nets, and already then there was hardly a quote from the whole of Shakespeare he could not pinpoint.

Menzies envied the cricketing ability of one of the students, Roy Park, who later became a doctor and represented Australia against England in 1921 in one Test match—in which he was bowled for a duck. Park likewise envied Menzies' knowledge of Shakespeare. While Park batted or bowled attractively at the nets, Menzies would regale him with suitable Shakespearean verses. Although he did not play the game much, Menzies liked it a great deal, and often put aside his book and became absorbed in the play.

Shakespeare played an important role in young Menzies' voracious appetite for reading. Often he went to a room by himself, and read plays aloud.

At the end of 1912 when eighteen, after three years at Wesley College, this curly haired, intense, quick witted young man won his way to Melbourne University with an exhibition, or scholarship, in the Senior Public Examination. To do so he beat all other Victorian entrants in his subject that year; several hundred of them. His subject was English Language and Literature. The scholarship meant a cash prize which would pay a substantial part of his university fees. Young Bob was on the way to fulfilling his dream of becoming a barrister.

Melbourne University, like Cambridge and Oxford and some American universities, has its halls of residence where the students live in, but they can also attend the classes and live outside. Naturally Bob continued to live at home.

The law student at that time followed a four-year course, the first two years studying Arts subjects. Menzies chose as his four subjects English, History, French, and Latin.

Menzies even found time to study law while reading his Arts course, although he was not to officially start on the law course for another two years. His interest in history and the desire for some outside activity apart from his course caused him to hit upon the idea of establishing an historical society. This he did with the aid of a friend and it soon became a lively forum where historical topics were debated, sometimes before an audience of hundreds.

Bob Menzies impressed other students with his ability to speak without notes. In fact, he made such a good showing with his easy gift of communication that he was elected a representative of the Students Council.

About this time Bob was beginning to take a look at the world around him. He was fond of a girl whose brother attended the Presbyterian Bible Class with him each Sunday, and each week the young worshippers took it in turn to read a paper on some subject of interest to the church. To impress the girl Bob used to write out the talk for her brother, who would then read it out as though it were his own work. Bob would address the group without a note and was always a hit.

Bob pleased the brother, though romance did not blossom fully with his sister. However, a sometimes reminiscent lady in Melbourne today still treasures a dressing table set, given to her in those days by Robert Menzies, as a reminder of the romance that might have been.

Bob often popped along to the Victorian House of Parliament to listen to the usually turbulent debates, taking his friends with him. He would remark on how few Members were in the House to listen.

A contemporary of Bob's at the time recalls that he had great ideas of what he intended doing in the future. "I'll finish up as Chief Justice or Prime Minister," Bob would say.

He seemed to have it in him to make a name for himself, was clearly ambitious and conscious of the fact that he was a very able young man, able to express himself fluently. But he never harped on the future that he thought Destiny held for him; passing it off in a more or less jocular way to get around what was interpreted as a perfectly serious remark.

Some other students regarded him as self-opinionated at university, but not offensively so. In the phrase of the time, he used to trail his coat a little.

Bob's boyhood experience with the *Jeparit Leader* proved useful when, with a student later to become a Judge, he was co-editor of the university magazine, "M.U.M." Not only did they write nearly all the articles to fill the space under various *noms-de-plume*, and composed verse, but they marked the type, took the material to the printers, and corrected the proofs. They canvassed tradesmen for advertisements to meet the cost of printing, collected the finished product, and sold it to the students for sixpence a copy.

Menzies in this period showed a capacity for dividing his brain into compartments, enabling him to do more than one thing at a time. While absorbing his lectures he wrote screeds of poetry.

By the time Menzies began his law studies he was already fairly well advanced in the subject. His knowledge and thirst for work surprised the Dean of the Faculty of Law, Professor Harrison Moore, himself an authority on constitutional law, who regarded Menzies as the most promising student the Faculty had ever taught.

While a student Menzies served his compulsory military training in the University Rifles, and after a short time was made a captain.

Soon after the first World War broke out and the situation grew grim in Europe, Frank Menzies decided to go straight into the Australian Infantry, the footsloggers. He joined up when the first casualty list was announced, believing he should be the first member of the family to do so.

James, his eldest brother and an intrinsically nervous type, also talked of joining up and a general family discussion was held. The result was that Frank went to the war, rising to captain and serving at Mouquet Farm and other parts of France, to be followed a few months later by James.

Bob stayed at home.

That fact was to give rise to bitter condemnation of him, with implications that he was a coward. And because he left the University Rifles, public phrases of contempt were used such as, "An otherwise brilliant military career was interrupted by the outbreak of war."

In later life this gave Bob Menzies a complex which caused him to act in strange ways, a complex on which he was more sensitive than any other point. Only once or twice could he even bring himself to defend his position publicly.

The truth is that although the decision to stay was finally his, it was based on the general wish of almost the whole Menzies family and in such a close group, that carried weight. The Menzies parents were in middle-age, with Jim Menzies not enjoying good health, and there was a prospect that in the not-too-distant future one son would be needed as the breadwinner.

Young Syd was only ten and at school—in his spare time he used to sell *Heralds* at Camberwell railway station. Bob had two years to go to finish his law course and the Menzies were already making a sacrifice with two sons at the war. Also, it was traditional at the time for one son to stay at home in a family of two or more.

But even more important than any of these considerations was the fact that the family at that time was undergoing a difficult domestic upset. These intimate details are mentioned here to prove that the criticisms of Bob Menzies over his action have been entirely unfair.

Kate and Jim Menzies were unhappy at that time over Isabel's choice of a future husband and this had led to angry scenes. It reached the stage where Isabel, a charming and gifted person but also a woman of strong feeling, had left home in order to show her determination. The family wanted Bob to stay home to sort out the situation and ease the burden of the parents who were unable to cope.

Bob Menzies did not resign his commission as some critics claimed. He served his full term as a compulsory trainee before his connection with the Army ended. To continue in the Army at that point he would have had to enlist for military service.

Among the many claims made on this issue is that when asked why he did not volunteer for service in the war after playing an enthusiastic role in peacetime, he replied: "Oh, it's all right for my pals to go to the war but a future Prime Minister of the

Commonwealth has to be protected." If he did in fact say this—which is extremely doubtful—it was obviously a bitter jest of the type which a man makes when he does not want to reveal his feelings. Unfortunately some people took the rumour seriously; perhaps because they wanted to.

But what is true is that soon after the first batch of 20,000 Australian troops left for Egypt at the end of 1914, Menzies composed a sonnet dedicating it to them and their sacrifice, which he read to his fellow officers in a tent while on a University exercise.

In the sonnet he declared his own life was "too valuable to be used for cannon fodder." The well-meant verse (Menzies was then only twenty), was not appreciated by one or two present and word of it leaked out, and it was used against him.

Men who feel they are destined for greatness usually place a high value on their lives. Winston Churchill, although he took enough risks, showed that he valued his life when galloping around South Africa as a young correspondent in the Boer War.

Writing in his despatch to the *Morning Post* about an incident in which he was fired on by a group of Boers and thrown from his horse, Churchill described how his position seemed hopeless. But then a scout from the Brigade of Imperial Yeomanry rode up and rescued him by taking him up behind him and riding out of the range of Boer bullets, but not before the scout's horse had been hit. "Oh, my poor horse," moaned the trooper.

"Never mind," said Churchill, "you've saved my life."

"Ah," rejoined the scout, "but it is the horse I'm thinking about."

Bob Menzies went on to sit for his final examination in law but not without some financial sacrifice on the part of the family. His scholarship helped considerably but it by no means met all his expenses and, of course, did not support him at home. Such were the filial bonds of the Menzies that the parents were saved from possible financial embarrassment by Frank making available from his Army pay an allotment of £200 a year.

Bob repaid his parents and brothers for their sacrifice and faith when at the end of 1916 he took first-class honours in Law, a reasonably rare achievement.

It was a brilliant year, a brilliant course for him, and he took off most of the prizes—the Sir John Madden Exhibition, Jessie Leggatt Scholarship, Bowen Essay Prize, and the Supreme Court Judges' prize.

In the opinion of Dr Thomas Coates, present headmaster of Wesley College, Bob Menzies with his achievements could have gone into university teaching, taken a Chair and become a Professor of Law with spectacular success.

"That stands out from his academic record," says Dr Coates. "My opinion is that he would have been a brilliant academic if he had chosen to follow a scholastic career."

After university the boy from Jeparit was on the way.

5

Before a law graduate in Australia can practise as a barrister he must first be articled to an established barrister or solicitor for at least a year. Bob Menzies was fortunate in being accepted as a pupil by Owen Dixon, a leading Victorian barrister later to be knighted and become Chief Justice of Australia.

In that first year the budding advocate was entrusted with a few briefs and appeared in court to represent clients before magistrates. He was paid a fee of £2 2 0 a time. Menzies gave a good account of himself and at the end of the year, when Owen Dixon took him before the Supreme Court and successfully moved that he be admitted to the Bar to practise as a barrister, he was beginning to build up a limited reputation—enough anyway, when admitted on 2 May 1918, to encourage him to begin his own legal business.

In the police and country courts he picked up modest guineas by defending many a misunderstood shoplifter, confidence man, and thug, taking on all kinds of cases for alleged offences against both property and the person.

And as barristers are not permitted to advertise, and must make their reputation in the courts and through Press reports, Bob in those days was not averse to the time-honoured practice of asking reporters to be sure to mention his name in their stories.

In his first year the junior had a lucky break. A solicitor came to him in a flap with a case he wanted argued before the High Court in two days' time. The case rested on a tricky point of constitutional law and, unable to get the barrister he wanted and knowing of Menzies' growing reputation, he offered it to him.

Menzies read the brief quickly—even then he could read and absorb a document with an astonishing speed, and said he'd take it.

Donning his wig and gown for the first time, Menzies argued his case before the judge, Mr Justice Gavin Duffy, and was subjected to a searching interrogation by the judge on the points he had made, and some he hadn't made. He matched wits with the judge and won the case, with the judge taking the unusual course of congratulating him in open court on his manner and ability in conducting the case.

Menzies' parents were at the court for this performance and Jim Menzies admitted to his wife that he had underestimated Bob.

Menzies became greatly in demand by the unions, balancing his advocacy between union, common law, and constitutional work. A Labor Party man and brilliant barrister named J. A. Arthur died prematurely and Bob took over a great deal of his work. As an honorary sideline, he tutored a group of returning soldiers who had interrupted their courses to go to war. Among them was Frank, who qualified for his examinations after nine months.

Menzies had all the qualities of the good barrister. He was tall, of commanding presence with a voice of strong timbre and a rare capacity for work, which some people tended to disregard because he was also a man of slow speech and in a way, quiet and unsuspected actions. Crafty in cross-examination he played along with a witness until he had all the information he needed, then turned the point back. Even expert witnesses often found themselves in trouble.

About the time Menzies first went to university his family had moved from East Melbourne to another suburb, Kew. The Leckie family also moved, to a neighbouring suburb, and once again the two families were attending the same Presbyterian Church in Kew.

Pattie Leckie, whose father was soon to become Senator Leckie, met Bob Menzies again in church, and this time they took more notice of each other. Early in 1919 they met at a party, were engaged about a year later and married at Kew Presbyterian Church on 27 September 1920.

They lived firstly in a flat in Kew because Menzies could not afford a house. It was to be the beginning of an enduring and happy married life, resulting in the birth of two sons and a daughter.

Menzies continued to work late into the night preparing his material for the next day, seldom going to bed until after midnight. He appeared to do this without fatigue, a prerequisite of the good student which most people seem able to do only when young.

After three years Menzies made the break which put the seal on his reputation. He argued the case of the Amalgamated Engineering Union, which challenged the Australian Constitutional law giving immunity to instruments of the Crown, such as the Railways, against decisions of the Arbitration Courts. A minority view had been expressed for years by such eminent legal minds as Isaac Isaacs that Commonwealth and State instrumentalities should not be immune from the court's decisions, but it had never been tested.

The Crown engaged several barristers of King's Counsel status to argue their case but Menzies, standing alone against them, won. The Chief Justice congratulated him on the handling of the case, a triumph because it changed the existing law right round. It altered the course of the Constitution and affected the awards of scores of unions, enabling them to bring the Crown to court, just like any ordinary employer, and sue for better conditions.

After that Menzies was in great demand, flourishing largely as a constitutional lawyer and earning a high reputation. All the early constitutional work in Australia centred about the industrial, conciliation, and arbitration power, and Menzies was to appear in all the cases that mattered. Later he was sought by Australian big business, arguing several cases before the Privy Council in England, including one for the Shell Oil Company.

Once, in 1927, he appeared as an arbitrator in a case between the Australian Journalists Association and metropolitan newspaper owners, and gave journalists the best conditions they'd ever had. Afterwards he was sometimes inclined to remind recalcitrant reporters with a grin that they needn't be so miserable, as he had got them their first decent pay!

Another time he defended a journalist in a libel action brought by a wrestler—colourful characters like wrestlers fascinated him.

Having paid proper tribute to Menzies as a barrister of outstanding class with his excellent diction, fluency, keen intelligence, and distinguished appearance, it must be said that in the early days he had one blemish: he was not always successful before juries. He could not get close to the jury, and contemporaries attributed this to an inclination to talk down to them.

Legal men who knew his work then are of the opinion that there was usually a gap between him and the jury, which allowed the opposing barrister, a man perhaps less distinguished than himself, to intervene and make the jury feel a little resentful against him. On one occasion in a hearing he omitted to give motion of mitigation of damages, and then could not call for cross-examination a witness against whom he had prepared a compendious file.

Menzies was as anxious to be successful before juries as he was before any judge, but it seems that in the early years he did not have that particular trait of making the jury feel close to him.

The defect caused him to lose a few cases. Menzies held a retainer for the *Truth* chain of newspapers and the proprietor, Ezra Norton, went from Sydney to Melbourne on one occasion to sit in on a case in which Menzies was appearing for *Truth*. Norton, a hard taskmaster who always wanted real value for money, wondered why Menzies had lost more than one case in a row. In that particular suit, £1,000 damages were awarded against *Truth*, and Menzies lost his retainer.

It was different in constitutional cases. He was acknowledged the outstanding young constitutional lawyer of his day in Victoria.

Within ten years his highly successful practice was earning him at least £10,000 a year, a figure that today would be worth not less than £50,000.

When seemingly at the top of the legal tree, Menzies decided to go into politics. He had made his mark in law, which now seemed a little narrow to him, and he wanted to try the wider political field, where new recognition was to be won.

Jim Menzies had lost his seat in the Victorian Legislative Assembly, or Lower House, in 1919, by only a handful of votes. This was after the Country Party, which had been formed to give farmers separate political representation, combined against him. But he was active behind the scenes as an organizer for many years after that.

Jim Menzies played a leading role in a political group which early in 1927 prevented a Melbourne man, Wilfred Kent Hughes, from gaining Liberal Party preselection for the seat of Kew in the Victorian Legislative Assembly. They favoured another candidate, Ted Reynolds, and he won the preselection. But Kent Hughes stood as an unendorsed candidate and won the seat just the same.

Bob Menzies in 1928 stood for the Upper House of the Victorian Parliament, the Legislative Council. This House is elected on limited franchise and corresponds roughly to the House of Lords. But he was easily beaten—a setback which he felt personally very acutely. However, the successful candidate died a few months later and Menzies tried again in the by-election and succeeded in being elected. He was then thirty-three.

In his first speech in the Victorian Parliament Menzies spoke in favour of justice for the underdog. It certainly could not be said that his views were Labor, for his party was the original Liberal Party, but his sympathies then were always with the man on the job.

On this occasion he strongly supported a proposal to increase the statutory amount for workers' compensation, after opposition had been expressed against the measure. Explaining that he had not intended to speak quite so soon, he pleaded with vigour and clarity the case for an increase so that the worker would not be denied justice.

Obviously, in that McPherson Liberal Government, a ministerial post could not be denied to a man of Menzies' talents and ambition for very long. He had the ability of a man marked down for promotion, and he was out to achieve it. After a few months he was appointed an Honorary Minister, or Minister without Portfolio.

It seemed inevitable that Menzies would run into a great deal of opposition and trouble wherever he went, by reason of his very ambition and also by his breadth of vision, which even then was quite outside the range of his acquaintance or background.

It wasn't long before he was stirring up some of those around him.

Just after he became Minister without Portfolio, the Cabinet was discussing a controversial issue on whether the Government should reopen an inland freezing works and spend a great deal of money. It was in the electorate of the Minister for Education, a Mr Pennington, who was putting up a fight for the reopening.

"Well, Mr Premier," Mr Pennington said, "I can assure you that unless these works are erected you can say goodbye to my seat."

Menzies, who hadn't previously spoken, declared: "The real question we are discussing, Mr Premier, is whether we are prepared to spend £400,000 of the State's money to keep Mr Pennington in Parliament."

The impudent young pup! was the impression created. He had taken a legal point, not necessarily a logical one, and used it with stunning effect. This was fairly typical of his technique with people and he would not hesitate to be personally offensive, though not directly so, if he thought he could win a point.

Menzies tried to be friendly with everybody but, in particular, he was cold-shouldered by the Labor Members of the Parliament. They thought him patronizing. To many of the older members in his own Party, too, he appeared to be arrogant and only just avoided being pompous.

Menzies was puzzled by the Labor Party attitude because he was very proud of the part played for the workers by Grandfather Sampson and he considered that he himself had quite a streak of radicalism in him.

John Cain the Labor leader, a pleasant and moderate fellow, came to him one day and said, "You know, Bob, the trouble with you is that you've come up from the Bar, where they all address one another by their surnames. But you can't do that in this place. If you do you'll run into trouble."

Menzies began calling everybody by their Christian names and there was quite a reform in attitude towards him from the Labor side. In fact, he got on better with Labor Members than those of his own Party.

But he would not hesitate to put a point across his opponents if he could. For instance, on one occasion a member of the Opposition raised a point of order on the absence of a quorum in the House and Menzies argued it was no point of order and quoted the Standing Orders to prove it.

But he quoted only the portion which suited his purpose, and got away with it because other members, unable to remember the Standing Orders, were bluffed. Even in those early political days Menzies was quick on the uptake, with the authority to say something and appear sure of his ground.

In 1929 Menzies decided he would like to become a King's Counsel, or "take silk." Only four or five K.C.s practised in Victoria then. The procedure is that before you take silk you notify all your seniors at the Bar so they may take precedence over you if they wish, and avoid being subordinated to you.

One of those he notified was Charles Low, an eminent member of the Bar (later to be Chief Justice of Victoria), who thought about it overnight and was reluctant to take it on. But Menzies, with all the enthusiasm of the time, went ahead and was appointed the youngest K.C. in Australia, beating H. V. (Bert) Evatt by a few months. Evatt, the man who at thirty-six was to make a unique passage from a career in State politics to become the youngest ever to be elevated to the High Court bench, and then step from the Bench into Federal politics, was Menzies' counterpart in legal precocity and brilliance at the Bar, although he took different sides in constitutional cases. Like Menzies, Evatt was born in 1894.

This elevation for Menzies meant fewer briefs but fatter fees. It also meant he could spend a little more time with his family.

By now he was living in a creeper-covered two-storey house at 10 Howard Street, Kew, having moved from the flat to another house in Kew which had been unsuitable. The first child, Kenneth Leckie, born in 1922, was in delicate health for most of his early childhood but the others, Robert Ian and Margery Heather, were as strong and healthy as their father. Pattie Menzies, in traditional Australian fashion, managed the home and children on her own without any outside help.

Menzies often called on his parents and took them for a drive in his car, remaining, as always, a staunch family man. And if he were engaged on a big case Jim Menzies, with all his old verve, would tell Bob how to conduct it, even though he did not know the complete background.

Those were turbulent times in Australian politics. Parties quite often changed their names, and in 1929 the approach of the depression gave a sharp edge to debates. Parliamentary salaries were low and a man had to be more or less dedicated to go into politics.

Today, almost anyone with the gift of the gab can go along and seek preselection. But in those days, outside the Labor Party, you almost had to have a deputation approach you and ask you to stand. Outside Labor the party machine system was hardly known, and members were free, or liked to feel free, to vote according to their consciences.

Debate in the Victorian Legislative Assembly was full of fire, but in the Upper House there was little action. It was really a House of review, most of the members were old and tired and here was Menzies, the bright young man, with virtually nothing to do. He wondered how he could get into the Lower House.

The opportunity arose, but not directly through his own efforts. Wilfrid (Billy) Kent Hughes, another bright young man, was beginning to make a name for himself in the Lower House. A Rhodes Scholar who had gone to Oxford, Kent Hughes had won a Military Cross in the first World War, was mentioned in despatches four times and, among other things, had represented Australia at the Olympic Games and the British Empire against the United States in 1920.

A man of ability and ambition, he had the idea of founding the Society of Young Nationalists of Victoria; to band together enterprising young men of generally liberal outlook in order to get things done. With this in mind, Kent Hughes called on Bob

Menzies one Sunday morning at his home in Kew. He was accompanied by Ted Greenwood, who was then the Member for the Melbourne electorate of Nunawading.

Greenwood had decided to retire, and he and Kent Hughes had discussed the possibility of Menzies resigning from the Upper House and standing for Nunawading in the Lower House. Kent Hughes considered that Menzies, with his knowledge and ability, would be an asset.

"Bob, you'd better get out of the Upper House," Hughes said. "You've got to take Ted's place. We're going to start a young people's political movement, called the Young Nationalists."

They spent the afternoon with Menzies and finally he agreed to resign and stand for Nunawading. The idea of joining in the young people's movement and going into the Lower House appealed to him.

Kent Hughes, as a lad of eight or nine, had had similar dreams to the young Bob Menzies. He once told a pal, while playing marbles on the way to his home at Kew, that when he grew up he was going to be Prime Minister.

The Young Nationalists began at his instigation. He and Menzies worked on it together, and Menzies became the first president. He resigned from the Liberal Party in 1929 after a disagreement on some issue, then resigned from the Upper House, and at the elections won the seat of Nunawading in the Legislative Assembly. But the Labor Party went into power on the economic issue, and Menzies and his colleagues sat in Opposition for the next two and a half years. The Young Nationalists flourished. Among the discontented young men who joined the ranks were John Spicer (later a Judge), R. G. Casey, and Harold Holt.

Number 10 Howard Street, Kew, became the venue of many a political discussion. At one Sunday meeting Joe Lyons talked over with Menzies and some other Young Nats his historic decision to make a switch from the Labor Party. He was the former Premier of Tasmania, whom the Federal Labor Leader, J. H. Scullin, had requested in 1929 to leave State politics and stand as a Labor candidate for the Federal Parliament. He became Postmaster-General and Minister for Works and Railways in the Scullin Government. With a handful of followers, he now allied himself with the Opposition and formed the United Australia Party.

That conspiratorial gathering was early in 1931. In the previous

41

year, as Acting Treasurer, Lyons had succeeded in floating a £25,000,000 conversion loan in spite of the Depression.

He resigned from the Federal Cabinet on 4 February 1931 as a protest against the return of Edward Theodore to the position of Treasurer; a colleague, J. E. Fenton, also resigned.

The leader of the Nationalist Party in the Federal Parliament, J. G. (later Sir John) Latham, changed his party's name and joined with Lyons in the United Australia Party, standing aside to allow Lyons to be elected as leader of the Opposition. Lyons' action is regarded as a factor in the Labor Party losing office at the elections of December 1931, when Lyons became Prime Minister and Treasurer.

In the Victorian elections of 1932 Labor was defeated there, too, and the majority of liberals returned to Parliament were members of Menzies' and Kent Hughes' Young Nationalists. This placed Sir Stanley Argyle, leader of the Victorian Liberal Party, in an embarrassing position.

He was the senior man, and a politician of considerable experience, but according to general practice the young ambitious Menzies, as leader of the numerically stronger Party, should have become Premier. However, the position was resolved when Menzies, feeling in that time of depression and difficulty that he was not quite ready to take the responsibility of leadership and realizing that to do so would cause friction among the older Liberals, went to Sir Stanley and diplomatically indicated that he was not seeking the Premiership.

The result was that Menzies became Deputy Premier, Minister for Railways, and Attorney General. For a time he did act as leader when Sir Stanley Argyle became ill, and proved a success.

A few days after Menzies became Attorney General and Minister for Railways, in May 1932, a young Melbourne reporter called on him in his office in the course of his rounds. He'd prepared a few questions. The new Minister sat him down and to his surprise not only answered his questions explicitly and without hedging, but made several newsworthy statements—new Ministers are like that.

Menzies asked him if he intended walking down Collins Street and strolled with him. The young reporter was very impressed with this unusual behaviour by a Minister of State. Menzies, in fact, was very friendly and affable towards all Pressmen.

A few months later when the young reporter called again Menzies was sitting in his office with a book in his hand.

"Look at this," said Menzies. "I got it for being dux of the fourth grade at Jeparit. My headmaster said to me when he gave it to me, 'Robert, you might be Prime Minister of Australia one of these days.' "

Looking up after a pause Menzies said, "Look at me. Minister for Railways! I ask you!"

"Cheer up," the reporter said brightly. "You might be some day."

"It doesn't seem likely," said Menzies, gloomily.

6

The scene: The Hotel Canberra set in lovely grounds in the national capital, near Federal Parliament House. Time: towards the end of 1934.

About to enter the dining room, separately, Robert Gordon Menzies, Wilfrid Kent Hughes, and William Victor McCall.

Menzies and Kent Hughes entered the room, but Bill McCall, the newly-elected member for the Sydney seat of Martin and at that time the youngest member ever elected to the Federal Parliament, stopped on the way into breakfast to bid good morning to an elderly gentleman sitting on a garden seat. The gentleman was Sir Stanley Argyle, Premier of Victoria.

Without ado the genteel Sir Stanley motioned towards Menzies after he passed, and said to McCall: "Well, thank God we got rid of him. You're welcome to him. Have some fun with him."

In the breakfast room McCall sat with Billy Kent Hughes who had some highly unflattering comments to add about the tall, impressive figure of Robert Menzies.

McCall, aged twenty-five, was soon to make his maiden speech before Parliament, which was to be opened by the Duke of Gloucester, and was receiving his baptismal first day in Federal politics. McCall had come up the hard way, spruiking from a soap box to critical crowds in the Sydney Domain and narrowly missing out in an earlier election against E. W. (Eddie) Ward, the radical young Labor man from East Sydney, and he'd been in some pretty tough political fights.

McCall had met Menzies and Kent Hughes in Melbourne when the two men were president and deputy president of the Young

Nationalists, at a State conference when the United Australia Party was formed. But now he felt he was really going to learn something, and wondered what he had let himself in for.

The scene reflects the worst misfortune Menzies had to fight against at the time—many people just didn't seem to like him.

From the time he turned to politics from law he was confidently named as a future Prime Minister. He towered above his Victorian contemporaries, making many of them look like country yokels against the brilliant and pertinently clever Young Nationalist. His transfer from State to Federal politics was inevitable, his rise unstoppable.

Menzies' opportunity to enter Federal politics came when the Prime Minister, Joe Lyons, invited him to contest the Melbourne seat of Kooyong, then held by the Federal Attorney General, John (later Sir John) Latham.

The Prime Minister sent for Menzies and later gave him an official letter explaining that Latham wished to resign because of ill health, and if Menzies agreed to contest the by-election for Kooyong he would, if he won, be appointed Attorney General.

Latham really resigned to become Chief Justice of Australia— a post which appealed to him and, as he had stood aside to enable Lyons to become Prime Minister, Lyons felt obliged to grant him his wish.

Menzies himself says he was reluctant to accept the opportunity, mainly for family reasons, but that his wife encouraged him to accept. That Joe Lyons invited Menzies there is no doubt, but it is doubtful if he was enthusiastic over the appointment. The impression Lyons created in some quarters was that he felt no urgent need to have young Bob around to develop politically.

Joe Lyons crossed over the Bass Strait from Tasmania as a Labor man, then crossed over the floor of the House of Representatives in the Federal Parliament and became a Conservative. He was accepted by Collins House and was a prisoner ever after.

Collins House, in Collins Street, Melbourne, was, and is, the headquarters for most of the big business interests of Australia. In those days, much more than at present, Collins House controlled the Melbourne financial world. And because the companies concerned were major contributors to Party political funds, Collins House had a considerable say in the affairs of Government, both in Canberra and Melbourne.

When Lyons, a practical and honest man, first became Prime Minister, many felt he had been handed the reins as a stop-gap leader to guide Australia through a difficult period. This he did with a sound financial policy, his main problem being to reduce unemployment.

But those who felt he was only a temporary leader underestimated him. Not only did everybody like Honest Joe, but he had a tact, shrewdness, humour, and commonsense which kept him unspoiled by power, plus a capacity to inspire confidence and loyalty. In short, a good Prime Minister. His one regret was that his former supporters never appreciated his reasons for breaking with the Labor Party.

Joe Lyons invited Menzies to enter Federal politics because, no doubt, he was asked to invite him. After Lyons was firmly established in Canberra, some Melbourne people thought here was a chance to push young Bob. Menzies had considerable support at this time from many top Melbourne businessmen. People like Walter Massey Green, Lyons' first Treasurer and an outstanding financial figure, were keen to see the brilliant young Menzies promoted, although some members of the political Old Guard might have felt like keeping an eye on him.

But at this time he did not have the support of the Melbourne aristocracy; the top drawer of society. They were suspicious of him, feeling he was a controversial young man; a bit of a problem. They felt too, that he might become another Lord Bruce—more English than the English.

Clive (later Sir Clive) Baillieu reputedly had little time for Menzies then. The Baillieus were something like the Rothschilds, with business interests in many parts of the world. W. S. Robinson, the head of the Collins House group, was also suspicious of Brilliant Bob.

But Menzies had plenty of influential friends. He was friendly for instance, with Staniforth Ricketson, the Melbourne proprietor of J. B. Were and Son, who had built up a chain of investment companies which bought stock exchange shares. Menzies had been made a director of some of Ricketson's companies, but he gave this up when politics became more serious than law for him.

Menzies did nothing in those days to court the people of wealth and position in Melbourne. It was not his style to court anybody. He was not, of course, a member of The Establishment by inheritance, as were such men as R. G. Casey. He had no means, no family background to recommend him, only sheer ability. And that was not enough for the aristocracy.

It was the combination of ability and driving ambition which got Menzies into trouble in the years after he went to Canberra to become Federal Attorney General in 1934.

From the comparative gentility of the Victorian Parliament he entered what could only be described as a jungle.

There were immensely strong and dominating characters in the Coalition Government, which had grown up like some hybrid mule out of a period of turbulence. The United Australia Party and the Country Party was a coalition party thrown into government by a crisis; by the passions that threw out the Scullin Government. It had also the background of the Bruce-Page Government splitting on arbitration policy in 1928, and the Labor Party splitting on conscription in 1917.

This gave colour and character to the individuals of the Party, to people like Lyons and Billy Hughes who had been imported from Labor. The Party was really a group of individuals who came together for convenience rather than for any particular philosophy. And it was not terribly sure what it stood for. Some members of the Party could only be described as merchant adventurers.

Menzies came up against such strong characters as Sir Earle Page, Larry Anthony, Arthur Fadden, John McEwen, and Percy Spender in those first few years and found himself in strange surroundings. He didn't know how to live within a coalition party, didn't understand most of his fellows, nor they him.

To succeed in such surroundings you have to prove yourself firstly as a human being, as a personality, and show others that you understand them. It is a personal thing. To be right, to win by reason of logic or power of oratory, is not enough.

Menzies, with his ambition and apparent superabundance of self-confidence gave the impression that he thought himself to be superior.

And so some of the characters and shrewd heads on his own side set out to cut the bright boy down to size. Menzies was to learn that in the game of politics you must protect not your front but your back, that the people who purport to be friends are often not so.

Almost immediately Menzies was appointed deputy leader of the United Australia Party, which firmly established him in a position of power. But generally he was seen as the brilliant amateur, who showed contempt for mediocrity; a person who, although a superbly logical debater who could tear an opponent's argument to shreds, rarely moved Parliament because he spoke with his head and not with his heart.

It was said and written of him that he believed he had made history when he made a speech. And although it was felt he had the intellect of a big man, he was sometimes suspected of having all the vanities of a little man; he did not like being contradicted.

He had a conservatism that had grown naturally out of his detailed study of British political history and he stood for political principles, not Party platforms. He had the courage, or the folly, to say unpopular things.

One of the first nicknames attached to him was Buck Menzies, because he seemed to be a hangover from 18th century English politics when most leading politicians were orators—a mildly flattering sobriquet which would not have displeased him.

But when Menzies spoke, his disciplined intellect was obvious to one and all and his ideas were so fluently expounded and tinged with wit that he stirred even the reluctant admiration of the Labor Opposition benches.

Add to these qualities a big frame, a greying mane, big bushy black eyebrows, strong features, a slow walk with a gentle swaying of the ample stomach and you had, even then, a magnificent Empire Statesman appearance—a figure with a great deal of personal magnetism about him.

Menzies by now had become a bon viveur—a lover of good wine, good food, good company, and good conversation. His greatest recreation was at a dinner party, particularly a mixed one, at which all of these were present.

Few, if any, knew him as a man, but if you could break down the reserve you found a charming companion of broad and culti-vated tastes; a Menzies who revelled in the good and pleasant things of life.

In 1935 Menzies travelled to London for the Jubilee Celebra-tions of King George V, a visit that was to develop into an annual affair. And these were not hurried or perfunctory visits, but more like pilgrimages.

Menzies found London to his liking. He knew that colonial politicians were duchessed by Whitehall and, overwhelmed by The Treatment, were often taken for a ride. And he set out to make a good impression, to show he was above this level in his own right.

He charmed the English with his culture, his appreciation for English institutions and history, and he showed that he loved a lord as much as the next man. He was at great ease in Britain where it became customary for him to be fêted in the best surroundings.

On his first visit to Britain he represented Australia in trade negotiations and argued a case before the Privy Council. He was back again the following year pleading a case before the Privy Council, involving an interpretation of the Australian constitution.

Menzies proved himself a King's man in 1936 with Churchill against the stand of the British Prime Minister, Stanley Baldwin, when he supported King Edward VIII who abdicated to marry the *divorcée* Mrs Wallace Simpson.

His comments at the time created the impression among colleagues that he believed the King could do no wrong.

When in England in 1937 as spokesman for the Australian delegation to the Imperial conference, Menzies received his first big public honour. He had made a powerful impression before the King's Privy Council and now he was appointed to the Council. At the same time, he was made an Honorary Bencher of Gray's Inn, an honour given to only the most distinguished lawyers who are not members of the Inn by practice.

The Privy Council accolade rebounded on Bob Menzies soon afterwards in a way that indicated his attitude at the time.

Menzies could not spare the *bon mot,* the opportunity to ridicule, the temptation to expose a fool; but as there's one born every minute, his technique was not calculated to win friends.

Menzies often hurt a man's dignity with his remarks, and few men forgive or forget if their dignity is hurt. The fact that they remember makes the hurt all the greater.

There are two ways of looking at this, depending on your sense of humour. Those who appreciated Menzies believed that he took an essentially common sense humorous attitude to everything that did not demand serious thought; that he got as much fun out of life as possible; that he'd enlighten certain situations with his wit and humour just as easily as the ordinary man could take a more sober approach. This point of view was to gain wider acceptance at a later period, but at this time it was very much a minority opinion. The other view, shared by the majority, was that Menzies' so-called wit was employed solely to ridicule people, and sprang from sheer arrogance.

An insight into Menzies' own sense of humour was given soon after he returned from England in 1937. He attended a convention of young U.A.P. members on the south coast of New South Wales, and among several members of the Federal Parliament present was Bill McCall.

McCall, who was very friendly with his deputy leader, had a habit of pouring large quantities of olive oil over his food and on cold train trips between Sydney and Canberra, a distance of 200 miles, he always carried a flask of hot Ovaltine.

As they sat at lunch at the convention Menzies, from the head of the table, said to the group, "I'll tell you a story. You know, Bill," looking at McCall, "I sometimes wake up at night with the horrors. I see Bill McCall in a bad dream with liquids pouring through him. They happen to be olive oil and Ovaltine."

Everybody laughed, including Bill McCall. Then he thought he'd have a crack back at Bob. Looking at the menu which carried the names of the U.A.P. hosts from Canberra he saw the newly-gained letters P.C., for Privy Councillor, after the deputy leader's name.

"Ah," he exclaimed. "P.C. This means something. Bob has been elevated. He's been made a probationary constable!"

Everybody laughed loudly. Everybody but one. The laughter died away nervously as they realized Bob was not amused.

When silence fell, he said with measured disdain: *"Not* very funny." The rejoinder completely demolished McCall, who was only trying to make a joke.

Menzies had a good sense of humour provided the joke was on someone else. Time and again he showed he could dish it out, but not take it.

But there were many times when Menzies entered into the spirit of things and enjoyed fun, particularly with Pressmen of the time.

In Canberra he often popped into hotels, where Pressmen were staying, for a drink with the boys. He liked to swap stories and match his ability as a raconteur with any who cared to join in from the Press gallery.

He was a first-class mimic; sometimes a pretty cruel one. One of his best efforts was to impersonate Billy Hughes' story of how Lord Forrest, the first Australian politician to be elevated to the peerage, became a peer. You could swear you were listening to Billy Hughes in all his colour and wit.

But Menzies often mimicked Hughes, and other people he didn't like, in a less kindly mood, and this was not appreciated by all the boys of the Press gallery.

On one occasion Menzies went in to the Hotel Canberra on his way home from Government House. He called in on the room occupied by the Sydney *Daily Telegraph* representative, Massey Stanley, for whom he had a great regard and who he knew was throwing a small party.

Menzies was dressed in a dinner jacket and starched shirt, and Stanley attacked him almost at once about his attire. Menzies would join in this sort of thing, relishing an encounter in which he might score with a witty remark. Any politician who ventured into a journalists' party at that stage must have expected a few home truths.

Massey Stanley accused him of aping Stanley Melbourne Bruce and told him if he continued along that path he would intensify the poor opinion which people had of him. Massey kept on insisting that Menzies was over-ambitious and was making his pace too fast. Bob defended himself and the repartee was quite amusing.

Stanley repeatedly poked his finger into Menzies' chest, declaring several times: "You'll never bloody well be Prime Minister, you'll never be the bloody Prime Minister." And as his finger jabbed, his cigarette burned a hole in the Attorney General's shirt front.

Unperturbed, his corpulent posterior resting on the wash basin and with a glass in one hand, the Attorney General flicked out the flames on his smouldering shirt front and replied: "I think I'll reverse that prophecy, Massey. I'll prove you wrong." That was in 1937 or 1938.

In this period many Pressmen used to visit Bob and Pattie Menzies in their holiday home at Mount Macedon, about 40 miles out of Melbourne. Menzies had bought the home, set in the midst of mountain bushlands, some years before as a week-end retreat and as a spot where the health of his son Kenneth might improve.

The house had been owned by Lady Clarke. It was old and had run to seed, was not lavishly furnished, and obviously the young Menzies couple were going to do something about it.

Although making a good deal of money through his occasional legal appearances, Menzies gave no impression of having much wealth. He always had a good supply of liquor around and he and Pattie, both splendid hosts, served up drinks in odd glasses.

Many people spent the week-end there, among them journalists like Harold Austin of *The Age,* Doug Gardener of the *Sydney Morning Herald,* and others from Canberra, and they often played tennis with Bob. Menzies at the time was making a point of getting to know people, and journalists found him very stimulating company.

An interesting aside around this time is that Menzies did not have a high regard for Churchill. Privately he used to say that Churchill was no statesman because he lacked judgment. He had made too many mistakes, such as at Gallipoli. A fact which Menzies would admit today, but no doubt adding the rider that "it was a long time ago."

A significant factor in the development of Menzies in the days when he was Attorney General is that not only did he have to struggle against resentment and dislike from within his own ranks, but he also had to make his way against a catchcry that he was a Fascist.

In this respect Menzies got off to an inauspicious start right from the time he became Attorney General. Within a month or two of his assuming office the Kisch case broke around his ears. The Duke of Gloucester had been invited to open the session of the Federal Parliament and to attend the celebrations for the 100th anniversary of Melbourne towards the end of 1934.

To coincide with the Melbourne celebrations a number of important Britishers were invited to attend, among them Sir Maurice Hankey, Secretary of the Committee of Imperial Defence; Field-Marshal Lord Milne, the British Army's mechanization expert; and Sir John Cadman who had organized British and Australian petroleum supplies in the first World War.

Naturally enough, the Communists and extreme left-wingers in Australia (there were about 70,000 Communist votes in Australian elections at the time), having in mind the growing tenseness of the world situation with the crisis in China, the Japanese threat to Russia and Manchuria, and the war between Bolivia and Paraguay in South America saw the Melbourne celebrations as a chauvinistic pageant of the imperialists. "A great patriotic and military display to attempt to re-establish the war-like sentiments in the minds of the people, disillusioned by the experiences following the first imperialist world war."

They played on the theme that before the eyes of 300,000 or so unemployed on the relief work pittance or the dole, tens of thousands of pounds were to be spent on decorations, displays, parties, an air race, and ceremonies by the very people who, for years, had said that no further money could be spent on relieving the conditions of the unemployed or to restore the depreciated wages of the working class. The situation was ripe for a fruitful protest. Miners on the south coast of New South Wales expressed themselves by demanding payment for a holiday proclaimed on the Duke's arrival.

The World Committee against War and Fascism decided to send the famous author, Egon Kisch, to represent it at a week-long anti-war congress organized in Melbourne to coincide with the centenary celebrations. The New Zealand movement was to send Gerald Griffin to Australia as its representative. Kisch, a cultured man, also intended to collect material for a book on Australia.

The Lyons Government refused to allow the men to land. Under the Immigration laws Griffin was given a dictation test, but as it was deliberately given in Dutch and he could not pass it, he was sent back to New Zealand. He returned immediately, and landed illegally by jumping from his ship. Kisch also jumped ashore from his ship but broke his leg and these events brought the issue before the public.

While the police searched high and low for Griffin he bobbed up in Melbourne and addressed a big crowd, and a similar protest meeting in the Sydney Domain was described by the *Sydney Morning Herald* as "an amazing one." Indeed, the campaign around Kisch and Griffin reached such proportions that newspapers at the time relegated the Duke of Gloucester and the grasshopper plague to the back pages. Embarrassed police and parliamentarians claimed that Griffin was being impersonated.

The case for deportation went before the High Court and Kisch won against the Federal Attorney General and the Government. Kisch and Griffin spoke to big meetings throughout Australia, attracting vastly more attention than if they had been allowed to land in the first place.

The case, to put it mildly, did little to enhance Menzies' standing as a progressive Liberal and Attorney General.

Then came the Freer case at the end of 1936. This, too, helped create an impression that Menzies, along with other Ministers in the Cabinet, was repressive. Details briefly were that a British subject, Mrs M. M. Freer, was prohibited under immigration laws from landing in Australia without any reason being given. She was allowed to land in New Zealand.

Then it transpired, as the case reached a point of public controversy in the Press and Parliament, that Mrs Freer had been banned purely because of her domestic circumstances by one man. This was the Minister for the Interior, Mr Paterson, who had not consulted Cabinet. The Minister took this action on information from a letter which was unofficial and from an interested party, and, according to his opponents, without even checking it.

When the Minister realized the public was demanding the facts he asked Cabinet to support him in a refusal to release them, and Cabinet made its conspiratorial decision to stick to a colleague while the Prime Minister was absent—in short, they realized a blunder had been made and tried to cover up.

The case finally resolved in favour of Mrs Freer, who was allowed into Australia. This was mainly due to a determined stand by one Government member: Bill McCall. Menzies, on one occasion, no doubt acting on instructions from the Prime Minister, asked McCall if he would drop his challenge to Cabinet on the issue, and received an emphatic "No." Widespread feeling mounted in Australia against the Attorney General and other Ministers, at what was considered to be an act of despotism.

Around 1938 the nickname "Ming" came into general use. This was partly through the Scottish custom of pronouncing Menzies' name as Meeng-us and partly through a repulsive comic-strip character of the time called Ming the Merciless. While Menzies' supporters called him Ming with some affection, his enemies and critics took delight in using the full comic-strip title.

Then came the appellation, Pig-Iron Bob.

This name, by which Menzies was to be known in many parts of the world, grew out of a dispute at Port Kembla, south of Sydney, when wharf labourers refused to load 23,000 tons of pig iron for Japan which was then waging war on China. The Government claimed it was Government policy to load the pig iron because of its trade contract with Japan, but the men, conscientiously believing that the pig iron would be used for bombs to be rained on the innocent Chinese, refused.

Through its Attorney General the Government introduced economic sanctions against the men through the Transport Workers Act, or Dog Collar Act as the wharf labourers called it, and the whole port ground to a halt with about 10,000 men out of work.

The League of Nations determined that Japan had resorted to war against China. On 16 September 1938, the League was told that 1,000,000 Chinese had been killed in the war and that about 30,000,000 Chinese had lost their homes or worldly possessions. The Japanese Air Force had made more than 2,000 attacks on open towns in China killing 100,000 and destroying 90,000 buildings.

Japan was not a member of the League of Nations, but China was. And legal minds argued that Australia as a member was bound by a League covenant to sever all trade and financial relations with Japan, a belligerent.

The dispute began at the end of 1938 when the first of three shipments of pig iron for Japan were to be loaded on a British tramp vessel, the *Dalfram*. The shipments amounted to 23,000 tons, and the wharf labourers learnt that Japan had contracts for 300,000 tons of pig iron altogether.

The secretary of the Port Kembla branch of the Waterside Workers Federation, Ted Roach, checked the intended cargo and learnt it was going to Kobe. The British and Lascar seamen then walked off, and the watersiders advised their employers that they objected to loading pig iron for the potential enemy of Australia. They expressed the opinion that pig iron to Japan could mean bombs on Australian cities.

The watersiders wanted to work on other ships but the employers after a few days decided that if they wouldn't load the pig iron, they couldn't work the other ships. Then the situation hotted up and nationwide attention was focused on the dispute.

Representatives of the men went to Canberra on the invitation of the Attorney General and conferred with him and the leader of the Labor Opposition, John Curtin. Ted Roach recalls that Curtin was even more dogmatic than Menzies.

Roach today says of that interview: "Curtin lay back on a big green divan, his hands under his head, staring into the ceiling. He spoke to us as though we were a team of naughty boys and said, 'If there was a Labor Government in power you would still have to load the pig iron. It is Government policy.'

"Bob Menzies became very upset when we told him we would not load the pig iron to a potentially hostile neighbour. He said it was the Government's policy and he would ensure it was carried out—he would not allow a group of unionists to dictate policy to the Government."

In Port Kembla police searched for the Lascars and British seamen who left the ship to show solidarity with the wharf labourers, and who were now technically illegal immigrants. Wharf labourers and their families kept moving them from house to house.

Various meetings were held at which a British seaman, and sometimes a Lascar would appear, make a speech and disappear again. The Lascars would speak only a few broken sentences but with strong effect. For instance at one meeting in the Sydney suburb of Balmain, a Lascar said: "Me very poor. Coloured. No pig iron for Japan!" and brought the house down. All other unions supported the wharf labourers and the stevedoring authority could not get labour from anywhere to man the ship. Moral and financial support poured in from many parts of Australia.

In desperation the Federal Attorney General declared Port Kembla a Transport Workers Act port, which meant everybody had to be registered to be employed and penalties imposed on those who refused to obey Government instructions. Workers had to pay one shilling to take out a licence.

Notices appeared in the Press and signboards went up notifying the workers to take out licences. But only one licence was issued—a member of the Port Kembla waterside workers branch bought his licence, then ceremoniously burnt it, with photographs of the burning appearing in the Press next day.

Then a Government Under-secretary named Lawson bobbed up in Port Kembla without warning, wanting to have a discussion with the watersiders' executive. He said he was in a hurry as he had to catch a plane to Melbourne from Sydney that evening at eight o'clock.

The Under-secretary was told: "Well, don't let us stop you. Catch your plane. We can get the executive together tomorrow morning, not before." He stayed—and the meeting was held next morning.

At the meeting all those purporting to come from the executive were introduced to the Government Under-secretary by name only. Mr Lawson did not realize that one man present, Bob Allan, was the south coast representative of the *Labor Daily* and that the notes he was furiously taking were not the minutes of the meeting, but for a sensational report in the next day's paper.

Finding himself outnumbered in debate the Under-secretary, after a discussion on the ethics and principles involved in the dispute, said: "I can understand the stand being made by your union while the world stands aghast at the atrocities being committed in China." When the Under-secretary asked Ted Roach if they could issue a joint statement, Roach replied it would be better if they made individual statements.

Next day a lengthy report of what went on appeared in the *Labor Daily* under the headline, "Lawson woos the Wharfies."

Repudiations followed quickly from Canberra about atrocities in China.

The Government was in a dilemma and Menzies decided he would go down to Port Kembla himself and beard the lions in their den. By now something like 10,000 men were out of work, and the steelworks were shut down and deserted except for a skeleton staff.

Those out of work were not suffering any hardship, because an all-out effort had been organized—co-operatives were set up all over the place and market gardens were providing fruit and vegetables.

On the day the Attorney General was to visit, wharfies, miners, and others declared an unofficial holiday from school for their children to "welcome Mr Menzies."

Two roads lead to Port Kembla, forking from the top of Bulli

Pass, and to ensure a decent "welcome" for the Attorney General the unionists had to know which road he was to take. A motor cyclist on a hot 4¼-horsepower Norton was stationed at the top of the Pass to race ahead on whatever road the Attorney General took, so that placard bearers could bustle into place.

A cat-and-mouse game followed in which Canberra officials, in telephone conversation to Port Kembla, altered the time of arrival of the Attorney General several times, obviously to disorganize the welcoming preparations.

But when Menzies drove down the Pass the motor cyclist roared ahead at breakneck speed and alerted the banner bearers. And all the way along the mining towns leading into Wollongong men, women, and children greeted him with slogans and hostile banners such as , "No Pig Iron for Japan!" "No Dog Collars for Wharfies!" and of course, "Pig-Iron Bob!"

In the main street of the South Coast city of Wollongong, where a luncheon had been arranged at the Wollongong Hotel, traffic could not move because of the blockage of people all carrying placards. A wharf labourer placed himself on point duty like a policeman and began directing traffic away from the area. There was even a dog in the act, a short-legged black half-breed named Mungo, who also carried a placard, "No Dog Collars."

As the luncheon drew to an end Inspector Rosa, who was in charge of the police, called through a loudspeaker for Ted Roach.

"Is there going to be any trouble?" asked Inspector Rosa.

"We're not here for any trouble," replied Roach. "We're not out to make trouble. We're just here to welcome the Attorney General."

"Look, as he finishes his lunch, would you be prepared to move through the crowds ahead of Mr Menzies and make a pathway through them?"

"Certainly."

When Menzies came out of the hotel to move across the street to the Town Hall for the important discussion, Ted Roach walked ahead to make a pathway. Women and children, with banners and placards on sticks, poked them at the Attorney General and shouted their defiance. Press photographs next day showed the Attorney General with a worried expression on his face.

While the meeting went on inside, one took place outside, rowdier, of course. People were slipping in and out of the meeting in the Town Hall to give those outside a report of proceeding. Little progress was made at the conference and Menzies departed to a spirited farewell and cries of, among other things, "Pig-Iron Bob."

At one stage of the dispute the Government considered bringing in outside labour to load the *Dalfram,* but with such a weight of public opinion against them this move was scrapped as being far too provocative.

While this consideration was thought to be a possibility, groups of unionists kept watch on the *Dalfram* around the clock to see what was happening. At one point the Master of the *Dalfram* turned the ship's propellor over as a boat load of wharf labourers were rowing around the stern, and this action was angrily resented.

While the *Dalfram* dispute raged, efforts were made to transport the bulk of the 23,000 tons of pig iron to Sydney for loading on to the other two ships in the contract. A small amount of pig iron did reach Sydney, but through co-operation with the Railways and other unions, the watersiders were able to prevent the rest being shipped or transported from Port Kembla; it was a community effort, and with the whole of the Wollongong area on their side, not a thing happened that the watersiders didn't know about.

These watersiders were accustomed to fighting for their rights. Up to 1936 working conditions on the waterfront in the Wollongong area were practically non-existent; there was no roster system, and while some unionists might get 24 hours work straight, others would stand around for 24 hours waiting unsuccessfully for a job, and without appearance money. They even had to take their own shovels aboard when working a ship.

These things were only bad memories at the time of the pig iron dispute, but the organization they built up in fighting for better conditions helped them in the *Dalfram* trouble. And the support of the public encouraged them to challenge the full might of the Government.

After about two months the Government and Attorney General Menzies were gravely embarrassed, and getting nowhere. Articles began appearing in some newspapers, particularly the *Sydney Morning Herald,* which were obvious kite-fliers or feelers, prompted from Canberra. They suggested, as a possible term of settlement, that if the current shipment of 23,000 tons was despatched the question of further shipments making up the 300,000-ton contract might be considered "in the light of the watersiders' objection."

It was on this basis that after about ten weeks the dispute was finally settled—the watersiders did not win outright, but they compromised and won a point, the 23,000 tons, but no more, being shipped.

An extraordinary dispute, as it was not one for better wages or working conditions or one involving party politics, but a struggle by a group of men and their families against the right of the State to violate individual conscience.

All types of organizations supported the watersiders and miners, with donations coming in even from pensioners. The Australian community as a whole was behind them. Certainly that dispute did more to undermine public confidence in a Liberal Government, and caused more damage to the image of Menzies, than anything else in Australia up to that time.

The Parliamentary Labor Party and the Labor leagues and branches everywhere were part of the movement against Menzies and his supporters, in spite of what Labor leader John Curtin said to the watersiders, and in spite of Curtin's action earlier that year in complaining to the Federal Government on behalf of his own State (Western Australia), that they had been refused permission to supply the Japanese with shipments of iron ore from Yampi Sound in the West.

Later the waterside workers received an officially stamped document signed by thirty-eight trade unions and cultural organizations in China thanking them, and the people of Australia, for their stand in helping the Chinese.

Sir Isaac Isaacs early in 1939 published a thesis on the pig iron dispute in which he honoured the men in their stand for the whole of the Australian community, and strongly deprecated the Government for what he termed one of the most regrettable episodes in the whole history of executive government in Australia.

Isaacs, an outstanding legal mind, who was first a member of the Victorian, then the Federal Government, and later the first Australian-born Governor General in history, was a member of the committee which drafted the Commonwealth Constitution. In 1930 he was Chief Justice of Australia.

Sir Isaac expressed the considered view that it was wholly contrary to British democracy to coerce a private citizen to do something not required of him by law but simply because it assisted the policy of the Government. That, he said, was a dictator's rule.

No industrial tribunal could decide such a dispute because it was Government policy versus individual conscience. What policy of Government, Sir Isaac asked, was entitled to coerce a man by the whip of starvation if he declined to take part in an action which he thought was conducive to inhumanity?

Sir Isaac said the Government's official estimation as set out by the Prime Minister was gravely disappointing. As a sop by way of appeasement it was both humiliating and futile. "And," he said, "when we remember we are told that peace is hanging by a thread, it even becomes conceivably dangerous to ourselves. The Prime Minister's latest broadcast in his reference to Japan gives excellent reasons for not stocking them up with ammunitions."

Sir Isaac said Australia had broken the customary right and the duty of neutrality, that she could have stopped exporting the pig iron not as an unfriendly act but as a normal sovereign act under international law, provided she remained impartial to both belligerents.

Testing that part of the Government's explanation which said it would be discrimination to single out one commodity and one nation which would be contrary to the Government's policy of preserving and maintaining friendly relations with all countries, and further that such an act might be fraught with grave consequences in the then unsettled state of the world, Sir Isaac pointed out that in this case the word "commodity" referred to pig iron which was for war purposes.

In effect, he said, the Government's policy was not to preserve friendly relations with all countries—certainly not with China which happened to be weak—because perfect neutrality could not be construed as an unfriendly act. When it took sides and intervened to compel the loading, the Government had been guilty of a "delinquency," offending against both the constitutional right of individual conscience and the recognized legal duty of neutrality.

"Is Australia afraid to stand up for her rights, her duty, and her honour?" he asked. "If what is happening is only a dispute, what would the Government require to make a war?"

Sir Isaac computed that from the 23,000 tons of pig iron there could be fashioned over 100,000 high-explosive bombs of more than 250 lb each, or more than 1,000,000 incendiary bombs of 50 lb each, according to whether the main object was the slaughter of population or destruction of property.

Dealing with the Government's statement that pig iron was comparable to wheat and other articles, he said it was in fact more comparable to shells, bombs, and chemicals for poison gas. The British list of contraband of 2 July 1917, had included iron, lead, and a long list of ordinary articles as absolute contraband which could assist a belligerent.

Sir Isaac Isaacs wound up his assessment with these words: "I conclude my consideration of this most unpleasant incident with unbounded admiration for the struggle for humanity and the freedom of conscience.

"I believe that Port Kembla with its studied, but peaceful and altogether disinterested attitude of the men concerned, will find a place in our history beside the Eureka Stockade with its more violent resistance of a less settled time, as a noble stand against executive dictatorship and against an attack on Australian democracy."

Bob Menzies was only one of the Cabinet members who made the decisions but as Attorney General he played a leading role. The name Pig-Iron Bob stuck to him and he was extremely sensitive of it for many years, constantly referring to it and even making a joke out of it as though it did not affect him, claiming it wasn't pig iron anyway, but scrap iron.

Ted Roach has the last word on that: "It was pig iron, all right. I lumped too much of it not to know. *Bob wouldn't know.*"

A few months after the Nazis occupied Austria in March 1938, and Anthony Eden resigned from the British Cabinet in protest against the policy of appeasement, Menzies made an overseas tour. He returned in mid-September and pointed out that having had the advantage of contact in London, Paris, and Berlin he was "disposed to discount the significance of German military demonstrations against Czechoslovakia."

He considered the state of Europe "in reality more balanced than it was six months ago." Even after the Czech crisis his faith in appeasement was not shaken; he still believed the door of negotiation should be kept "wide open."

In a broadcast on the international situation early in 1939 Menzies said he could see "no sufficient cause for anything approaching panic."

The *Sydney Morning Herald* criticized the Attorney General for this statement, saying there was no panic in Australia but a firm resolve borne of recent tragic and alarming events to make Australia ready for war; Mr Menzies' comfortable words, said the *Herald,* would have carried more conviction if in the past he had proved a sounder guide to European affairs.

The newspaper said: "It is difficult to negotiate with or appease a Hitler who has consistently refused to say what he wants, but whose policy has made it starkly clear that he is determined to win everything that can be won by violence and chicanery. Mr Menzies' views on the injustices of the Versailles Treaty and the

61

unwisdom of subsequent Franco-British treatment of Germany are familiar enough, and, with some reservations are widely shared.

"But surely it is the business of the democratic world, if it hopes to survive, to face the harsh and dangerous reality of Nazism, not to repine over the Germany that might—or might not—have been."

In some quarters the Attorney General's statements on Germany were distorted and interpreted to mean that he was an admirer of Hitler.

Statements were made publicly and appeared in print about Menzies being the man "whose brilliant military career was suddenly cut short by the outbreak of the world war."

The old story about his not going to the war was exhumed by critics and played up at a time when the Government, of which he was a leading member, was considering conscripting youth for military training, and this gave impetus to the story.

The old frustration for not having enlisted raised its head. Bob Menzies wanted to prove himself even more, to give service, a term he had heard his father use since he was a child.

It had the effect of making him even more determined.

7

The Lyons Government supported Neville Chamberlain and appeasement at the time of the Munich crisis. But its fears over Hitler's intentions were not entirely lulled.

William Morris Hughes, then the Minister for Health and Repatriation, after having had a long exile from Ministerial benches, summed up the Government's views when he said in the House of Representatives on the Munich debate: "We have stood loyally and firmly behind Great Britain, believing that in that way and that way only could peace be preserved. The dark clouds that lay overseas a week ago have for a moment been swept away, but actually nothing is changed. The danger is still there. In a little while the clouds will gather again."

However, John Curtin, the Labor Party leader, criticized the Government over its decision to increase armaments and for taking part in the disputes of Great Britain and Europe. Although he did not reflect the extreme isolationism of previous Labor leaders, he thought Australia should attend to its own affairs but be able to defend itself if an emergency arose.

Australia, of course, was woefully ill-prepared for any kind of a war. She was tied completely to Britain's coat tails, to the idea of sending, in Army nomenclature of the time, so many "bodies" overseas, these to receive their supplies from Britain. The fact of being under Britain's protective wing was criticized many times in Parliament from 1937 onwards by a number of Government members, among them Percy Spender, the new member for Warringah, in Sydney.

Near the end of 1937 the Government, on the recommendation of the Imperial Conference, adopted a policy of building up munitions supplies and of making their own munitions for the first time. Plans for an aircraft industry were devised, tentative plans for war organization of industry and manpower drawn up, and the Royal Military College at Duntroon, Canberra, reopened for the training of Army officers.

But the whole atmosphere was unrealistic.

After Munich the Government did increase its efforts at war preparation. Defence spending in the Federal Budget of 1938-39 for the next three years was £44,500,000, but this was increased to £63,000,000. By the end of 1938 the Minister for Defence, Mr Street, outlined the Government's proposal.

The peace-time establishment was being increased to 70,000 front line troops with an increase in the militia forces. The Air Force was to be increased to 212 front line planes, and pending deliveries from Britain, Avro-Ansons were being lent. The production of Wirraways was being increased and orders had been placed in the United States for fifty Lockheed Hudsons. Strategic aerodromes were being built in many places, and a base was to be provided at Port Moresby for mobile naval and air forces.

By 1940-41 a total of £3,355,000 was to have been spent on munitions production, a plan for industrial mobilization was being surveyed, and a manpower organization had been set up under General Blamey. The Minister emphasized the need for a fleet at Singapore to protect sea communications, with a strong Army and Air Force there.

Coastal and aircraft defences, he said, were being provided in Australia on the scale recommended by the Committee of Imperial Defence. A few months earlier a plan had been worked out with the British Food Controller, Sir Henry French, for the movement of Australian foodstuffs to Britain if war broke out.

But if there was *talk* of a war on the international front there was a *real* war going on within the ranks of the Government. The fight for the Prime Ministership was on.

Rumblings of discontent had been heard for several months up to October 1938, in the U.A.P. and the Country Party. Seven members who had held Ministerial posts in the Government, among them Frederic Stewart, Henry Gullett, Charles Marr, and J. A. Perkins, were now sitting on the back benches.

Some had lost their positions in Cabinet reshuffles, others had resigned because of disagreements. The Country Party, the minority party of the coalition Government, contained some overpowering personalities who played a brand of politics that could only be described as horse trading in order to get their own way.

The real crux of the discontent was a struggle for the leadership. Everyone in Parliament believed Menzies wanted to become Prime Minister and some others, too, were out to improve their status.

The Premier of New South Wales, B. S. Stevens, was named as a contestant for the battle to take over the Prime Ministership, and Sydney newspapers speculated on his proposed entry into the Federal political sphere. However, a reappraisal of the situation today among Federal members of the time indicates that he had no chance.

An influential section of the Melbourne financial aristocracy had the idea that Joe Lyons had out-served his usefulness. He was, in their opinion, after all only a Labor turncoat and this didn't really suit them. He had performed a first-class job for his country through a difficult period, but now they were looking to new blood.

To some of the interests then supporting the U.A.P., Joe Lyons had stayed too long; but to most of Joe's Parliamentary supporters, he couldn't stay long enough.

Menzies by now had the patronage of some wealthy interests behind him. Members were saying he wanted Joe Lyon's job. And there were many supporters in the U.A.P. who felt that he was the ideal man to assume the Prime Minister's role. Those who supported Menzies were of the opinion that with all his ability he was being made to suffer because Joe Lyons was clinging on to power too long.

But Joe Lyons retained a majority of support from his followers, who almost without exception regarded him as being a capable, kindly, and understanding man.

Joe Lyons' health was not good at the begining of October 1938, and in his absence the Government was led by Sir Earle Page, the Country Party leader and a tough, consummate politician. In the following weeks speculation was rife as to what might happen if Lyons were forced to retire.

As Acting Prime Minister, Page, who had just returned from Europe where he saw the war clouds gathering, persuaded the Federal Government to call a meeting of all State Premiers to discuss finance and development, and to decide the urgency of the various works in the light of the war threat.

Page had in mind that an advisory committee should be set up from the best men in the community and with Cabinet approval he approached Essington Lewis, the chief general manager of The Broken Hill Proprietary Company, and several others, who agreed to go on these committees provided their views were heeded. With this promise of assistance Page arranged with the Secretary of the Commerce Department, K. J. Murphy, the Commonwealth Statistician, Roland Wilson, and the Secretary of the Treasury, Stuart McFarlane, to help him draw up a proposal for submission to the Premiers.

The proposal, setting out the best economic means of achieving State and Commonwealth co-operation in national security and the expansion of secondary and primary industries over the next ten years, was sent to the six Premiers. Page, to demonstrate his loyalty to Lyons and believing it was necessary in the dogfight going on, arranged for Lyons to preside over the Premiers' meeting and to deliver the official speech. Lyons agreed with this view, in spite of his poor health.

Page then asked Menzies and R. G. Casey, the Minister for Supply and Development, to help him prepare his speech for the conference. Page later stated that when he told them he had arranged for a Broken Hill Proprietary areoplane to fly Lyons to the meeting in Canberra from his home in Melbourne, Menzies "threw down his pencil and declared that he would not write another word for Lyons to deliver as his own."

Page said that Menzies left it to him and Casey to finish the speech. But by the time the Prime Minister was due to arrive they had not finished it. When he met Lyons at the airport he explained the details of his proposal, and just before the conference opened handed the Prime Minister about half the completed text, advising him to read it slowly while the rest was typed and handed to him slip by slip as he addressed the meeting.

Page wrote later that Menzies adopted an aloof attitude at the conference, which ended without practical results. Lyons declined to accept any amendments, and no council was set up to plan the development of industries and migration.

A few days later the internal power struggle in the Party erupted to public notice. Addressing a meeting of the Constitutional Association in Sydney, which was attended by several members of Cabinet, Menzies gave a talk on leadership. As he was deputy-leader of the U.A.P. his remarks were interpreted as an overt attack on his own leader. Many Party members commented that they regarded it as a "stab in the back."

Joe Lyons was deeply hurt by the public and Party members' discussion over these remarks, so much so that he suggested to Page that he might help him and the Government if he made a speech on leadership in a forthcoming scheduled broadcast.

Page was concerned because the Country Party was wondering whether it could continue its alliance with a Party which was so clearly riven by personal and political issues, so he agreed to do so. Page had great respect for Lyons, and in his broadcast he paid tribute to his qualities of leadership, supporting them with details from his distinguished career in State and Federal politics.

The Labor Opposition wasted no time in capitalizing on the split and on 2 November 1938, Curtin moved a censure motion in the House of Representatives against the Government's "lamentable want of leadership in regard to urgent national problems" and failure to implement the plans discussed ⁿᵗ the State Premiers' meeting.

Joe Lyons is said to have confided to some of his intimates that in his efforts to stay in office he had had to break up a partnership between Menzies and R. G. Casey, the Melbourne blueblood who had graduated from Cambridge University with honours in mechanical science, and who won a Military Cross in the first World War.

Lyons is reported to have said that Menzies and Casey had ganged up on him and he was determined to break the partnership. Lyons is alleged to have told Casey he had him in mind as his natural successor and that he intended nominating him for elevation to the Privy Council.

Reports circulating in the lobby and among Pressmen in Canberra at the time intimated that a great coolness subsequently developed between Menzies and Casey. Casey was appointed to the Privy Council in 1939.

A distinguished parliamentary source of the time discloses that the rows in Cabinet about this time were furious. He reveals that little was accomplished in Cabinet during this period because Menzies would occupy a great deal of time in baiting and arguing with the Country Party ministers such as Thorby, Hunter, and Paterson. Lyons in desperation used to leave the Cabinet Room because of Menzies' conduct.

Sir Earle Page wrote later that at the end of the 1938 session of Parliament Menzies sought him out for an intimate talk. During a car trip from Canberra to Sydney, Menzies told him he felt that for some reason he was out of step in Cabinet, often finding himself voting in opposition to all other ministers. Did he think Menzies should retire from the Government and from politics entirely?

Page wrote: "He said that the opportunity had arisen to secure a high appointment of great distinction for life and he wished my advice whether he should accept or remain in politics. I urged him to remain . . .

"I instanced that only two doctors of eminence had entered Federal politics during my term and that since the Parliament had transferred from Melbourne to Canberra in 1927, only four distinguished lawyers had been elected. If Menzies retired, having held high office in State and Federal Parliament, his action would tend to discourage other political aspirants of like quality.

"I suggested that his difficulty seemed to be that he expected 150 per cent reaction from other people in politics, whereas one did well to secure 50 per cent. Sir Austin Chapman after forty years in politics, was even less generous. He considered himself lucky if he got 20 per cent.

"I pointed out that every section of the community was represented by the various men who comprised the Cabinet. If they agreed in general then there was a good chance that the people would accept their decisions as sound. If we were to arrange a dinner to which each diner contributed something, it would be a good dinner if Lyons brought the roast beef, I brought the vegetables, someone else the pudding and Menzies the champagne. But if everyone brought champagne it might be a bright party but would scarcely be regarded as a sustaining meal.

"Menzies admitted that he had never thought of Cabinet in that way. He decided to reconsider the whole question and wire me his decision on Christmas Eve. He duly telegraphed me that he would carry on as a member of the Government and remain in Parliament. When, early in the New Year, Lyons arranged a Cabinet tour of Tasmania, Menzies accompanied the party and worked harmoniously with his colleagues both on the tour and in the Cabinet."

Then, without warning, Menzies resigned. He resigned his Ministerial post and his position as deputy leader of the U.A.P.

That was on 14 March 1939, the day Hitler's troops marched into Czechoslovakia. It was an extraordinary decision, especially in view of the possibility that Australia could have been at war that night.

Ostensibly his reason was Cabinet's decision to repeal certain provisions of the National Insurance Act, to which he was committed.

The *Sydney Morning Herald* in an editorial, after pointing out that Menzies had delayed his resignation until the last possible moment, knowing it must have been deeply embarrassing to the Prime Minister and Government, declared: "Mr Menzies entered Federal politics and the Lyons Ministry with a brilliant State record and every augury for advancement to the highest political post in the Commonwealth.

"If he did not fulfil all the expectations of his admirers, and if it seemed sometimes as if success and political preferment had come to him too easily, the action which he took yesterday shows that he possesses what is becoming increasingly rare in public life —a devotion to principle and a refusal to cling to office when convictions, strongly and honestly held, counsel a contrary course.

"For that example the public everywhere will honour him. It will also discern in Mr Menzies those qualities of courage and determination which are the blood and bone of true leadership."

However, some saw Menzies' reason in a different light. Many political discussions were dominated by a belief that his real reason was frustration at Lyons' refusal to step down, that he intended to challenge Lyons for the leadership, and the challenge was to be a test of strength between the traditional right-wing Conservatives—the backbone of the U.A.P.—and the group represented by Lyons as a former Labor man. Some influential Melbourne people were of the opinion that Lyons did not go along entirely with their views because of his old Labor principles.

Among other disgruntled members who were critical of the U.A.P. leadership were the former Ministers for Trade and Customs, Mr Thomas White and Sir Henry Gullett, both of whom left the Ministry in an atmosphere of bitterness. White had resigned over a petty thing—the order of precedence at a Government House function.

Sir Frederic Stewart, another former Minister, was far from satisfied with the Government's policy on social questions, particularly national insurance.

Percy Spender, a King's Counsel, was seen as the obvious choice to succeed Menzies.

A great deal of work had gone into the National Insurance scheme and it was frustrating to the majority of Government members to see it take so long to be introduced. As early as 1937 Sir Ralph Kinnear and Sir Godfrey Ince, who produced the British National Insurance Scheme, came to Australia as advisers, to help prevent the recurrence of defects which had occurred in the British scheme.

Menzies fought strenuously in Cabinet, early in 1939, for retention of the scheme approved by Parliament at the end of the previous year. But a section of Cabinet, headed by Sir Earle Page, pressed for modification and Menzies and his supporters were finally overruled. The fact was that Page and Casey were the only ones who had shown real interest in the scheme right throughout.

After his resignation, Menzies issued a statement saying: "The Prime Minister would be the first to agree that my allegiance to him could not very well be counted upon as breach of faith on my part.

"On the strength of a declaration by the Treasurer, Mr Casey, on 8 December that 'National insurance will definitely be proceeded with' and with a view to answering what I considered ill-founded criticism, I circularized thousands of my electors stating among other things: 'I am so utterly convinced of the essential qualities of National Insurance that I am prepared to incur any quantity of temporary unpopularity to see it made effective. I am not unaware of the manner in which certain interests which would seek to defeat me, or to take my place in the representation of Kooyong, are using National Insurance against me. I stand by National Insurance and I say that a defeat in defending it would, in my opinion, be an honourable one.'

"It is clear that I cannot, with self respect, abandon today what I wrote only a few weeks ago. I am bound, not only by my real belief that the best interests of Australia would be served by going on with the scheme, but by my categorical statement to my constituents.

"I make no cheap criticism of the position of the Prime Minister or any other of my colleagues. In particular, I make no attack upon my friend and colleague the Treasurer, who has worked manfully on this matter. Each of us must determine his own line of action according to his own rights and obligations.

"It might possibly have afforded me a way out of this impasse if I had been able sincerely to state that the carrying out of a defence programme rendered necessary the postponement or abandonment of National Insurance. But the facts are that on 8 December when the Government's insurance announcement was made, our new three-year defence programme of £63,000,000 had been approved by Parliament.

"By 24 January the financial effects of the drought on the current financial prospects were known. No new financial circumstances have arisen since 24 January which could possibly release me from statements made on that date.

"The funds which are created under national insurance are not spirited away from the country. The bulk of them amounting to nearly £10,000,000 a year during the next few years, would have constituted a community fund which would have been available for investment in public loans for defence purposes. These are the reasons for my resignation."

Three days later the man who held one of the three most important posts in the Federal Government, the man regarded as one of the best intellects and debaters ever to appear in Parliament and who on a visit to England in 1938 had been described by the *Sunday Times* as "an inevitable Prime Minister," resumed his legal career in Melbourne and took a back bench in Canberra.

Two weeks later, after an absence of nearly three years from the Courts, he made his reappearance in the High Court presided over by the Chief Justice, Sir John Latham, who had preceded him both as Federal Member for Kooyong and as Federal Attorney General.

Menzies appeared as senior counsel for the respondent in a case relating to letters patent on the use of containers for jelly crystals.

8

Working behind the scenes at the end of March 1939, Joe Lyons put out feelers for a combined Ministry from the three Parties represented in Parliament as a possible means of overcoming the crisis and staying in power.

Sir Earle Page gave his approval for the move on behalf of the Country Party. But John Curtin refused for Labor.

In the face of the pressures that had built up, Lyons decided to resign. But he was waiting for the U.A.P. and the Country Party to find a position for him before he announced his decision.

However, while waiting for his position to be resolved and before the public or Press had any hint that the Prime Minister intended stepping down, he collapsed, and died in St Vincent's Hospital, Sydney, on 7 April.

On the Tuesday night two days before his death, Lyons attended a Cabinet meeting in Canberra, then travelled to Sydney in the evening. On Wednesday about 10 a.m. he told Page he did not feel well enough to attend a luncheon to mark the opening of the Royal Easter Show and asked him to take his place. That day he was admitted to the hospital with what appeared to be a severe chill.

The next day, accompanied by the Treasurer, R. G. Casey, Page visited Lyons who appeared to be much better. Lyons' doctors believed he had a very reasonable chance of recovering quickly.

About ten minutes after leaving the hospital at 1 p.m. and arriving home, Page was called back to the hospital. Joe Lyons had become unconscious from a heart attack. His wife, Dame Enid Lyons, was also called to the hospital and until he died early next morning he was unconscious most of the time, but was occasionally able to recognize her.

The Governor General, Lord Gowrie, spoke to Sir Earle Page on the afternoon Lyons collapsed, to ask if he could get some advice on whom the Prime Minister wished to nominate as his successor. Two doctors told Lord Gowrie that that was impossible.

And when he died no advice had been given to the Governor General, by the only person constitutionally able to do it, as to whom the new Prime Minister should be. The position then was that the U.A.P. which was in Government with the Country Party, was left without a leader or a deputy leader.

The Prime Minister's death not only shocked the nation, it caused bitterness and distress in Parliamentary circles, in the confusion that followed.

Before losing consciousness, Joe Lyons had some hard things to say about certain of his colleagues, and these remarks were discreetly repeated around the Parliamentary lobbies.

The Lyons family, particularly Dame Enid, was bitter towards the former Federal Attorney General. She alleged to a number of people that Menzies had not been loyal to the Prime Minister.

Sir Earle Page, himself a doctor, wrote later that the crisis in Joe Lyons' political relations and the severe strain of international events caused him great mental perturbation, and undoubtedly hastened his end.

A Parliamentary official told this writer that in his opinion Menzies' tactics had turned Lyons into a nervous wreck.

"I talked to him and had a drink with him a few hours before his collapse," he said, "and I saw that he was in a highly emotional state, and desperate."

The death of Joseph Aloysius Lyons, Australia's "financial recovery" leader, from worry and exhaustion on a Good Friday within a few days of a record term of office, showed how mean a nation could be towards its chief executive.

Lyons, who died in his early fifties, was not a wealthy man, leaving only a few hundred pounds in his bank account. When the Lyons' estate was sworn, Dame Enid and her eleven children had nothing, apart from outstanding salary and reimbursement of expenses, but their cottage in Devonport, Tasmania.

And added to the bereavement of the Lyons family was the humiliation of a wrangle in Parliament over the Government's £1,000 a year pension proposal. It was a field day of sordid, provincial malice.

James Scullin was another example of a Prime Minister being repaid with little more than prestige for the burden of office because of the absence of a proper pension plan. Scullin, Prime Minister from October 1929 to November 1931, was overwhelmed by the Depression immediately he took office, and legislatively crippled by a hostile Senate. His hair turned snow white half way through his term, and within three years his health was broken.

Such was the price these men paid for getting to the top of "the greasy pole."

The death of Lyons meant a renewed contest for the Prime Ministership.

Sir Earle, as deputy Prime Minister, immediately called together the Ministers available in Sydney at noon on Friday, 7 April, to discuss the constitutional procedure. Billy Hughes, who had succeeded to Menzies' portfolio of Attorney General, was of the opinion that the Prime Minister's death meant that the commissions of all Ministers automatically lapsed.

As the U.A.P. had no deputy leader he considered that the Governor General should be advised to ask Page to form a Government with full authority. Hughes recommended this because he felt that a Government with full power was needed to deal with the critical international situation. All Ministers agreed.

Page called on Lord Gowrie and told him he would accept a commission only if it were free of all undertakings, and the Governor General agreed that he could form a Government on this basis. The coalition of the Country Party and U.A.P. was maintained and no changes were made in the Cabinet.

But Page laid down two conditions to Cabinet in accepting the Governor General's commission. One was that as soon as the U.A.P. had chosen a leader he would not be prepared to go on as Prime Minister. The second, and most important was that if Menzies was elected leader of the U.A.P., he would refuse to remain a member of Cabinet.

In this way Page expected to exclude Menzies from the Prime Ministership, and, of course, he hoped that with his following he might somehow retain the role himself, although his main objective was to obstruct Menzies.

The Page Government took office on 7 April 1939.

Page wrote later that he felt that if Menzies should be elected leader of the U.A.P., he could not recommend to his Party to place itself in pawn with a Prime Minister who he believed could not achieve the necessary stability of Government to effectively approach the pressing problems of a coming war.

The immediate period that followed was one of confusion and frenzied organizing behind the scenes. When it became obvious that Menzies intended standing for leadership of the U.A.P. and, if elected, would automatically become Prime Minister on the basis that it was customary for the leader of the numerically strongest Party to assume the role, Sir Earle and his supporters got busy trying to arrange a solution to what was, to them, a distasteful situation.

Curtin made it plain that the Labor Party would not join in a National Government, but said he was prepared to support a Government led by Page until that session of Parliament ran out in eighteen months, on condition that conscription was not introduced. Page knew that such a Government, lacking its own majority in Parliament, was hardly likely to succeed.

Assisted by R. G. Casey, Sir Earle tried desperately to co-opt as a leader S. M. Bruce, Australia's Resident Minister and High Commissioner in London. Bruce had been Prime Minister from 1923 till 1929, when he lost his Victorian seat of Flinders.

Page felt he had the qualities to fill the role of a national leader—and it could also be a way of keeping Menzies out.

Lord Bruce, who had just visited Australia, was on his way back to England and was now in the United States to see President Roosevelt. In a radio-telephone hook-up between Page, Casey, and Bruce, Page put the proposal that if he consented to return to Australian politics, he would be prepared to stand down and make his own safe seat available to Bruce.

Bruce made it plain that he would return only on the understanding that he would have freedom to form a National Government with representatives of all Parties.

The Parliamentary Country Party met in Canberra on 18 April and carried this resolution: "That in spite of past harmonious co-operation in Government with the United Australia Party and a willingness to continue similar co-operation to maintain stable Government, the Party is definitely unable to co-operate in a Government with the Hon. R. G. Menzies, K.C., as its Prime Minister; nor is it willing to give any undertaking to support such a Government if it be formed."

The following day the U.A.P. met.

While walking from the Hotel Canberra to Parliament House to attend the meeting which had been called to elect a new U.A.P. leader, Menzies fell over and injured one of his arms.

He was taken at once to Canberra Hospital where an elbow was X-rayed. Although he did not suffer any broken bones he was in pain from a severely jarred arm, slightly strained back, and abrasions to one of his knees.

When news of his accident reached the Party meeting it was suspended and resumed later in the day so that he could attend. When he turned up, he carried his right arm in a sling.

Later a joke went around among Party members and journalists that Menzies was in such a hurry to get to the Party meeting and be elected leader that he had tripped over.

Casey outlined the proposal that had been made to Bruce and his reactions, but the Party decided to go ahead and elect a leader.

Billy Hughes had mustered his forces and was a keen contender, as was Menzies. Casey and Thomas White also ran for the leadership, but were defeated in early ballots.

The final result was a narrow win by Menzies over Hughes by twenty-three votes to nineteen.

Taking the bit between his teeth, and expecting to become Prime Minister, Menzies immediately called on Page to ask him about Country Party co-operation. Menzies insisted on the right to pick his Country Party colleagues instead of automatically accepting the Country Party leader's nominations and, at the same time, made it clear that he was not enthusiastic over Bruce's proposed return.

In a heated interview Page told Menzies that neither he nor the Country Party would serve under him, and the wily doctor refused to hand over the reins. A further meeting of the Country Party supported Page's stand.

Various alternatives were discussed to break the impasse, one that a leader of the Government should be chosen by a vote of the combined Parties, and lobbying began for likely contenders, among them Casey and Percy Spender. Menzies' position was made difficult by the refusal of the Country Party to co-operate with him.

That Sir Earle Page wanted to hold on to the Prime Ministership himself there is no doubt, but Menzies refused to yield.

In fact, the hiatus became so pronounced that Wilfrid Kent Hughes, who was still a member of the Victorian Parliament, wrote a personal letter to Menzies in which he said: "I think that if you are wise you will put Earle Page in the place which he deserves as Prime Minister until the next elections, when the leader of the U.A.P. will become Prime Minister and you will get your turn then."

Page had a further telephone conversation with Bruce on 19 April but nothing definite was arrived at. Page had already indicated to Cabinet that he would resign the Prime Ministership when the U.A.P. had elected its leader, and now he wanted to discuss this with the Governor General. But Curtin would not agree to an adjournment of Parliament, to allow him to discuss his resignation with the Governor General, without first giving a full explanation of the course he intended following.

When Parliament met after a recess, on Tuesday, 19 April 1939, Page formally announced the death of Joe Lyons to the House of Representatives. He spoke at length with affection and admiration for his late Prime Minister and friend, and also paid tribute to Dame Enid.

Page told the House: "They made an appeal to the fundamentals of human society and contact. They had the common touch and understood the needs and wishes and aspirations of the poorest and simplest of their fellows. No matter in what exalted circles they were called upon to move, their affection and understanding of the ordinary man remained lively and unchanged.

"They spoke to the hearts as much as to the heads of the people and at a time when immense sacrifices and extraordinary individual efforts were necessary on the parts of the people of Australia to meet the crisis of the Depression, their unfailing courage, their cheerfulness in all circumstances, their consideration, and endeavours to ameliorate conditions of the women and children, of the sick and the poor, their aptness in expressing the mind of the common man, their loyalty to the ideals of service, assure them of a special place in the hearts and memories of the people."

Then Page quoted from the poet Lowell:

> His magic was not far to seek
> He was so human with the strong or weak
> Far from his time he neither sank nor soared
> But sate an equal guest at every board.
> No beggar ever felt him condescend
> No prince presume, for still himself he bear
> At a manhood simple level and where'er
> He met a stranger, there he left a friend.

Billy Hughes in his tribute said of Lyons: "He was a true patriot, he never posed nor boasted of his service. Not for him the tinsel and the glitter that served the pinchbeck patriot and poseur.

"He served his country zealously but without ostentation. A firm believer in the Empire, he was first and foremost an Australian and retained throughout his public career an Australian outlook."

Menzies said: "For myself I would like briefly to mention what I believe to have been the central feature in the character and the statesmanship of the late Prime Minister. As I understand it, it was this: the problems of Government were to him the problems of humanity and not the problems of blue-book or even primarily problems of economics or science.

"Because he understood that so clearly and so instinctively, because that great truth was in him, he brought to all his public actions a simplicity, a sympathy, and a loving kindness which marked him out in the political affairs of this country. His example remains with us and I am sure we will all carry our own memories of him with us until our own time has come.

"I know of no consolation more apt and true at this time than that which can be given by reminding you of the words of the greatest of all Consolers: 'Blessed are the merciful, for they shall obtain mercy. Blessed are the pure in heart for they shall see God.' "

On the following day, 10 April, Sir Earle Page in the House of Representatives tendered the resignation of his Ministry, which had remained in office only nineteen days.

Perhaps, to understand what followed, it may help to know what manner of man Page was. He had changed little over the years since he first appeared in politics wearing a blue suit and a new (soldier's) badge. He still interlarded his sentences with "Y'see," and despite a knighthood and membership of the Privy Council, he still longed for the day when he could retire to a farm and play godfather to a district; he owned two farms.

His outstanding quality was tenacity. He was still plugging away at ideas he expounded almost thirty years previously. A man solid in friendship and determined in his feuds, his first row with Billy Hughes resulted swiftly in the Little Digger's discomfiture.

Page's first and most enduring friendship in politics was with S. M. Bruce. A stranger pair never walked the boards, but they proved an ideal combination. Bruce's diagnosis of Page was: "It is no use dissenting from him. You can tell him his ideas are iniquitous and his proposals impractical, and all he does is to murmur, 'Y'see, y'see, I knew you'd agree with me.' "

The most characteristic thing about his political technique was his method of making a statement. It was usually long and rambling and tedious. Nobody was sure what it was all about, but usually everybody caved in.

Thus did he persuade the Government, and helped to persuade the country, into the formation of the Loan Council, which was a first step towards the undermining of the State's powers and the consolidation of Commonwealth national authority; thus, too, did he gradually revolutionize overseas marketing plans; and thus did he create rural hydro-electric schemes and various other changes of great importance in rural life.

On the other hand, when he wanted to make an incisive speech or talk to a Government concisely on some issue, he could do so in a way which made the Government squirm.

Sir Earle Page was now in such a mood, backed by strong emotion, because behind his feelings lurked the implications of his strong friendship for Joe Lyons.

After briefly outlining the reasons which brought about his Government being formed, he led up to the reasons for his resignation. The result was an attack on Menzies which not only made Members embarrassed, but shocked the nation.

Sir Earle's widow excluded these details from his autobiography after his death in 1961, and Dame Enid Lyons pulled her punches in her own autobiography; so, in that sense, it can be said that the widows of the two men who perhaps had most reason to resent Menzies, censored books relating to him. The facts are set down in these pages.

Page told Parliament that the change in leadership of the U.A.P. had resulted in a change in the relationship of his Party and the U.A.P., while the successful functioning of a composite Government must rest on the fullest mutual confidence and loyalty between the Parties.

Sir Earle said: "For twelve years in this Parliament I have sat in composite Governments, with Mr Bruce and Mr Lyons, under such conditions and have by my co-operation been able to give stability to the Government in this Chamber. During that period no Party had a majority.

"Mutual confidence and loyalty are still essential conditions for the existence and proper functioning of a composite Government. But at present, unfortunately, there is another consideration which overrides, but does not dislodge, these conditions.

"Everyone realizes that today we are perhaps on a threshold of war. During the last four or five weeks action has been taken by certain aggressor countries which, if permitted to continue, would undoubtedly finally lead to Australia having to fight in self-defence. More recently extraordinary steps have been taken by other nations, such as the United States, for instance, to endeavour to ensure the peace of the world.

"It seems to me that if a wartime Government is to function, and that may be the position at any time, although I hope not, it must function in such a way as to secure the greatest possible measure of co-operation in the community.

"The Australian Government needs a leader with not merely the qualities I have mentioned, but also three essential qualities of courage, loyalty, and judgment, in such a degree as will ensure that the people of Australia will give the last ounce of their energies and resources in the united national effort to ensure our preservation.

"Therefore, as the leader of the Country Party which has been associated for so many years with the U.A.P. in the Government of this country, I was compelled to consider the qualities of the new leader of the U.A.P., not that the Country Party is interested in the personnel of the Ministerial members of the U.A.P., or of its representatives in this Parliament.

"It is entirely a Party domestic matter, but if the leader of that Party was to become the leader of united national effort, I was entitled to consider whether he possessed the qualities necessary for his high office, and to ask myself whether his public record was such that it would inspire the people of Australia to the maximum unstinted effort in a time of national emergency.

"Because of that I was reminded of three incidents in the career of the new leader of the U.A.P.

"The first of three happened only twenty-four days previously when Honourable Members will remember the Right Honourable gentleman tendered his resignation as Attorney General in the Lyons' administration. His country is spending many millions of pounds in preparations for defensive war and we are endeavouring to get every industry to put forward the maximum effort in order that Australia may be prepared for any eventuality.

"At this time, when all efforts were being strained to put the defences of this country in order, the Right Honourable gentleman insisted on resigning from the Government because he differed from its attitude towards national insurance.

"I shall quote one sentence from the letter of resignation to the late Prime Minister. He said, 'I frankly do not think we can expect to be taken seriously if we start off again with conferences and draft committees at a time when we have already so notoriously failed to go on with an Act which represents two years of labour, a vast amount of organization, and a considerable expenditure of public and private funds.' Now, the Right Honourable gentleman says that that is exactly what he intends to do.

"The second incident is this: some twenty-four weeks ago he went to Sydney where he made a speech on leadership. That pronouncement was regarded by the public and the Press of Australia as an attack upon his own leader. I do not say that it was, but I merely say it was construed in that way."

Mr John Lawton: "His leader did not regard it as such."

Sir Earle Page: "I spoke to Mr Lyons and he was very distressed about the matter."

Sir Frederic Stewart: "At least six members of this House had an assurance from Mr Lyons that he did not regard it as such."

The Speaker: "Order. The Chair must insist that the Prime Minister be heard. These interruptions are distinctly disorderly and unfair to the Right Honourable gentleman and to other members who wish to hear him."

Sir Earle Page: "I come now to the third incident. Some twenty-four years ago the Right Honourable Member for Kooyong was a member of the Australian Military Forces and held the King's Commission. In 1915, after having been in the military forces for some years, he resigned his commission and did not go overseas."

Mr James: "That is dirt."

Sir Earle Page: "I am not suggesting that the Right Honourable gentleman had not the best possible reasons for his action. I am not calling into question the reason for the Right Honourable gentleman's action, nor would I question the reason of any other individual in similar circumstances.

"All I say is that the Right Honourable gentleman has not explained to the satisfaction of the great body of people who did participate in the war his reasons, and because of this I am afraid he will not be able to get that maximum effort from the people of Australia to which I have referred.

"I personally have been very considerably perturbed in regard to the whole position. I believe that the present is a time when we should be in a position to pull our whole weight in a combined national effort to ensure the defence of Australia."

After outlining to Parliament the proposals that had been made to Bruce, Sir Earle said if the leaders of the two Parties could agree on the choice of a national leader, either in or outside Parliament, he would serve under him and his Party would co-operate. He made one stipulation—in order that bona fides would not be questioned, neither he nor any member of his Party should be regarded as a candidate for leadership.

He said he would see the Governor General that afternoon and resign his position as Prime Minister.

Menzies looked distressed when he rose to reply before a silent House, and he spoke with restraint. The attack had been delivered with such stunning effect, that Menzies actually had the sympathy of a majority in the House.

"It was an extraordinary speech," Menzies said, "if I may say so, at a most inappropriate time.

"We all agree irrespective of Party associations that the Commonwealth is at the moment called upon to deal with difficult problems. Most of us believe those problems can be attacked successfully only by a concerted effort.

"I kept silent in the past two days, though I've heard whispers about why the Country Party refused to co-operate with me in the formation of a Government. I should have been very glad to avoid saying anything about the matter, even if refusal had been persisted in.

"My own view is that in the interests of Australia the door might have been kept open. If that door had been closed for reasons of high policy, I could have respected those reasons. The door has been closed, bolted, and barred presumably for reasons which are not only offensive and personal, but also paltry.

"The first reason that has been adduced for the refusal of the Country Party to co-operate with me as leader of the United Australia Party is that I resigned from the Lyons Government on the issue of national insurance. But honourable members know that I resigned from that Government because only a few weeks ago I had given a specific pledge in writing to my electors."

Mr Brennan: "Irrespective of the honourable gentleman's Cabinet colleagues, did he have no responsibility to them?"

Mr Menzies: "I am stating my views. In due course the honourable gentleman may have an opportunity to give his. I . . . am the person who has been attacked . . . I resigned from the Lyons Government because as I told the House I gave a specific pledge to my electors in connection with the insurance scheme.

"Is it a contemptible thing for a man to keep his word? Is it the mark of a coward for a man to keep his word on an issue which is far from popular? I have no apologies to offer for my resignation. On the contrary, I regard it as one of the more respectable actions of my public life.

"The second reason given exhibits an amazing effort at ingenuity on the part of the Right Honourable gentleman. Having, I think he said, looked the matter up he said that twenty-four weeks ago I made a speech to the Constitutional Club in Sydney on the subject of leadership.

"I do not know whether any honourable gentleman was present on that occasion, but I can say now that not one word of it do I wish to retract. The burden of my remarks was that dictatorships owed no small portion of their success to two things—one was the leadership, the undivided leadership we can enjoy, the other was the undivided loyalty to that leadership which existed inside the country.

"I went on to say that whilst I despise the doctrines of dictatorship and would resist them to the utmost, the test of a successful democracy was leadership and loyalty to that leadership. After I'd said that, I went out of my way to say that it was an Australian homily which I was addressing to myself and every other person who occupied a position of leadership of the people.

"I am not responsible for the manner in which my views may have been twisted. But the Honourable the Prime Minister has refrained from saying that he thought my speech was an attack on my late leader. All I can say on that point, that conversations which I've had with my late leader and friend were completely inconsistent with any suggestion that he regarded my speech as an attack on him.

"After all, is this not getting down pretty low? If we are to be held responsible not only for what we say, and I'm always prepared to accept responsibilities for my utterances, but also for the gloss which some person who may not have heard a speech puts upon it, that will be the end of all pleasure in public life. I invite every honourable gentleman in this Chamber to ask himself, 'How should I like that standard of judgment to be applied to me?'

"I come now to the third ground of attack which, I may add, is no novelty. It represents a stream of mud through which I have waded at every election campaign in which I have participated. The attack is, 'You did not go to the war.' That is a statement that I daresay has been directed to some members of the Party led by the Right Honourable gentleman.

"There are certain people who regard it as their ordained mission in life to pry into the private reasons for other people; to put them up against the wall and say why didn't you do so and so? Presumably prying in this fashion, the Right Honourable gentleman discovered some facts concerning my action at the time he mentioned, but failed to discover others. He said, all with deadly implication, that I resigned a military commission a year after the Great War broke out.

"If he had investigated a little further he would have discovered, in common with other young men of my age, I was a trainee under the then existing system of compulsory training and as such, in common with other young men, I took my chance at being a private, a sergeant, a lieutenant or an officer of any other rank.

"When my period of universal training expired my activity in connection with the system also expired. I did not resign anything. I served the ordinary term of a compulsory trainee. I was in exactly the same position as any other person who at that time had to answer the extremely important question—is it my duty to go to the war or is it my duty not to go?

"The answers to those questions cannot be made on a public platform. They relate to a man's intimate and personal family affairs and I, facing those problems, problems of intense difficulties, found myself for reasons which were and are compelling, unable to join my two brothers in the Australian Imperial Force.

"I say that, after all, this kind of attack is very disagreeable, it is the sort of attack that is made and in my case has been made time and again. But I am foolish enough to believe that the only judgment as to a man's capacity, a man's courage, a man's fortitude that has any relevancy to his public conduct, in the judgment of the people, is the judgment of the people who've known him and worked with him.

"Members of the United Australia Party are familiar with me, they know my many faults, they are acquainted with such poor qualities as they think I might possess. They believe, and I am conscious of the honour they have done me, that I am capable of leading them, and I am vain enough to hope that I have the capacity to discharge that trust, and that, in the discharge of it, I will exhibit none of those miserable attributes suggested by the Prime Minister in the most remarkable attack I have ever heard in the whole of my career."

From the other side of the House John Curtin was quick to take full advantage of the attack, claiming that Australia could have no confidence now in either the Country Party or the U.A.P. to lead the Government. Curtin's remarks, too, are quoted because they reflect the tense atmosphere over the struggle for the Prime Ministership.

"The two leaders," said Curtin, "have convicted each other of offences which make the good government of Australia not only difficult, but indeed so long as they exhibit this attitude towards one another, impossible. My position is that we have no confidence whatever in either the United Australia Party or the Country Party, separately or corporately.

"We told the people that the Labor Party was the only Party whose principles were consistent and whose elements were homogeneous. The Right Honourable gentlemen behind me and other recruits who will come to the ranks of my Party, sit in this Parliament as members of a completely solid and consistent Party.

"It appears to me that the solution to this difficulty is that the people of Australia should be heard. One suggestion by the Prime Minister was he would be prepared to recommend that the three Party leaders in this House should consult with a view to forming a government.

"Presumably the Right Honourable gentlemen meant an all-Party Government. If there could be anything worse than a government consisting of two Parties, it would be a government consisting of three Parties.

"Such a combination would not be a government, it would be a society of disputation and debate. Decisions would never be reached, determinations could not be arrived at, let alone carried out.

"I say to Australia quite seriously that however good a government may be, it will be all the better if it is composed of men who subscribe to the one set of political principles, who are united in their outlook upon the problems of the country and who may, as a team, translate into reality ideas that they have, as to the way in which the government should be administered.

"That government would be a government of leadership in action and any government, even if it has the best policy, would do far better service to the nation if there were arrayed against it in Parliament an Opposition courageous, intelligent, and patriotic.

"It is not a good thing for democracy to have governments that are unchecked by criticism or by honest opposition. We have to preserve the validity of democracy, therefore all this talk about an all-Party Government is not really a contribution to the safety of the nation. It is designed merely to ensure the safety of the Government against internal criticism, however necessary it may be in the interests of the nation that that criticism should be levelled.

"Let us not leave the reality of totalitarianism while pretending to maintain democratic institution. For myself and my Party, I say that either in peace or war, we are prepared to take the responsibility of governing this country on the basis of our own programme.

"We shall not attempt to govern this country on any other platform than that of Labor, and we shall make no presumptuous endeavour to become the government, until the people of Australia give us a majority in this House. So long as the people of Australia give to Labor in this Parliament a minority of votes, we shall accept the duty cast upon us as that of Opposition.

"But when the people of Australia, as I hope and think they will, thrust on us the responsibility of government, then we shall accept the responsibility of government on our own policy, a policy which the people will have first approved and we shall not be involved in struggles for portfolios and leadership.

"The Prime Minister as leader of the Country Party says that what is required is a leader of courage, loyalty, and judgment. He has by implication said that the United Australia Party had such a leader in the deceased Prime Minister. In effect, he says that the present choice of the United Australia Party does not possess those attributes. Otherwise his speech was meaningless.

"The Country Party accuses the United Australia Party, its political collaborator for years, of having reached the stage of complete bankruptcy in leadership. That is the charge implicit in everything said by the leader of the Country Party against the United Australia Party.

"I repeat that the leaders of both Parties have convicted each other of unfitness to be leaders of this coalition. Therefore, as the leaders of this coalition cannot agree and because of the divergence of policy and principle which emerges from the discussions between the collaborators, it must be palpable that separately or together, they are no longer fitted to be entrusted with the government of this Commonwealth."

Notwithstanding all the sharp differences, the Menzies Ministry was formed, on 26 April.

A few days later two proud parents flew from Melbourne to Canberra. For Kate Menzies, aged seventy-three, it was the first time she had ever flown. She celebrated the occasion by giving a newspaper interview in which she described Bob as the bravest member of her family.

When the new session of Parliament opened on 3 May 1939, they were in the gallery to see Robert Gordon Menzies as Prime Minister.

He had finally made it.

9

Bob and Pattie Menzies moved into the Prime Minister's Lodge in Canberra soon after the appointment.

Mrs Menzies enjoyed formal entertaining at dinner parties, but social duties on the large scale falling to the lot of a Prime Minister's wife were to be a new experience. A home-maker by preference, Mrs Menzies' good taste was shown in the solid friendliness of their Kew residence in Melbourne, with its big rooms furnished in dark polished wood and vivid with flowers. It was a place of warm peace and quiet where the woman's touch was everywhere apparent. The walls were friendly with original water colours and some outstanding oils.

Although Mrs Menzies played tennis and kept garden, her main interest centred in her husband and three children. The two boys, Kenneth aged seventeen, then studying law, and Ian aged fifteen, who planned to take up farming, were boarders at Geelong College.

She loved children and when she and her family went off to their holiday retreat at Mount Macedon they took as many of the young visitors from Kew as they could crowd in. The new mistress of the Lodge was no stranger to the exigencies of political life—her father J. W. Leckie was then a Senator in Canberra.

Moving into the Lodge, Mrs Menzies paid a tribute to her predecessor, Dame Enid Lyons. "I consider her one of the finest personalities I have ever met," she said. "And the most able woman in Australia today. Because of the sad association, I cannot feel any of the joy I should in my own position."

Bob Menzies soon settled into his role. In his first speech broadcast to the nation on 26 April, he spoke of the Empire's duty if England was involved in a war. "The peace of Great Britain," he said, "is precious to us because her peace is our peace; if she is at war we are at war even though that war finds us not in European battlefields, but defending our own shores.

"Let me be clear on this; I cannot have a defence of Australia which depends upon British sea power as its first element, I cannot envisage a vital foreign trade on sea routes kept free by British sea power, and, at the same time, refuse to Britain Australian co-operation at a time of common danger. The British countries of the world must stand or fall together."

When he and his Cabinet colleagues met for the first time he told them they'd have to get down to business as a team. He said, in effect: "We are in the position of an executive of a business. We direct what is to be done; we accept that our subordinates have the capacity to carry out our decisions. In future we will deal with major problems, we will waste no time on details."

The staid *Sydney Morning Herald* evidently thought Menzies had made a good start, declaring that he was likely to be an outstanding Prime Minister who had recaptured something of the Bruce tradition. It praised what it described as the Prime Minister's obvious efficiency, his clearness of mind, and his anxiety to give to the public, as far as possible, a knowledge of what was going on.

The *Herald* then went out on a limb on his behalf: "Mr Menzies has been accused of aloofness, a superior manner, a Fascist mentality, and sometimes indolence. The true picture of him when one knows him is that he, like most intellectuals, realizes just how much he does not know and because of an inverted type of modesty he gives the impression of patronage. That explains his air of aloofness and superiority. And to some extent it explains the suggestion that he has a Fascist mentality.

"He has the capacity to look abstractly at any argument or theory whatever his personal ideas, and he realizes that, however unsound the Fascist ideology may be from the point of view of a democracy, it produces some results that would be an advantage to any system. The fact that he sees attractive features in another system does not mean that he is prepared to submerge his democratic background in a new and revolutionary ideal.

"On the score of indolence, Mr Menzies can do no other than concede its truth in certain circumstances. If he is not interested, he is indolent. But when he is interested he shows no lack of energy and vitality. Today he is not only interested but sincerely moved by a desire to do his best for Australia—with all the gifts he has at his command."

In the House of Representatives on 9 May, the Prime Minister echoed a Chamberlain-like philosophy when he rejected the idea that the world would inevitably drift into war because in some countries there was a democratic form of Government and in others a totalitarian government.

And he was later proved rather wide of the mark in a reference then to the U.S. and Japan, "those two great and friendly powers in the Pacific."

But he did speak with a more accurate sense of history when he appealed to Australians to do everything in their power to improve mutual understanding with the American people, because he believed that on an association and understanding with them a great deal of future happiness for Australia could be built.

Menzies showed his great love for Whitehall and the British people, a love that was not to diminish over the years: "Were I charged with the responsibility of Government in the United States of America, I should not care to contemplate a world in which the strength, the liberal thought, and the genius of self-Government of the British people had been extinguished. I should regard myself as having been left quite lonely in a strange world. . . ."

The Prime Minister had some real problems on the home front. The breakaway of the Country Party from the coalition meant that the U.A.P. did not have any clear majority. Sir Earle Page's stand received wide support from Country Party groups in the States, although two Queensland Members of the Federal Parliamentary Party, Arthur Fadden and Bernie Corser, dissociated themselves from his reasons for not arriving at a working basis with Menzies, and Tom Collins from New South Wales and another Parliamentary Country Party man, from South Australia, joined them.

The Cabinet was drawn entirely from the U.A.P. Percy Spender became Assistant Treasurer in the Government, and a youngish Harold Holt, Minister without Portfolio.

Menzies tried to submit the whole question of the national insurance scheme to a committee of parliamentary members for consideration, but the move was rejected by Parliament. Naturally, Menzies' critics did not fail to point out that on this occasion when he failed to implement the measure himself, he did not resign. In fact, national insurance was shelved.

An atmosphere of unreality continued over the war threat.

As late as 17 August, Menzies expressed hopes of peace when he told a Sydney meeting: "Let us give up talking of the inevitability of war, let us be optimistic and talk about peace and happiness."

When war finally came on 3 September, Menzies followed Neville Chamberlain by a few minutes in declaring war on Germany, the first Dominion Prime Minister to do so. He led Australia into the war with the words: "Australia's frontiers are on the Rhine and on the East Coast of England."

All Parties immediately pledged their support for Britain, and Sir Earle Page, offering to sink his differences with Menzies, sought a composite Government with the U.A.P., and if possible the Labor Party.

Menzies replied that Curtin, while prepared to support necessary war measures, did not want a composite Government and he himself could not have any Minister in his Cabinet whom he himself had not selected.

Page resigned leadership of the Country Party on 13 September in the hope that in the absence of personal differences between the two leaders of the Government Parties, the way might be cleared for negotiations for Country Party members to enter Cabinet.

Two candidates, John McEwen of Victoria and Archie Cameron of South Australia, stood for his post and Cameron was elected. Cameron declared that negotiations between the Country Party and the U.A.P. should be based on a principle of equality, but Menzies insisted on his right to choose his own Ministers, and negotiations lapsed.

Australia's war effort lagged. Although the Sixth Division of the Second Australian Infantry Forces was formed about a month after war was declared and the first contingent left Australia for the Middle East on 9 January 1940—three months before the end of the Phoney War—recruiting was slow.

In the early stages there was no equipment for recruits or the organization to handle them. Like Britain, Australia did not realize a long war was at hand until the fall of France, and in the interim the nation wallowed.

Admittedly Australia had to start its war effort virtually from scratch. She was, after all, only a small community in a vast land area, not a particularly rich country compared with say, the United States, and with only 7,000,000 people, less than half of whom were effective for war between the ages of fifteen and sixty-five.

Australia had no experience in the complex technique of modern mass production industry, or the plant for it. She had no Dearborn, and in fact, had only three organizations with any extensive experience in mass production industries when the war began—The B.H.P., General Motors, and Australian Consolidated Industries.

When war came there were only nine Government munitions factories in the whole country and four firms producing machines and tools. Industry, broken up into small factories, was scattered around the continent.

And yet, when Australia settled down to war production, it proposed not only to build such intricate machines of war as Bristol Beaufort Bombers and Beaufighters, anti-aircraft predictors and tanks and aero engines, but also as the main manufacturing agency of the Empire east of Suez, to export millions of pounds worth of equipment. To produce the Beauforts, three Railway workshops had to be used in three different States, plus 150 sub-contractors all over Australia.

The story of the Beaufort shows some of the problems a totally unprepared Australia had to face. Early in 1939 the British Government promised to give Australia the 33,000 jigs and tools and fixtures needed to build this complex machine. The Bristol Aeroplane Company undertook to ship to Australia, before the end of December 1939, ten sets of fabricated parts and ten sets of raw materials and equipment needed for the first twenty planes.

Because these plans were not fulfilled Australia had to manufacture 26,000 of these jigs and other items. In most of those that did arrive, specifications were wrong—the holes were in the wrong places, and so on. When Britain embargoed the export of aircraft and aircraft material, Australia turned to America for raw materials and had to fight other countries in the mad scramble, with Great Britain her main competitor there.

Trouble occurred over the engines, too. Originally the plane was to have Bristol Taurus engines and Britain promised 250. This promise was reduced to 100 and as the Taurus engine wasn't so good anyway, Australia decided to build the twin-row Pratt and Whitney Wasp, and Britain promised 100 of these to start off with. But because of the confusion, the plane had to be redesigned twice in Australia.

Australia couldn't get vital aluminium from Britain but arranged for a plant from her. When the plant arrived at the wharf, Britain found she needed it herself, and when Australia got another plant in America, Britain took that too.

The division of labour had to be organized in a wild rush when, at the fall of France, the Government gave production departments permission to go ahead. Perhaps unavoidably, there were some wasteful anomalies: canvas, woven in Sydney, went to Melbourne for inspection, to Adelaide to be made into knapsacks, back to Melbourne again for inspection; tracks for tanks were made in three places when they could be produced more cheaply in one. But even these problems did not begin until the war was well under way.

Like the rest of the Empire, Australia dithered through the early days of the war waiting for Germany to collapse. The engineers, administrators, and technicians equipped to organize Australia's production wanted to go ahead, but they were held up by political indecisions—by sheer inefficiency or through politicians taking an electoral rather than a national or international view of history's greatest war.

The Menzies Government in the first few months of the war generally had the support of the Australian Press, including that of Sir Keith Murdoch, boss of the Melbourne *Herald*. But demands soon grew for greater action. The situation called for strong and inspired leadership, but it was soon felt that too much time was being spent on political in-fighting and not enough on getting the country mobilized.

The *Sydney Morning Herald*, which had always been strongly anti-Labor, emerged as a sharp critic of Menzies. This was the result of a personal feud between Menzies and Warwick Fairfax, the proprietor. The cause of this feud is puzzling because Menzies, when Attorney General, had been friendly with the Fairfaxes.

In January 1940, Menzies appointed the Treasurer, R. G. Casey, as Australian Minister to Washington, making it the country's first diplomatic appointment overseas. Although Mr Casey did not fully realize it at the time, he was being eased out and wished Godspeed all the way—notwithstanding the most cheerful and amiable of farewells. Such are the vicissitudes of political fortune that this distinguished Australian, who had stood out against Menzies' election and tried to prevent it, was now on seemingly friendly terms with the Prime Minister and referred to him as "my friend Bob."

In the following months the Government's popularity took a tumble when the Labor Party was able to make great capital out of the circumstances surrounding the resignation of the Minister for Trade and Customs, Jack Lawson. A hot topic at the time was whether approval for the complete manufacture of motor vehicles in Australia should be given to General Motors or Australian Consolidated Industries. The Government proposed to give a monopoly to A.C.I., in the face of Country Party opposition. The managing director of A.C.I. was W. J. (Knockout) Smith.

The facts leading up to that resignation have not previously been stated publicly, but it can be plainly said that the association between Lawson and Knockout Smith, although often alleged to have scandalous undertones, was entirely innocent.

Menzies, knowing the truth, and describing it as a stupid bungle, stood by Lawson in the face of hostile criticism, showing a quality which not everybody believed he possessed—loyalty to a colleague. Menzies showed great loyalty to people who were Menzies' men. Being a Menzies' man, according to many parliamentarians of the time, meant that you had to accept him entirely and show your loyalty to him, and not criticize or make jokes about him.

The storm broke with all sorts of innuendoes about bribery and corruption when a horse leased to Lawson by Smith won a race in Sydney carrying Lawson's colours.

The leasing arose purely out of an informal conversation at a U.A.P. meeting one day between Lawson and his colleague, Bill McCall. McCall had been to Knockout Smith's stud at Scone in New South Wales and was telling Lawson about Smith's horses. Lawson, whose brother was a horse trainer and who liked to bet in a modest way, casually asked McCall if he thought Smith might lease him a mare. McCall said he'd ask Smith next time he saw him, and nothing more was mentioned about the matter for some months.

McCall asked Smith, and one Friday Lawson telephoned McCall at his home and said: "I've got some news for you. Bill Smith has leased me a mare. It's name is Billy." Lawson asked McCall if he and his wife would accompany him to Randwick the following day because the horse was to be tried out.

They had a look at the horse on the course and Lawson's trainer brother remarked that he thought it was carrying a bit too much weight to be much good as a galloper.

Lawson handed McCall £2 to wager for him, his normal betting amount, and McCall, noticing Knockout Smith put a wad of notes on, himself put something like £20 on. Betting was 33-1, the horse bolted down the straight carrying Lawson's colours and Knockout Smith won £1,500.

In the public outcry that followed, Lawson decided he would have to resign from the Menzies Cabinet and talked it over with McCall, who agreed there was little else he could do. Lawson, who was distressed over the upset to his family at the publicity, wanted to go to Melbourne to see Menzies, but he would not take a plane or a train for fear of being questioned by reporters. He asked McCall to drive him to Melbourne, about 700 miles away, and he was in such an emotional state that McCall agreed.

Lawson would not leave the Customs Office in Sydney until after dark and had a dinner of meat pies from an out-of-the-way shop to avoid reporters, whom he imagined to lurk to every turn. They arrived in Melbourne at 8 o'clock next morning, saw Menzies at the Australian Club where he was all set to preside over a meeting of the War Council, and handed him his resignation, which was accepted.

Lawson would not travel back to Sydney by train or plane so they set out by car with Lawson driving the first leg. However, after nearly running into a horse and cart and going off the road about 50 miles out of Melbourne, he fell asleep and McCall had to drive all the way back to Sydney, arriving there at 1 o'clock the next morning.

The Federal Parliament was composed very largely of individuals, especially on the Government side, who were colourful and strong minded. Debunking of their fellows was their favourite pastime and they were pervaded by a spirit of fun. It required a strong personality to lead them; a man who understood those around him and who in turn was understood and respected.

Apart from the "Old Doc"—Sir Earle Page—who had the reputation of never burying the political hatchet except in an opponent, there was, of course, Billy Hughes. He had been born in London, of Welsh extraction, in 1864, and flourished in Australian conflict in the storms of the first World War. One of the great wits of his time, he was an architect of modern Australia. As a youngster he had been a tramp, boundary rider, drover, sea cook, pantryman, shopkeeper, a stonebreaker, school teacher, and stage extra. A trade union organizer, he was also a qualified lawyer, and for more than forty years up to this time had been a parliamentarian, including eight years as Prime Minister.

Then there was Arthur (call me Artie) Fadden. His university had been the little wooden school at Walkerston, one of the few places in Queensland where there were remnants of the kanakas who stayed in Australia after the abolition of coloured labour in the canefields.

He left school at fifteen to become "offsider" for a gang of cane cutters, boiling their billies, sweeping the barracks where they slept, and generally making himself useful. A cane inspector, who liked his willingness and broad grin, gave him a job as office boy at a sugar mill, and he was in danger of permanently slipping into a clerical chair when he heard of a job in the Mackay City Council as assistant to the Town Clerk—"Smart boy with flair for figures."

At eighteen he took this job, played football from Rockhampton to Townsville, and cricket for Mackay. Young Fadden was a district champion in boxing, and his followers won stakes on him until someone rang in a professional tough from a wandering troupe and he was knocked cold. At twenty-one having passed his accountancy examination, he was made Town Clerk of Mackay.

Fadden went to Townsville on a holiday at twenty-four, saw an opening there for his own accountancy and tax agency business, and resigned his municipal office. Big companies, pastoral concerns, mining syndicates, and sugar interests gave their business to the young man to unravel their taxation problems and put their accounts in order. By the time he was in his early thirties Fadden controlled one of the largest businesses of its kind in Australia.

He entered the Queensland Parliament in 1932, lost his seat in the next election, and vowed he was finished with politics forever, but came back for the Country Party in 1936 in the Federal Parliament.

A jesting, jovial character with a zest for living, Fadden soon earned himself the reputation of being the best raconteur of the rambunctious type in the business.

All politicians claim they are motivated by a desire to serve their country. And no doubt with most of them these professions are sincere. A rarity indeed is the politician who will admit, or even be prepared to consider it possible for one minute, that the welfare of the country is identified with his own welfare.

Such a rarity is W. V. ("Big Bill") McCall. He went into politics to save himself, not the nation—not so extraordinary in itself, but what is refreshing is that he readily admits it.

McCall was a student at Sydney Grammar School when his father died in 1924. He was fifteen, his mother had only £2 a week pension, the Depression was coming on, and without passing an examination, he left school to support her.

His first job was with the firm of Wilcox Mofflin Limited, raw-hide and skin dealers. For two years he worked in their store as a labourer then went to Glen Innes in northern New South Wales and as far north as Rockhampton trading in skins. In all, McCall bought 1,000,000 possum skins and 250,000 koala skins in Queensland.

Trappers came in with skins or he went out on to the properties to buy them. The main topic of conversation in the wool stores was sex, horse racing, and politics, a formula which hasn't changed much since then.

McCall wanted to be independent, so just before he was twenty-one, with £76 capital, he started his own business. Registering as William McCall and Company, he bought and exported rawhides and skins to Florence, rabbit skins to London, and lambskins to New York. He built up £1,600 capital but went broke, started again as the Depression hit and went bust again.

McCall took stock of his position. He decided his best feature was that he could talk fluently, and that the only place where this could be of any value and get him somewhere, was Parliament. But not State Parliament. After all, he was presentable and while he talked to advantage he would be assured of his salary of £875 a year. This was the way to eat.

Wilcox Mofflin offered him his old job back but he declined it. He tried to make his own way and was struggling with his own company again as he set out to get into politics.

He mustered a few supporters together and, being a keen student of economics, started an organization known as the Economic Reconstruction League, which was little more than a name, and then the Sound Finance League of Australia. Elections were coming up and Jack Worth, the Member for East Sydney, had died and it was an open contest for the seat.

McCall persuaded a friend, J. J. Clasby, who had more political experience, to nominate for East Sydney in the Federal elections at the end of 1931. Clasby had £25 in a savings bank account, but his bank had been closed by the Depression and they couldn't use that money as a nomination deposit for the newly-formed United Australia Party. So McCall took the hat around among their subscribers and supporters to raise the money.

Clasby was a good speaker, and they talked in the Sydney Domain and at Kings Cross, standing up on the police call boxes. or horse troughs, opposing the Douglas Credit Scheme, Communism, racialism, the nationalization of banking, and a few other things. Sometimes as many as 3,000 people listened to them.

Clasby had a weak heart and fearing he might collapse if he talked for too long, McCall would wait until he made a sound start, then he would take over. Rested, Clasby would resume when McCall's arguments began to wear a bit thin or the crowd started to drift away. That way they kept going for long periods.

Clasby won the election but died immediately after his victory and never took his place in Parliament. McCall succeeded in taking over his preselection for the by-election but was narrowly beaten by a Labor candidate, Eddie Ward, by only 173 out of 64,000 votes.

He then ran for the electorate of Mosman when the sitting Member Dr Arthur died, but was beaten on preferences and finally in 1934, after going broke for the third time, got into the House of Representatives for Martin when W. A. Holman died.

McCall wanted to succeed, to make money. While reading the book *Think and Grow Rich,* he discovered what he believed to be the secret of that success, through conscious auto-suggestion. In this sense conscious auto-suggestion to him was the agency of control through which an individual could voluntarily feed his subconscious mind on thoughts of a creative nature.

Using this theory, Bill McCall began a twice-daily reading, with emotion and concentrated attention of a written statement of his desire for money. By communicating the object of his desire directly to his subconscious mind, he could already see and feel himself in possession of the money. He believed that habits favourable to translating his desires into money would be voluntarily created through repeating this over and over again.

Bill McCall each day read aloud the statement of his desire to develop a money consciousness, and to set himself a specific target, he wrote down: "My definite major aim is to be a millionaire by 1960."

When McCall got into politics in 1934 at the age of twenty-five he was already a man of strong determination with an ability to concentrate. He had developed a positive mental approach to any problem that confronted him, and having already sold 100,000 shares forward in the Depression years, in share dealings, he was learning the pros and cons of business the hard way.

Tall, dark, and good looking, and the best dresser in the Federal Parliament, Bill McCall had something of a film star quality about him; an Australian counterpart in the physical sense of handsome Anthony Eden.

He was no lightweight in any direction, especially when it came to work. He tackled everything that came his way in Parliament, and indeed at one stage asked one tired Minister in his own Party so many questions that the irritated gentleman walked around the Canberra lobbies bleating, "Who will rid me of this man?"

McCall had a fanatical desire to keep fit. Every morning he ran around the Royal Canberra golf links for two-and-a-half hours, often accompanied by the man who became Minister for Defence, Jeffrey Street. Street was killed with two other Ministers in an air crash in Canberra in August, 1940.

Often, in singlet and shorts, McCall would run around the roof of Parliament House, much to the annoyance of Honourable Senators drowsily pondering the affairs of the nation below.

As one of a number of characters in the Federal Parliament, McCall symbolized the twilight of the lively, free and easy days of Australian national politics before the rigidity of Party control killed this atmosphere.

For instance, a year or so after going to Canberra, McCall decided it would be better to sleep on the job so he could be closer to the centre of activity. He would book in to the Hotel Canberra until the session of Parliament began, then he used to move to Parliament House.

He found a room which had been allocated to the *Labor Daily* but not used, and h_re, at the back of the plush, red-carpeted Senate Chamber, he made himself at home. Commandeering one of Dick Casey's comfortable leather rumble chairs and a radiator from somewhere round the House, he was nicely ensconced in quarters that had a shower and toilet as well.

Towards the end of 1938, Bill McCall returned to his room one day and found that his furniture had been removed and the room occupied by H. Thorby, the newly-appointed Minister for Works. Thorby and McCall did not have any great liking for each other and this takeover was tantamount to a declaration of war.

Not long before Thorby, an ex-policeman, had addressed an election meeting in New South Wales and when a member of the audience called him a liar he had jumped down from the platform and punched him.

McCall, although he appreciated that Thorby had to find another office on vacating the one he had occupied as Minister for Defence, was angry that Thorby had not mentioned it to him before moving it. McCall waited until Thorby's redheaded typist had gone to lunch then confronted him at the door leading to the Parliament House roof, and called him out.

"You must be able to punch," said McCall. "You hit that fellow on the jaw down in the Riverina. Now you kill me or I'll kill you. Either I throw you off the roof or you throw me."

The Minister for Works went white. He'd had enough, and agreed without demur to return the McCall ministerial furniture from an adjoining office.

The Minister got stuck in the doorway with Dick Casey's comfortable rumble chair. "Give me a hand," he asked McCall.

"Give you a hand nothing. You got it *out*, now get it *back*." And he looked on while the Minister struggled—and restored the room to its former state. McCall slept in the room uninterrupted for another five years.

McCall was one of a number of practical jokers who kept the House of Representatives laughing, even into the war years. Artie Fadden was one of the most persistent jesters, together with Tom Collins and Bernie Corser from the Country Party. They teamed up with McCall and were known as the "Terrible Four".

Any Minister who took himself too seriously or was obviously vain was a sitting target for this quartet, who tried to raise a laugh whenever absolute seriousness was not required. They played jokes on just about everybody except Bob Menzies.

With Menzies, even before he became Prime Minister, it was much the same as with Henry Ford. According to a biography of the car magnate they never called him Henry, it was always Mr Ford. In the same way they never played jokes on Menzies because they felt they would not be appreciated.

Fadden, though, would often ape Menzies in private as a means of scoring off him. For instance, in the Parliamentary dining room he would sometimes order a bottle of wine and imitating Bob, would say somewhat pompously, "It's not room temperature," and painfully screw up his face.

Artie Fadden would go round to the bedrooms of some of his more formal fellow members and pour Condy's crystals or cochineal into their bed chambers. The honourable gentlemen would think from the discolouration that they were bleeding to death and Doc Page would be urgently called in. Several times the Old Doc went to the humourists and cautioned: "Lay off, boys, you've done enough, you've gone far enough."

Sometimes in the Parliamentary dining room, when a new waiter was on duty, they would order large quantities of champagne and wine and sign the chit "Harry Knox", a teetotal member of the House, or with the name of some other member present, then watch the fun when he was asked to pay.

On one occasion a Member audibly fell asleep in the House, his sonorous snores providing a fitting background to the debate. Bill McCall approached the outstretched form, delicately removed his dentures and quickly popped them into Treasurer Dick Casey's pocket. Casey was very embarrassed as the House guffawed.

In a sequel soon afterwards, McCall went into the Parliamentary lavatory just outside the Cabinet Room and discovered the cleaners were using a most evil-smelling disinfectant. He got a paper bag, picked up several pieces of the disinfectant which looked like rock salt, and sauntered into the House.

Because it was felt the Treasurer had no sense of humour, but could take a joke on himself well, he sidled up to him on the front benches and slipped a piece of the offensive substance in his coat pocket. Then ambling over to the other side of the House he struck up a conversation with Rowley James and saluted him in the same way.

The fun started as he was lining up a third victim. Evidently someone had complained and the House attendant was racing around trying to find where the smell came from. For some odd reason one of the first places he went to look was the Press gallery.

McCall then went to sit near Casey again, looking sideways at him with frowning suspicion. The Treasurer looked back, puzzled.

These were only some of the members who got fun out of politics whenever possible, and the variety of their jokes was almost limitless.

One night late in a wartime blackout Artie Fadden, Bernie Corser, and Bill McCall were walking near Parliament House when they heard two fellows thrashing about in a rose garden cursing furiously that they were getting scratched. They recognized the voices of two Members of the House. The honourable gentlemen had had a very good night out, were as tight as drums, and were trying, with considerable difficulty, to find their way either home or back to the House.

The situation was too good to miss. Next day the Terrible Four alerted "the boys" who were peering from doorways and casually standing around in Kings Hall, Parliament House, to watch the fun.

Someone got on the telephone to the Government Whip with several handkerchiefs over the receiver to disguise his voice and said: "Mr ——? Post Office here. Canberra Post Office. Now, how are you going to fix this matter up because we don't want any scandal about it?"

"Scandal? Scandal? About what?"

"About that window you broke in the Post Office last night."

"Window? Window? What window . . . ?"

To cut the story short, they had the Party official standing in King's Hall, "where the King signed the Constitution," waiting for the "postmaster" to turn up. And after he had gone to the Hall searching for the right spot they recalled him to an attendant's telephone several times, accusing him of not being there until the honourable gentleman, who was a little vague about his movements of the previous night, finally woke up to the joke.

On another occasion, to protest against late night sittings during which most Members fell asleep, Bill McCall told some of his friends with boyish good humour: "Tonight I'll smoke these bastards out."

He went to great pains in the tea adjournment to pack waste paper bins with plenty of paper and putting camphor in to make them smoke well, placed them strategically around the Chamber, one almost behind the Speaker's chair.

Then late at night when the House was drowsy he went round and lit them. Jack Perkins, the Minister for Trade and Customs, was sound asleep with a rug over him. When smoke began spiralling through the Chamber, Perkins was seen to rush out with the rug around him looking like a Red Indian shouting, "Fire, fire!" The fire alarm sounded to add to the din.

Some jokes had a cruel cut to them. One Member, not noted for his brilliant intellect, would get up and make a harmless speech, then there would be some startling reaction, such as a telegram allegedly from officials in his electorate telling him his speech had caused a great disturbance and asking him to return immediately. In one instance this Member actually boarded a plane because of a similar hoax.

This robust fun, of course, tapered off with the seriousness of the war and the ascension to the Prime Ministership of Menzies. But it remained in the background as a recognizable thread, adding a touch of lightness to the Parliamentary scene.

A leader, to handle this type of thing, needed to be a man's man. Menzies did not quite meet this description, being somewhat withdrawn and having had a reserved upbringing. Humour of the colloquial style was quite foreign to him. Though he would not tell a blue joke himself, he would sometimes listen to one and while not using bad language himself, he did not object to others using strong words.

He usually appreciated a wit, provided crudeness wasn't apparent. For instance, one of his favourite journalists in the early war period was John Fisher, a Communist who worked on the *Tribune* newspaper. Fisher, son of Andrew Fisher the former Labor Prime Minister, was a whimsical fellow who often amused Menzies. One sample of his wit concerned Forgan Smith, the Queensland Premier: "He can quell his political opponents with shafts of wit, and vice versa," Fisher wrote in the *Tribune* on one occasion.

But Menzies did not always communicate with the down-to-earth men around him as he perhaps should have done. For though they might have been characters, they had their contributions to make, were intelligent and resourceful and good workers.

Menzies underestimated one of these men and made the mistake of his life.

IO

Prime Minister Menzies and his Government knew from early in 1940 they must face a general election before the end of the year.

Confronted by revolt from some back benchers in his own United Australia Party which did not have a majority in the House, the Prime Minister received a fright in March that year which caused him to change his unremitting attitude toward the Country Party. In a by-election for the Victorian seat of Corio, vacated by Richard Casey on his departure for Washington, the U.A.P. was thrown out and Labor candidate J. J. Dedman roared in with a majority of 10,000.

Menzies immediately offered the Country Party five Cabinet posts in a coalition Government with the two leaders mutually selecting them. Among those who went in were Archie Cameron, Artie Fadden, and John McEwen. Doc Page remained in the cold, still plugging away for a national government.

Menzies finally suggested to Curtin that a national government be formed, even offering to serve under Curtin as Prime Minister. But Curtin maintained his stand, saying he would govern on no other basis than that of Labor.

Doc Page then suggested a National War Council as an alternative but that too was rejected, although later an advisory body was set up with four Government and four Opposition members.

Menzies came under fire from the back benchers for tardy war production. Bill McCall was the first man to attack and for a time he was the only U.A.P. member asking the Prime Minister embarrassing questions in Parliament. Then other Government back benchers like Jack Jennings, Albert Lane, and Jack Lawson joined in.

Behind the persistent criticism by McCall lay, initially, a personal undertone. In the contest for leadership on the death of Lyons, McCall backed Billy Hughes. And the inevitable that happens to any man who backs the wrong horse happened to him.

McCall, in a way, was Hughes' Man Friday. He had known Hughes since he was a youngster, had been his branch secretary and branch president. He was a close friend and the Little Digger was godfather to his young son, Bill Jnr.

McCall organized strenuously for the old man in the Party election against Menzies. Living on the premises, as it were, he was always in the House; continually coming in and out of parliamentary doors and drumming up support for Hughes.

In fact, so zealous an organizer was he that he often took short cuts through the empty chambers of the Parliament: late one night he swung open a door leading into the august and presumably empty Senate chamber—and an honourable Senator and his lady friend fell to the floor!

Menzies would have liked to have won by a comfortable majority but he only just scraped in. And he did not forgive McCall for whittling down his majority. Immediately the election was over he laid down a barrier of coolness towards him.

Menzies and McCall had always been friendly until then. So were their wives. When Attorney-General, Menzies advised McCall: "Bill, you've got to persuade; unless you can persuade, you cannot hope to succeed," a tip that could not have been more friendly.

Menzies expected McCall to support him in spite of his close association with Hughes. But McCall was a little upset at the way things developed. He thought everybody was entitled to his own opinion and felt the new Prime Minister's attitude was petty. However, there was no outward show of hostility between them, just an air of brooding resentment from the Prime Minister.

When the war committees were set up, McCall became a member of the Parliamentary War Expenditure Committee, which gave him access and entry into all Air Force, Navy, and Military establishments and factories around the clock seven days a week. Keen to do his part he threw himself into the work with his customary zeal and pretty soon, finding out things that weren't being done, he began to prod the Prime Minister with them.

One of the points on which he locked horns with Menzies was the manufacture of hand grenades. He asked about these and the

Prime Minister made a statement saying a certain number had already been produced.

McCall was then a director of Emmco and R. B. Davies Pty Ltd, the two companies making grenades. He checked, and found that one company had not even tooled up and that the other had just got the first grenade off the assembly line, a dummy given to him as a souvenir.

With this information McCall went back and assailed the Prime Minister. He ferreted out other things that weren't being done and with this knowledge fired a stream of questions at Menzies and his Ministers, organizing other back benchers to keep up the attack.

The Prime Minister instructed his Ministers to say as little as possible and not to try to score off any questioner because that, he believed, only encouraged further criticism. Even Percy Spender, who loved to snap back and match wits with anybody, drew rein.

McCall's complaint was that the Prime Minister resented being asked awkward questions by the War Committee. And when he did not have the answers he simply glared.

McCall used to say to members that Menzies was just like a big polar bear when he got mad—he used to sit there swinging his head from side to side when he did not have the answers and glowering at the deputation. "When Bob starts the polar bear act," McCall would tell other members, "you might as well get up and go."

Publicly McCall referred to the Prime Minister as being like a typical barrister who, after his junior has done the donkey work, picks up the brief and studies it, gives his address and gathering up his flowing gown, walks off to another case, leaving the administrative duties to others.

This, of course, was an exaggerated parallel, but it enabled McCall to make his point that he did not think the Prime Minister was firmly at the helm.

Billy Hughes, like many others at this time around the parliamentary lobbies, was giving his own inimitable summing up of the position: "That Menzies, brother, he's long on words but short on action."

Having failed to draw Curtin in on a national government Menzies told Parliament in July, 1940, that the general elections would be held later in the year when that session of Parliament ended, unless circumstances rendered it impossible or dangerous in the national interest.

Curtin, a true patriot, replied that Labor would not object to a suspension of the Constitution in an emergency, to allow Parliament to continue as a Constituent Assembly until the emergency passed. But Menzies did not accept this offer and the elections were set down for 21 September.

About a month before the elections, however, Parliament suffered a grievous loss when three of its best Ministers were killed in an air crash at Canberra. The Prime Minister decided to recall Harold Holt, who had resigned as Minister without Portfolio in order to go into the Army.

Allan Dawes, a distinguished journalist who had been Press Secretary to Jeffrey Street, one of the Ministers killed in the crash, was sent to see Holt with the message that the Prime Minister wanted him in the Government.

Holt was then an enthusiastic gunner at Puckapunyal in Victoria, and was soon to go overseas. At this time, when he was asked if he were willing to be conscripted as a Minister of the Crown, all the best Army fatigues had been selected for him, including the celebrated latrine one. And he was just taking a well-earned breather after cleaning several rows of latrines when the Menzies' missive arrived. Holt went back into the Government.

The election campaign was bitterly fought. Strikes were becoming a serious problem and the decision of the Menzies Government on 15 June to ban the Communist Party had touched off a fierce controversy. The police had been mobilized beforehand and late one Saturday night raided the homes of reputed Communists, carrying away books and papers and seizing printing plants.

But police action didn't end there. They were zealous to the point of being ludicrous, even raiding the homes and libraries of many liberals who were thus virtually branded as undesirables. This caused resentment against the Government and with extreme left wing papers appearing in illegal form, and increased activity by the trade union movement, it all gave evidence that the Communist Party was settling down to illegal conditions.

Although the Prime Minister increased his own personal majority in the election, his Government almost toppled. Official Labor went back with thirty-two seats and a new Labor group, the Non-Communist or Lang Labor, with four. The U.A.P. was reduced to twenty-three and the Country Party to fourteen.

Victoria returned two Independents, Arthur Coles who was inclined towards the U.A.P., and Alec Wilson, who described himself as Independent Country Party.

Thus, in the midst of the war, the Government had a majority of only one, with the balance of power resting with two independent members.

Immediately after that election, when reshaping his Cabinet, Menzies made a move which, if it had worked out the way he envisaged, would probably have altered the course of his political future.

The Prime Minister called on Bill McCall at his Sydney seaside home at Harbord. He went inside, leaving his driver, Ray Tracey, sitting outside in his Cadillac. After giving McCall's young son a two-shilling piece as a spontaneous gesture because of his liking for children, he found McCall dressed in shorts pulling the heads off a plate of prawns.

After a discussion, Menzies said to McCall: "Will you join me?" —an invitation to become a member of Cabinet.

McCall declined. He felt he was being bought off, that the Cabinet post was being offered to keep him quiet, and that if he accepted he would have to remain under the Prime Minister's thumb, a situation which a man of McCall's strong character would have found intolerable.

Arthur Coles was to make a significant contribution. Lord Mayor of Melbourne for two years, Coles was a wealthy man who had joined a partnership with his brother and an uncle to launch the big chain store group of G. J. Coles in 1921. He went in on a policy that all possible action and direction should be taken, including conscription, to gear Australia at once for war—at that time there was not even any restraint on the common use of critical war material.

Coles had fought at Gallipoli and in France in the first World War, had been to Europe before 1939, had seen the Nazis strutting, and was convinced this was going to be a long war.

While Lord Mayor and before going into Parliament, Coles held a communion breakfast at the Athenæum Club for seventy leading people from the business, manufacturing, and newspaper world and made them all speak on what they thought was needed to produce a maximum war effort in Australia. Then with two others he had gone to the Prime Minister's home the following Sunday morning and given him a report on the substance of these views, pledging the support of the responsible community.

This helped in no small measure towards major reorganization of industrial war effort in mid-1940 by Essington Lewis of the B.H.P. Company, who had direct access to the War Cabinet to help him form a Department of Munitions.

Coles, generally regarded as a vain man, was one of Australia's top business brains and a man of outstanding principle and integrity.

But if Menzies had troubles previously, they were nothing compared to now. It had been difficult enough trying to mobilize the country for war, a fact shown in a weary observation by Menzies to a Victorian colleague early in the war, when he was trying to sort out the Army and the various organizations: "What do I do with this amorphous mass?"

The Opposition now was sharpened by the addition of Dr H. V. Evatt, a compelling force. The Prime Minister conferred with all Party leaders trying to secure stability, and this meeting once more ruled out a national government. But Labor appealed to all members and all Parties for their co-operation to enable the Parliament to work effectively.

Perched as he was on a tightrope, Menzies finally came to the conclusion that he could not afford to have such a powerful personality as Doc Page cooling his heels outside Cabinet any longer. Several Ministers convinced Menzies of this although he was not enthusiastic over making peace. Archie Cameron arranged a handshaking between the pair in Melbourne, and Menzies agreed that if Page joined the Cabinet he would seek a national government once more, but as Curtin somewhat predictably rejected it again, Page rejoined Cabinet in his old spot as Minister of Commerce and Transport.

Cameron himself at this stage fell victim to yet another side issue of intrigue. He was expected to go back as leader of the Parliamentary Country Party, although John McEwen was also a candidate. But at the elections a Country Party group attacked him, ostensibly over some speech he had made. The real reason was that Cameron was a Catholic, and as Protestants they ganged up on him.

Cameron's temper rose and he rushed from the Party room, refusing to vote or to be a candidate. Finally a deputy leader was chosen in Artie Fadden. Cameron resigned from the Party and his portfolio, and stayed as a waspish critic on the back benches, later to be a stern Speaker of the House of Representatives.

It must have been with some feeling of relief that Menzies was able to get away from this maelstrom early in 1941 to visit his spiritual home of London, after working fourteen to sixteen hours a day seven days a week before he left Australia.

Labor had given its pledge to co-operate in his absence. The Prime Minister wanted to discuss policy at the highest level and to visit Australian troops, then fighting the Italians in the Western Desert. Australia desperately needed aircraft, having then as a fighter only a handful of Wirraways, which were mythically deemed by the experts to be the equal of anything Japan might unleash if she declared war. Britain was not playing the game with its promised aircraft deliveries to Australia and Menzies was going over to find out why; it was to be something of a show-down.

On the way to London in February the Prime Minister made a highly popular and successful visit to Australian troops at the scene of their recent victories at Bardia and Tobruk. From the air he could follow the course both battles had taken.

From his plane Tobruk Harbour seemed filled with sunken Italian shipping, ghostlike under the water's surface. At Tobruk, in the early morning inside the steeply rising banks of the Wadi Auda oasis, the first green spot for hundreds of miles since leaving the Nile delta, the Prime Minister met the battle-stained Diggers and raised a cheer with his first words, "Sit down and smoke."

In a few ringing sentences he conveyed to the men the pride of their families and of Australia, and the shortness and sincerity of his speech raised thunderous cheers.

Following the Prime Minister's Tobruk visit an amusing after-math occurred over publication of a joke in the *Tobruk Truth*, the daily news sheet circulating among the Diggers and known as the Dinkum Oil. The *Truth* was brought out by a former Mel-bourne newspaperman, Bill Williams, using the back of Italian Army forms as paper and a busted Italian duplicator which he managed to get working.

Williams published seven days a week, taking shorthand notes from B.B.C. broadcasts, but was restricted by a shortage of paper. Fortunately one day there was a hell of an air raid and presuming the Tommies in the stationery store would be in an air raid shelter, Williams ran to the store and removed all their duplicat-ing paper, thinking the Tommies would put down the disappear-ance of the paper to "enemy action."

The extra paper enabled him to produce a special four-page edition on Sundays with a few cartoons, jokes, and local items, liberally laced with Diggers' language one heard not infrequently in their hide-outs. One of the earliest special editions followed the Prime Minister's visit. The published joke, censored here, was based on the Prime Minister's speech and ran something like:—

"Mr. Menzies, addressing troops in the Western Desert: 'Men, I have flown over 700 miles of desert to see you. . . .'

"Bluey, from Back of Bourke: 'You're —— lucky, we had to —— —— walk!' "

An order came from Tobruk Headquarters to the men in the bombed area that in future there would be no more special issues, that the *Tobruk Truth* would restrict itself to reporting B.B.C. broadcasts, and further, that all copies of the special edition would be destroyed under supervision of an officer.

A fire was duly lit and witnessed and some copies burnt. But, of course, somehow not *all* copies were destroyed, the remainder achieving a greatly enhanced value on the souvenir market.

It was really a very mild joke compared to some in the Dinkum Oil, and had Menzies known about it he would probably have laughed—and requested a souvenir.

In London, with the blitz on, Menzies set out to pay tribute to British courage and succeeded in arousing a popular enthusiasm second only to Churchill.

Apart from the official side of his visit the Australian Prime Minister leapt out of bomb shelters to watch rescue squads and firefighters, even lending a hand at times himself, and drank beer with firemen on the job to see the way England was doing things at first hand.

In his first speech, an Empire broadcast, he told the hard-pressed British that Australia was in it with them to the end of the fight. "I am here to tell you in your own lovely country that we are with you," he said. "You must never think yourselves alone. Everything we have of manpower, treasure, skill, and determination is pledged to work and fight for you and with you until victory is attained, and a better and juster day dawns for the world in which our children are to live."

Menzies soon learnt why Britain hadn't kept all her promises regarding aircraft—she didn't have any to spare. When Menzies and Churchill met they sat up until 3 a.m. on the first two nights discussing the war and all its ramifications.

On the first occasion Menzies, a man quite prodigal of speech, could hardly get a word in until well after midnight because Churchill paused only to take breath, and it was several hours before Menzies had a chance even to begin putting Australia's point of view.

Already Menzies was a statesman acclaimed by *The Times* as "courageous and uncompromising in matters of high principle." Another London newspaper described him as one of the world's three greatest statesmen, placing him after Churchill and Roosevelt.

And there were eight week-ends in a row with Winston at Chequers!—eight week-ends in which both men apparently changed their previously-held views on each other and came to terms of great mutual respect.

The British were saying at the time that when Churchill made his famous speech about fighting them on the beaches and in the streets, he really had whispered under his breath, "what with?"

The main point Churchill made to Menzies in their early meetings, naturally not intimated to the public was: "I think Australia will have to be mauled a little." Clearly, in Britain's view Australia would have to largely fend for herself if war came to the Pacific, but Menzies fought a strong case for Empire unity.

Menzies sat in on the British War Cabinet, the first Dominion Prime Minister to do so in that war—Billy Hughes had attended the Imperial War Cabinet in the first World War. He was a guest of the King and Queen, staying overnight and sleeping in a huge antique four-poster bed so big, he told newsmen, it was like a four-roomed apartment. Asked by some detail-conscious reporter what period the bed belonged to he said, "I do not know, but there was certainly a lot of it."

Hanging his gas mask and tin hat in his office at Australia House, the Prime Minister went to work. One speech he made had an unfortunate reverberation back in Australia. In his remarks on Australian-Japanese relations he said, among other things, that he discounted the idea that war in the Pacific was inevitable.

This caused a rumpus in Canberra where many Labor men claimed it was appeasement talk. The Prime Minister's record in this regard was not good—his assurance that it was "business as usual" in the phoney war meant that the fall of France came as a shock, and this was still fresh in many minds.

One Labor man, Mr Beasley, declared publicly what was to turn out later a clear insight into history: "If there has been any change in British policy about the Dominion, it is vital that Mr Menzies should tell us. We want to know whether the Dominions are being let go. Have we reached the stage forecast by Mr Chamberlain that the Dominions must look after themselves and be won back later?"

In Canberra it was felt that Britain was keeping the Australian Government in the dark over war information from theatres of war in which Australia was concerned. Most parliamentarians hoped that an Imperial War Cabinet, now being suggested in London to include Dominion representatives, would be set up.

At the request of Churchill, Menzies stayed an extra two weeks in London. There he met Arthur Coles, who had gone to London

111

independently to see the war effort for himself, and to attend to some G. J. Coles' business. The Prime Minister gave Coles a number of assignments, mainly on aircraft production, and for the first time Australians got details which they had been awaiting for twelve months.

Menzies made a week's tour of country districts under their wartime "disguise" and himself had many conferences on aircraft production, which were expected to result in the employment of 70,000 Australians in the following two years.

Prior to his visit Australia's part in the war was little known. Cable news from Australia had been swamped by the war news from various fronts and the bombing descriptions. Menzies' visit made Britain realize Australia was playing her part with supplies and armed forces. It was a pity Menzies was not brought into touch more often with the mass of Londoners and that some of his best speeches were at private functions, and therefore not reported.

When he addressed the British Parliament privately, he had the largest audience any overseas visitor to the House of Commons has ever commanded. The only news the British public read about it was a paragraph written by a gossip writer, a member of the Commons, in a Sunday paper diary. He voiced the regret that such an inspiring talk had been given behind closed doors.

Menzies too, must have felt this for he began giving off-the-cuff talks inside air raid shelters and moving about unofficially among the bomb ruins. Once, after Jerry bombed heavily one night while he was entertaining Lady Astor and other guests, he walked around the ruins of countless Plymouth homes early next morning while delayed-action bombs were still exploding in the background. One went off about 40 yards away.

While the bombs were falling he had gone out and helped householders clear their furniture and other belongings from the path of flames.

Several times in his stay he and his party gave up their hotel rooms for blitz refugees, and frequently he made his car available for them.

Some people might have felt the Prime Minister was taking unnecessary risks in strolling out of air raid shelters and having a look around blazing streets while the bombing was still going on. Menzies revelled in this and, almost certainly, it was a reaction from his complex for not having gone to the previous war.

An intimate friend who has known Menzies for more than thirty years later expressed the view: "I am certain Bob did this to prove to himself he was no coward—although nobody has ever said he was a coward. I am sure this was his reason for taking what were, for a Prime Minister, definite risks."

A London columnist who attended a dinner in the Pinafore Room in the Savoy where twenty-five prominent people—a queer crowd in the columnist's view, but not uninteresting—gathered to meet Australia's Pig-Iron Bob, had this to say of the Prime Minister: "Menzies of course, is superb.

"Standing nonchalantly at his place and with polished effrontery he alternately moves us to laughter and to thrills. He has the mind and something of the style of the famous Lord Birkenhead, with just a suggestion of Australian accent.

"Churchill is his only Empire rival as a speaker.

"His irony, his wit, his powers of quotation are superb. His brilliance has made him distrusted in Australia, but rouses the deepest enthusiasm in London. Oddly enough, no Premier has so precarious a foothold as he, not even in the Balkans.

"Listen to him: 'Why not look at the worst and be thankful if it turns out less than that. Spain may come in against us, and France and Japan. Russia might—one must allow for that. We have been envied too long by others to be able to rely upon them when trouble overtakes us. But no combination of nations is powerful enough to defeat a British Empire thoroughly roused to its task.

"'War is an evil thing, but it is a great builder as well as destroyer. Because of the immense demands for war material, our industries are being speeded up and equipped to meet it. Why say that we shall emerge from the war exhausted? On the contrary, the British Empire should emerge like a giant that has renewed its strength.'

"A big man this . . . a flashing mind and a vaulting spirit. . . . and Smuts should be here now as the nucleus of a War Cabinet. We need men whose horizons girdle the globe."

To show his British spirit Menzies even called on the Irish to tell them they weren't playing the game by staying out of the war. Churchill didn't want him to go and tried to stop him, believing the mission was hopeless. Menzies didn't succeed in convincing de Valera, but he gave Menzies a long hearing.

When Menzies left London he had made everybody feel a lot better for the visit. And before leaving he gave British hearts a final boost: "Hitler might break London to pieces but he could never destroy London's unquenchable spirit. I would lose all my belief in the true spirit of mankind if ever I should doubt the result.

"This is why the British Prime Minister is certain of victory—
'Not so much because we are men but because the nature of man
will not be put down by the beast.' I would like to see Mr Churchill Prime Minister of all British people throughout the world."

In the usually unemotional Canadian House of Commons in
Ottawa, members broke all tradition by honouring him with fists
thumping their desks and wild applause, an amateur piper broke
out his bagpipes and honourable members went cheering, tooting,
and parading in a grand march down the chamber after he spoke.

In the United States, short of telling Americans they should
enter the war, he gave them a stirring call for arms production and
received one of the best receptions ever by a foreign visitor. Even
the sceptical Council of Foreign Relations in Chicago gave him a
standing ovation.

He went from one speech and conference to another, had an
hour's talk by the sickbed of President Roosevelt, and *Time
Magazine* recorded that not since Lord Lothian's death had
Americans heard so much plain talk from a British official as in
the two-week visit of Bob Menzies.

When, after three months he arrived home from his 30,000-odd
miles tour, the anxious restless Members in Canberra hoped he
had a message for *them*.

I I

Stares. Hard, silent stares.

"Ming's different."

MPs who hadn't seen him since he left on his travels nearly four months previously were saying it. Heads of departments, Parliament House attendants, messenger boys, cab drivers were saying it.

Only a dozen or so people had seen him since he had returned to Canberra, and so everybody's eyes worked overtime.

Menzies knew everyone in Australia was demanding a national government, and that some of his own "supporters" had been talking of pushing him out of office. He had been told of a plot to dethrone him. Some plotters (or were they?) had told him of other "plotters."

Nobody knew exactly why, but the word had gone out and they all heard: "Ming's different." So now, when Menzies came into Parliament for his first appearance since the papers in Britain and America had lauded him, everybody sat silent. And stared.

Menzies got up to move a condolence motion. "The Right Honourable the Prime Minister," announced the Speaker.

"Hear, hear," murmured a handful of ambitious supporters and loyal followers. That was the Prime Minister's Parliamentary welcome home.

Parliament adjourned after the condolences, and Menzies met the U.A.P. and Country Party members of the Government in a conference. He wanted to make a speech in the evening about his trip, then adjourn Parliament till next day.

Old tactics, those. A newsprint-rationed editor with limited

115

space would have to boil the Prime Minister's remarks down if he were to use details from a full debate. And if the Opposition were going to attack they would do so more savagely in hot blood than if they had to wait until next day.

A Party wrangle developed. Some said there should not be an immediated debate, but most argued it was no use haranguing the workers to step up production if the Government itself set a leisurely pace. Menzies fought back, and trotted out the old threat of an election if the lack of support continued because of the close division of Parliament.

He spoke heatedly, rebuking Members for their lack of support, and their criticisms during his absence from Australia. That was the atmosphere that evening, when Parliament resumed below the great chandeliers in the House of Representatives to hear Ming the Merciless make a leader's speech about the Empire at war.

Only half his Ministers attended, and the benches were silent when he earnestly began his message warning of an Empire beset with perils never faced before in its history. Members put elbows on desks, chins on hands, and after ten minutes Doc Page, the Minister for Commerce, appeared to be sleeping.

Perhaps a little compliment to Fadden, the man who had minded the shop, might have warmed the House and a joke with the Labor Party would certainly have helped things. But the Prime Minister ploughed on with his travelogue of war—a vision of what he'd seen in Palestine, Libya, and elsewhere floating before his eyes—and his earnest words fell flat.

He raised his voice and began to glare at his audience. Suddenly, towards the end of his 110-minute speech, he poked his face out at Labor leader Curtin and said he had felt sick at heart at having to come back to Australia and play at Party politics, and to find there had been a by-election which could have unseated the Government.

Heckling and interjections broke out and Curtin, red-faced, condemned the Prime Minister, accusing him of an ungracious act. The Prime Minister sat with his face in his hands, then walked out refusing to see reporters.

The Prime Minister, of course, had received a stirring welcome home in Melbourne. He had seen the British war effort, knew Australians must do more, and he inspired all Melburnians who heard him.

A couple of days later in Sydney Town Hall he made a tremendous speech about the people of Britain and their greatness, and was cheered for minutes on end.

116

TOP: *The general store at Jeparit owned by James Menzies, father of Sir Robert Menzies, who was born in the little house attached to the rear of the store*

BOTTOM: *The serious-faced boy on the left is young Bob Menzies as a pupil in Jeparit State School in 1901*

*The Menzies children in Jeparit, taken by a travelling photographer. Isabel Menzies has her arm round Les,
Frank is on the left, and Bob is sitting on the ground*

The Herald, Melbourn

Sydney Morning He

TOP: *In the garden of his Kew home*

BOTTOM: *He talks over his favourite sport with cricketers Ian Johnson and Peter May*

Sydney Morning Herald

Associated Press

TOP: *The Queen's Man. Sir Robert Gordon Menzies with Queen Elizabeth, during Her Majesty's visit to Australia*

BOTTOM: *He is capped by the Duke of Edinburgh, at the University of Edinburgh's McEwan Hall, while being awarded an Honorary Doctor of Laws degree*

United Pre

Australian News and Information Bur

TOP: *During the Suez Canal crisis, Menzies has his first meeting with the Egyptian President, Gamal Abdel Nasser*

BOTTOM: *Rain falls as Menzies prepares to inspect a Guard of Honour at Jogjakarta during his visit to Indonesia*

Reuters

United Press International

TOP: *With Sir Anthony Eden and Earl Attlee in London, 1956*

BOTTOM: *Washington 1957. Arriving to attend the funeral service for John Foster Dulles, Menzies is welcomed by President Eisenhower*

TOP: *The smile before the storm—Menzies with the Indian Prime Minister, Jawaharlal Nehru, in 1960*

BOTTOM: *In the White House, 1962. On his way home from a Commonwealth Prime Ministers' Conference, Menzies calls on President Kennedy*

*William McCall
in 1940*

Sydney Morning Herald

Sydney Morning Herald

"Billy" Hughes was godfather to Bill McCall's daughter Annabelle, and is seen here at her christening. Bill McCall at right

TOP: *With General Sir Thomas Blamey in the Middle East, 1941*

BOTTOM: *Addressing 2nd A.I.F. troops in Benghazi, 1941*

TOP: *Ambition realized. With his father and mother outside Parliament House, Canberra, when he first became Prime Minister*

BOTTOM: *With his family in 1940, in the garden of his home at Kew, Victoria. From left: Ian Menzies, Mrs (now Lady) Pattie Menzies, R. G. Menzies, Heather Menzies, Ken Menzies*

In his Privy Councillor's uniform, after appointment to the Council in 1937

Menzies after graduating from Melbourne University in 1916, with first-class honours in Law

Menzies (second from right in the third row) in the Melbourne University Rifles. Also in the photograph is Arthur Calwell (second from right in the second row)

Robert Gordon Menzies as a 13 year-old schoolboy

Kate Menzies, mother of Sir Robert

Planet News

June 1953. An important moment in Anglo-Australian relations. Churchill signs the agreement concerning Social Security benefits, such as Old Age Pensions, which now apply on a reciprocal basis between the two countries

Honours. TOP LEFT: *Sir Robert Menzies in the Mantle of Knight of the Thistle.* TOP RIGHT: *The gown of Honorary Doctor of Civil Law, Oxford.* BOTTOM LEFT: *Doctor of Laws, University of Sussex.* BOTTOM RIGHT: *In the uniform of Warden of the Cinque Ports.*

Perhaps the whole matter, he said, was summed up in the best remark that he thought had been made in Great Britain since the war began: "The King, who, with the Queen, is seen in every stricken field in Great Britain, and who grows in vigour and in force as she grows in charm, was visiting an area in which bombs had fallen and homes had been stricken.

"As she moved among the people with words of encouragement and sympathy, one man put his hand on the King's shoulder, in an Australian sort of manner, and said, 'Thank God for a good King.'

"The King turned like a flash and made one of those great remarks of history—'Thank God for a good people.' "

It can be disclosed that a day or so before Menzies made that magnificent speech, he had been shown a letter making it plain that a plot was afoot to remove him. Written on a Country Party letterhead, it pointed to a conspiracy being hatched within the Country Party.

The letter had been addressed on the envelope to Sir Sidney Snow, president of the U.A.P., but the letter itself inside was set out to a certain colonel. Obviously the wrong letter had gone into the envelope, and this letter was not intended for Sir Sidney.

Several U.A.P. officials and members had a hurried conference and although some suggested it was a "plant," Sir Sidney Snow was convinced the plot was genuine. Percy Spender passed the letter on to the Prime Minister with a written explanation of the circumstances.

In Menzies' absence overseas the whisperings and consultations that went on gave every indication of a sedulously cultivated campaign to unseat the Prime Minister. This came from the Country Party. A number of members were continually talking about the Big Fella.

Their statements were along these lines: The public does not react to the Big Fella; how are we to win with him? We'll never win an election with him; Fadden's the man who gets on well with everyone. Fadden will get the support of the public; we will definitely go out with Menzies. . . .

Fadden, of course, was loyal to Menzies in his absence and made it plain to everyone that he did not want the job. He was merely a caretaker. To keep the team together in the Big Fella's absence Fadden had encouraged joint meetings between the Country Party and U.A.P. and this was regarded as being singularly good and appreciated by every member.

Fadden was not organizing or promoting himself in order to get Menzies' job, but others were interested in pushing him.

Politics is very much a business of people and personalities and in the clash of ambitions and cross interests, reputations often come in for severe drubbings, even if only as an accumulation of passing jabs. If there was a campaign to push Arthur Fadden (and there was), or any other member who might be acceptable to a majority of people, there had also to be a campaign to belt other leading contenders if a change of leadership was to come about.

Percy Spender was involved in this way. A first-class Minister, he came into the reckoning by virtue of his own ability and the fact that he was a senior Minister from New South Wales, with only Billy Hughes senior to him in Cabinet.

Spender had the confidence and support of New South Wales interests, and if there was to be a change in the Prime Ministership, it was only natural that New South Wales, which had long suffered from Victorian domination at Canberra, would push its representative.

Accordingly, a coterie from the Country Party busily began to discredit him. As Minister for the Army, Spender toured the Western Desert and on 2 January 1941, he inspected elements of the Sixth Division A.I.F., the day before the troops captured Bardia, taking 40,000 Italian prisoners. The commanders showed him their plans and outlined their tactics for the coming battle.

Spender, like every other Australian, was proud of the Bardia achievement. When he returned, an Australian Broadcasting Commission reporter asked him to comment. In the interview the Minister used the words: "I remember very well the day before Bardia discussing the plans of attack. . . ."

His opponents at once cultivated the idea that he had tried to tell the public he had taken part in the plans and strategy which brought about the Bardia victory.

Spender was nicknamed the Baron of Bardia, and jokes went round that he was an opportunist; that he was always looking for public acclaim and would not keep out of the front lines. And when Menzies returned the word went out that Spender had been plotting.

Spender, who was a leading King's Counsel, could certainly take care of himself but he was not plotting—if he were going to cut your throat he would do so in a good open style.

And so, it is hardly surprising that privately Menzies was sceptical when Percy Spender, in addition to handing him the Country Party letter which the U.A.P. president had received, mentioned

118

in a general way that he suspected a certain Country Party mastermind was at work.

After the Prime Minister received his extraordinary ovation at Sydney Town Hall and there were speeches of loyalty to him, especially from Fadden, at the Lord Mayor's reception later, Menzies walked across to Spender.

"What about that grave you told me about *now*?" he asked.

"The grave is there, all you have to do now is go to Canberra and you'll find you will be walking into it," he was told.

"Oh," said the Prime Minister, "I think you have a fertile imagination."

The Prime Minister was a man who had recently trodden with mighty steps over the terrain of England and the United States and more recently, Australia. And after this tumultuous ovation he could not believe he had lost the confidence of a large number of people, and particularly, of many of his colleagues.

But after his welcome home, when he went to Canberra his experience at his first speech in Parliament when everyone stared, confirmed what he could not bring himself to believe.

The next day in Parliament everyone was surprised to hear Doc Page bury the hatchet, though exactly where he buried it is not quite certain. He made a statement of unqualified admiration for the work done for Australia and the Empire by Menzies on his world tour. It was widely regarded as putting an end to the bitter enmity which had existed since Page attacked Menzies about two years previously following Joe Lyons' death, although there were those who believed Page had not changed his real attitude.

Labor members were suspicious, interjecting with phrases such as, "What's this puff for?" "Who made you do this?" and "Cut out the soft soap." Eddie Ward of Sydney called out, "What a somersault! You should have put your tights on first."

Speculations began appearing in the Press that many Ministers believed Menzies intended returning to England, in the belief that the presence of an Australian Minister there was "essential" and that only the Prime Minister had the necessary influence and authority.

Menzies had been awakened by what he'd seen in England and he was a little frightened at what might befall Australia. He did his best to rouse the nation to maximum war effort and delivered a series of ringing speeches urging the mobilization of machines and manpower.

He announced sweeping powers for the prohibition of strikes in war industries, the internment of all "dangerous Communists and agitators," and action against employers who indulged in irritation tactics, even to the extent of taking over their businesses if necessary. The new order included a drastic overhaul of reserved occupation lists, rearrangement of munitions and supply departments, and overall control of transport to include the requisitioning of interstate merchant ships.

In most of his "heart to heart" addresses he had a word about the people of Britain as a note of inspiration. On one occasion he said at Melbourne Town Hall: "There was a time when one hoped to be worthy of the traditions of some ancestral home in England.

"But these are days when, for myself, I am content to try to be worthy of the glorious 1941 traditions of Bermondsey, Shoreditch, and the London docks. I ask nothing but the privilege to try to give my country some leadership worthy of the suffering, ordinary, grey man and woman of Britain. I was never so sure I was standing among the aristocracy of Britain as when I was with them."

British newspapers demanded that Churchill copy the all-in war programme of the Australian Prime Minister.

Menzies tried hard—but it was too late.

An impression had already been firmly created of delay, vacillation, and indecision. The Government had been guilty of indefinite policies on many problems affecting the general organization of war effort. This was partly because the politicians, owing to the delicate balance of Parliament were timid in the face of sectional interests which caused them to back down on vital decisions.

The Public Service and heads of war departments were overloaded with decisions that Cabinet should have made; the Government had dithered in resolving awkward problems such as petrol rationing, manpower, and industrial relations; time had also been wasted in Cabinet promises to placate sectional interests, followed by unproductive rearguard action to stall off fulfilment of the promises.

Because of a lack of clear policy, departmental heads often did not know which way to turn. As the Minister concerned would not take a stand the public servant had to fix it up some way himself, probably in an illegal, undemocratic, and even unconstitutional manner.

Petrol rationing is a case in point. The Government began looking into petrol rationing soon after the war began, and Press articles forecast rationing at least nine months before any rationing was introduced. Federal Ministers, including Supply Minister Sir Frederic Stewart, denied that the Government intended

120

rationing for civilians' use, stating privately that political considerations were the main reason.

An election was in the air and the politicians did not want to offend their electors, but Cabinet asked the Supply Department to draw up a rationing scheme. A drastic scheme was prepared allowing private motorists 2,000 miles a year, and commercial vehicles between 2,500 and 15,000 miles. Sir Frederic Stewart announced the scheme on 11 July 1940, to operate from 1 September.

Uproar followed from private motorists and petrol traders, with the Minister spending the next few days trying to square off. Eventually he said that the scheme as announced had not been approved entirely by Cabinet.

Cabinet got the jitters and the Minister asked the department to prepare another and more liberal scheme. Menzies then tried to soothe ruffled feathers by saying that all Cabinet had decided was that petrol rationing cutting consumption by one-third was to be introduced, adding that the particular method of achieving this result had never been before Cabinet.

On 17 August Cabinet decided to introduce a petrol scheme allowing private motorists 4,000 miles a year to begin on 1 October, instead of 1 September as was originally announced. A further cut was introduced on 31 March 1941 under the tougher Senator Phillip McBride who had replaced Sir Frederic Stewart, but he said the latest cut had not resulted in a one-third reduction. As the situation worsened, more cuts were planned.

Long before France fell a group of Government departmental heads and economists drew up a review of national resources, making recommendations to increase them, but many of these suggestions were not implemented until a year later. After nearly two years of war, departments were still preparing plans for increasing munitions production, mobilizing manpower, improving price control, and other urgent problems. Public servants were hoping for a Government strong enough to get these things done.

The public servants and production chiefs were responsible for much of what had been achieved since the 1940 election. Administration was being held up by political considerations at almost every turn, and some departmental heads were simply pressing on, doing the best they could without even referring to Cabinet.

Added to this was a tendency by a large section of the Australian community to not take the war seriously, and to make sacrifices reluctantly. In other quarters there was a tendency to make as much money out of the war as possible.

The situation called for powerful leadership and control of the Canberra factions and rugged individualists.

Menzies, in the opinion of some of his Ministers and many members of the time, did not help in what was an explosive situation.

They say a characteristic of his at the time was his lawyer's sense which frequently caused him to see both sides of an argument, often resulting in a postponement. Instead of action through a decision, he postponed issues to have second looks at them.

Those who opposed the issues had further time to compile an argument and this resulted in delay. Positive action in a time of war being essential, the delays enabled some people to spread dissatisfaction among the public.

Menzies' Ministers in the most part were afraid of him. With his gift for rapidly grasping anything set before him, Menzies would impatiently ask questions and expect all the answers. If a Minister was ill-prepared and could not provide them, he tended to be short with them, treating them in a schoolmasterly way, and they went away with a flea in their ear—annoyed because they were inclined to feel the fault lay with Menzies and not themselves.

They felt Menzies was overbearing. He had few friends; mainly supporters.

Ministers and Members were saying Menzies' capacity for speeches was not always accompanied by administrative action, that he was indifferent and superior and reluctant to give them interviews.

"You can't get to see the Big Fella," they were saying.

And he still could not spare the cutting remark. Soon after his return in 1941 he had dinner at Parliament House with several Ministers. It was a good meal, with wine and bright conversation and one Minister, feeling he was getting to know the Prime Minister for the first time, thought he would show a friendly front as they returned to the House and said, poking Menzies in the chest: "Well, Bob, you're a different man tonight. I've never known you before. I am even convinced you *could* suffer fools gladly."

Said Ming, with sting: "What do you think I'm doing now?"

He had already made a similar remark to one of a group of Pressmen who commented, "The trouble with you is, you don't tolerate fools easily." "Oh, I don't know," replied Menzies, "I've put up with you for a long time."

In Canberra they were saying that Menzies had been spending more time with Curtin trying to form a national government than with his own Ministers.

Some were also saying, whether justly or not, that Menzies wore the coat and the others wore the dandruff.

With a majority of only one, something had to give.

12

One of the things that Bill McCall learnt to do when he set out to achieve success through "a positive mental attitude" was to try to "divine" things; to read signs or portents before they materialized as being obvious, and so recognize opportunity.

One of the ways he did this was reading the signs on the stock exchanges at Sydney, Melbourne, and Brisbane. And he was beginning to make money out of it.

One day in July, 1941 he boarded a train in Sydney to go to Canberra while Parliament was out of session. He was joined in an oldfashioned, self-contained "dog box" compartment by three men he knew, all members of the Consultative Council of the U.A.P. The council was the New South Wales money-raising branch of the Party which held power from the outside in much the same way as the thirty-six "faceless" men (until recently) did in the Parliamentary Labor Party in Australia—they raised the money from various organizations, then told the Party what to do.

Naturally the subject of politics came up and one of the council members mentioned that they had just been addressed by the Prime Minister who had told them of his British experiences. McCall showed interest because the meetings of the council, always confidential, were important.

Suddenly one of the men said to him: "I say Bill, you'd better get those big signs of yours out from under your house."

"Why?"

"Oh well, I'm just giving you the tip, that's all. You'd better get them out." The other men nodded in agreement.

McCall knew the council member well—they had quite often visited each other's homes—and he believed he was telling him in as direct a way as possible that an election was imminent. The committeeman knew McCall kept his large canvas election signs under his house.

He recalled the Prime Minister's statement to the Party meeting on his return to Canberra and came to the conclusion, "Menzies is going to hold an election."

McCall thought this over and decided that what was needed was not an election but a change of leadership. He telephoned his U.A.P. colleague, Bill Hutchinson, in Melbourne and arranged to meet him at the Federal Members' Rooms there.

He acted this way in order to divert suspicion from the fact that a move to unseat Menzies was originating in New South Wales, particularly in Sydney.

Hutchinson issued a statement prepared by McCall, criticizing the Government over its prosecution of the war effort and declaring that there should be a change in leadership. He suggested Arthur Fadden (who had not then been consulted), as a new leader.

The statement, widely published in Australia, included the comments: "There is no use denying that things have come to a crisis with the U.A.P. at Canberra. Discontent is rife.

"I believe it is widely held among members that the time has come when a new leader should be appointed, not only to achieve the maximum degree of unity among Government members at Canberra, but also to obtain the maximum unity among the Australian people."

Menzies countered by saying he had attended a meeting of the council but leadership was not discussed. "Who are the members of the Party in Parliament who make this demand that a new leader should be appointed?" he asked.

"They should be candid enough to announce their names. Otherwise it is Mr Hutchinson alone. His bitter personal hostility to me and political disloyalty to my leadership have been well known at Canberra ever since I became Prime Minister. There is no novelty in that."

Back in Sydney, McCall told the Press that "in view of Mr Hutchinson's statement," he believed a meeting of the Party should be called to discuss the question of leadership.

Privately he organized another U.A.P. Member, Sir Charles Marr, in Sydney to call for a special meeting, with Marr adding

125

the comment that Menzies expected Party members to be a "band of 'yes' men."

The situation then hotted up. Menzies declared he would not resign, Fadden pledged his loyalty to the Prime Minister, and Menzies tried to dismiss the rebels with the comment that "after all, everybody cannot be in the Cabinet"—an adroit political tactic calculated to quell his critics, but hardly true in view of his unsuccessful approach to McCall.

McCall then announced the challenge to the leadership came after Menzies suggested to the Consultative Council that a "law and order" election be held as soon as possible.

That evening, having dinner with his family in the Sydney suburb of Manly, he heard the Prime Minister's rejoinder as the special item of national news, read by announcer Heath Burdock: "I have only two things to say in answer to Mr McCall.

"First, his statement is untrue. Second, for a member of a Party even to profess to make a statement in public about a private discussion between the leader of his Party and the executive of the Party organization—a meeting at which he was not present— seems to me to set a new standard of public indecency. I do not believe that such attempted treachery will commend Mr McCall either to his own Party or to the Labor Party."

Angered, McCall immediately drafted a reply, his wife typing several copies, and hurried into the city to make the morning Press with these comments: "As a representative of the people, I am not entitled to withhold from them knowledge of great concern. Mr Menzies has shifted his ground from politics to morals. He accuses me of indecency and treachery for disclosing the proceedings of a private meeting. I was not at the meeting in question, therefore I broke no confidence.

"The discussion on forcing an election was recounted to me by three people. This disclosure was not made in confidence. I am merely calling for inspiring leadership, as Mr Menzies himself did some years ago at a public meeting in Sydney.

"But there are these differences—firstly, the need for inspiring leadership was not nearly so vital then as it is now. Secondly, Mr Menzies was at the time a member of Cabinet, while I am only a private member and have no Cabinet loyalty to consider."

From that point on Menzies was doomed.

Employing the aphorism of Euripides that whom the gods destroy they first make mad, McCall set out to bait, organize against, and cause the downfall of the Prime Minister in a vigorous and open way that has probably not been excelled by one man in a democracy anywhere else in the world.

McCall, who today looks pure Hemingway without the beard, declared to U.A.P. members and everybody concerned: "Menzies must go!"

What went on behind the scenes in Menzies' downfall has never before been recounted in detail.

McCall is the man who forced the Lyons Government to back down on its stubborn refusal to allow Mrs Freer to enter Australia. When Menzies, as Attorney General, asked him if he would drop it, McCall said no; an injustice had been done. Finally, at the end of a bitter six months' campaign, Lyons called him to his office and said, "You realize you could wreck the Government?"

"It won't be me, you will be the one to do that," McCall answered.

"Bill, you can't do this to me," the Prime Minister pleaded.

McCall, who had travelled around most of Australia at his own expense organizing support from back benchers, replied: "Joe, it all depends who's got the numbers." And Mrs Freer got her permit.

On another occasion in the Lyons Government, believing it was unfair to the older Members to hold late night sittings, McCall spoke against this idiocy, and to demonstrate his point he began leaving early during late night debates and went to the hotel where he was booked in. When the Party Whip wanted him in order to make up the number for a quorum in the House, he would look in the hotel for him. To beat the system McCall would sleep in an unoccupied room other than his own.

The Party Whip, Siddie Gardiner, woke up to this, found a waiter with a master key and one night ferreted him out. As the waiter entered the darkened room he ran into McCall's fist, and fell back on the carpet at the feet of the startled Whip.

Reversing the traditional phrase, Siddie Gardiner said, "Joe wants you."

"You can tell Joe to —— ——," said McCall and slammed the door.

Next morning McCall was in the Party room in Parliament House when Gardiner came up. "The boss wants to see you," he said.

McCall went straight into the Prime Minister's office. "You wanted me, Joe?" "Oh, Bill," Lyons said. "About last night. I'm a bit concerned. Siddie Gardiner got very upset. I don't want to know what happened (nearly everyone in Canberra knew), but

Siddie came to me and said that you said I could ——— ———. Did you say that?"

"Yes, Joe, that's what I told him to tell you."

"Oh . . . that's all right then. I just wanted to know."

McCall organized strenuously to encourage confrontation of Menzies at a meeting which the Prime Minister finally agreed to call to discuss leadership. But it was not a joint meeting of the two Government Parties, only of the U.A.P. The other declared rebels, Sir Charles Marr and Bill Hutchinson, refused to attend on this basis.

The Party steamroller, or Party *panzer,* worked overtime trying to force McCall into submission, with the threat that he would never again get Party preselection. Even the U.A.P. president, Sir Sidney Snow, fought with him on the issue.

McCall stood alone at the meeting and made a long attack on Menzies' administration, after Menzies, speaking first, charged him with treachery and moved that he be excluded from the meeting. The attempt at expulsion was supported by Menzies' father-in-law, Senator J. Leckie, but had no support from the meeting.

McCall likened himself to Cortez, declaring, "I have burned my boats and on this rock I stand until we get a new leader."

The Prime Minister frequently interjected, but finally McCall was able to put his views without hindrance by telling him: "Don't try to put me in the witness box. I'm awake to you. I heard you in silence and I expect you to extend the same courtesy to me."

Two or three other rebels, previously undeclared, caused a sensation by joining in then and attacking Menzies but the meeting ended without any change in the leadership—the Party steamroller had done its job well and the numbers simply weren't there to force a showdown.

McCall went to the newspapers to get support. Sir Keith Murdoch of the *Melbourne Herald* had now changed his mind about Menzies. He considered Menzies ineffectual and believed a new leader would have to be found, but he did not have Artie Fadden in mind. McCall had discussions with him and when he was not in Melbourne, Hutchinson would see Murdoch or one of his executives.

With evangelical fervour McCall threw himself into the campaign. He had many discussions with R. A. G. ("Rags") Henderson, the managing director of the *Sydney Morning Herald,* on ways and means of getting rid of Menzies.

McCall fed anti-Menzies stories to Henderson, and Hutchinson would do the same with the *Herald* in Melbourne. Some of the discussions with Henderson took place at Henderson's home, some at McCall's, others in the *Herald* office. Getting rid of Menzies was a mutual interest, and Henderson too, was a real fighter.

These were not the only forces at work to boot Menzies out. Attempted bribery also played a part.

McCall was leaving the Federal Members Room at the Commonwealth Bank building in Sydney one afternoon around this time, when a man stood in his path just inside the entrance. He had been waiting around for days.

"Look, Mr McCall, the boss wants to put a proposition to you," he said.

"Who's the boss?" McCall asked.

"Oh," said the fellow, who had no front teeth, "you know who I work for." McCall said he didn't know and the man mentioned the name of a wealthy businessman and sportsman who was in trouble with the authorities.

Asked what the proposition was, the man said, "Well, I might as well tell you although he wanted to see you himself. There's £3,500 in it for you if you cross the floor of the House."

The fellow said his boss would go to £5,000 if it wasn't enough. He also mentioned the name of a prominent Federal Parliamentary Labor Party member who, he said, had asked his boss to put up the money so that the Labor Party could govern and enable him to get the boss out of trouble.

When an alderman of the Sydney City Council, between 1935 and 1938, McCall gave several would-be bribers short shift, reporting them at once. Apart from the fact that he would never even consider entering into any such arrangement, McCall knew that the go-between in these transactions is always the dangerous man —not only can he keep a cut for himself but he is in a position to blackmail as well, which makes bribery not only morally reprehensible, but plainly unsound as a practical venture.

McCall announced the bribery attempt at the next meeting of the U.A.P. in Canberra, leaving out, of course, the names involved because of slander (the name of the Labor member mentioned was *not* Curtin or his deputy, Ben Chifley), and told the Prime Minister that he would be prepared to give him all the details privately.

Menzies never asked McCall to elaborate.

The leadership row continued with Hutchinson using Keith Murdoch's columns for such statements as, "Mr Menzies taunts me about my loyalty—Mr Menzies himself did not give a very splendid exhibition of loyalty in the late days of the Lyons Government."

The Prime Minister declared: "There is a tangled web of partisanship, intrigue, and prejudice through which I have to break my way in order to do my job day by day."

As the situation grew more tense, McCall approached Arthur Fadden and asked him if he would be prepared to become Prime Minister if the situation arose. McCall made the approach on behalf of Sir Charles Marr, Hutchinson, and himself—nobody else.

Fadden, who had not been angling for the post, received a shock at first when he realized the suggestion was serious. He was not enthusiastic; he was frightened of the job, and doubted his ability to meet the challenge should it come his way.

As a last resort Cabinet discussed the proposal that Menzies should go to London and join the British War Cabinet to present Australia's views.

That was not Menzies' idea—it was fed to him in Cabinet by Sir Earle Page. But it was felt by many in Cabinet that Menzies responded to the idea with alacrity, that he saw himself as the Smuts of the second World War, that he thought rightly or wrongly that his place was in England. It is a characteristic of men of power, of course, that they like to walk with people of influence.

Billy Hughes with all his oldtime vigour made an amazing defence of Menzies in Cabinet and Parliament, urging in the strongest possible terms that he should be the man to go to London. Naturally he did not say what he was proclaiming privately, that they shouldn't miss the opportunity of getting rid of Menzies, that Menzies would not lead, yet would not follow.

In this respect Hughes clashed with McCall on the issue, claiming that only a Prime Minister would be acceptable to the British War Cabinet. But McCall, declaring that Menzies' place was in Australia, asserted that this was not so, and he produced the memoirs of Lloyd George, British Prime Minister towards the end of the first World War, to point out that when General Smuts sat for two years in the British War Cabinet it was as the South African Minister for War, not as Prime Minister.

Menzies wanted to go as Prime Minister, promising to resign after he entered the War Cabinet, but this was not acceptable to McCall—if Menzies wanted to go he had to resign first, he told the Party, and besides, McCall declared, "the Prime Minister will only be padding around Lady Astor's garden if he goes."

130

Billy Hughes was extremely sore at his young friend McCall for standing in the way.

Labor opposed the idea and it was dropped, the deputy leader Mr Ford saying it was shameful to unload an unpopular leader on the other side of the world.

But in London, where the British Cabinet reputedly was not in favour of Dominion representation, newspapers were hostile at the Australian Labor Party's stand. The *Daily Express* said: "Mr Menzies, one of the ablest Empire Statesmen, has to devote to the Australian Opposition the attention which should be concentrated against the Axis."

It all had to end somewhere.

After a month of bitterness in which Menzies' leadership was repeatedly challenged, the showdown came at a joint meeting of the U.A.P. and Country Parties. But first, on 27 August when that session of Parliament was almost at an end, Menzies took the Labor Opposition by surprise by announcing that a Minister other than the Prime Minister would go to London.

He also replied by letter to a Labor Party demand that he step down by saying that he "did not propose to accentuate the political uncertainties from which this unhappy country is suffering by handing over the Government to the Labor Party."

This phrase caused deep resentment in the Labor Party, members saying the Prime Minister was maintaining the superior attitude that had contributed to the crisis.

In the House that same day a member drew attention to a statement in Melbourne by the Australian Minister for China, Sir Frederick Eggleston, that he preferred the bombs of Chungking to the stink bombs of Australian politicians.

Asked if he thought an Australian diplomat should make a statement like that Menzies replied he could hardly be expected to disavow the sentiments expressed by Sir Frederic, as "they find an echo in my mind."

In a discussion on a statement by the Prime Minister that he could not command a constant majority in the House, Eddie Ward shouted out: "Will we have to blow you out?"

The Party machine had done its work so effectively that when the joint Government Parties met to discuss the leadership only three rebels remained—at least in the open. These were McCall, Marr, and Hutchinson. Others such as Archie Cameron, Senator Sampson, Duncan Hughes, and Tommy White had been pulled into line.

But a test of feeling had been going on behind the scenes. About a week previously Eric Spooner, the Minister for War Organization of Industry, who had been attacking the Prime Minister's aloofness on New South Wales' problems, called Arthur Coles into his office and asked him what his reaction would be if the Prime Minister resigned.

"Has Bob indicated that he is going to resign?" asked Coles.

"No, not as yet," said Spooner.

"That means a group of Cabinet Ministers are going to force his resignation?"

Spooner would not agree with this view but Coles immediately came to the conclusion that a conspiracy was afoot and declared that if anyone forced the Prime Minister out, they would lose his support in Parliament. And he walked out.

At the joint Party meeting, on 27 August, the three remaining rebels were as critical as ever of Menzies' leadership but McCall made the main attack. He said in effect that if Menzies did not resign, he would see that the Government would not have a majority in the House of Representatives, and all attempts to make him change his attitude failed. McCall emphasized that his object was to remove Menzies from the Prime Ministership, not to deprive the Government of its majority.

McCall accepted the pleas of Ministers not to make his inflexible attitude known outside the Party room because of the danger that the Labor Opposition, if they heard a whisper of it, might bring down a censure motion on the Government.

Hutchinson and Marr demanded a review of the Government leadership and with McCall demanding an assurance that there would be another joint-party meeting to discuss the leadership, a Cabinet meeting was called for 11 a.m. next day to discuss the crisis. At that meeting it became clear there was a majority of opinion against Menzies, that he had lost the confidence of the Parliament and a large section of the Australian people as a leader, and that in the interests of the nation he should step down to make way for a new leader—they asked him to resign.

This was no conspiratorial criticism but criticism based on the view that he was not giving leadership to the Party.

Claims made later that he had been forced out by New South Wales interests were not correct. Expressions of a loss of confidence did come from New South Wales Ministers, but they also came from Queensland, and from his own State of Victoria.

It is interesting to note today that one of the Ministers who stood out from the remaining small group of Menzies' followers and called for his resignation was Harold Holt. Holt had gone to the same school, was a member of the Young Nats with Menzies in the early days, and had been with him all through, and, even at that time, was being groomed for more important things because of his loyalty and support. But Holt was convinced a new leader was required.

Percy Spender was one of the Ministers who criticized Menzies at the meeting. He said the Prime Minister had been away from Australia too long, had lost the confidence of the people and his colleagues, and was not giving leadership to the country.

A few supporters, among them Senator Leckie, Senator Collett, Senator McBride, and Senator McLeay (known to members as "Mr Pickwick"), felt he should not relinquish the reins—all had hitched their waggons to the Menzies' star, now on the downward path.

In view of the weight of opinion against him, Menzies agreed to resign. Word of his intentions went round Parliament House.

But a dramatic thing happened just before Cabinet finally dispersed. Eric Harrison, the Minister for Trade and Customs, and a devoted Menzies supporter, had not been in Cabinet because he had the sad duty of attending the funeral of his wife, Mary, in Sydney.

Immediately the funeral was over he began a high-speed dash by road to Canberra in a Commonwealth Humber Super Snipe car. He covered the 200 miles in three and three-quarter hours and burst into the meeting.

"Boss!" he cried, having got an intimation of the trend of things, "what are they doing to you?"

"Don't do this thing," he shouted. And in the emotional state he was in Harrison delivered an impassioned defence of Menzies, calling some of his fellow Ministers a torrent of abusive and derogatory names, included in which was the unsettling term "traitors."

The strength of his attack came as something of a thunderclap and with murmurings of support, this turned the tide Menzies' way. He was able to pull the fat out of the fire and the meeting dispersed with the Prime Minister saying he would reconsider the position and announce his decision at another meeting that evening. He walked alone to the Lodge.

The strong bonds of the Menzies' family then showed. The Prime Minister rang his father in Melbourne, told him something of the situation and said, "I think I should step down, but before

I do I'd like you to give it consideration and, if possible, get the opinion of other members of the family."

The old gentleman—he was then eighty-one—telephoned all the family and summoned them to his home for the early evening. To his daughter, Mrs Green, he said: "Isabel, I want you to be here at seven o'clock, not a minute later."

When Mrs Green asked why, he said simply, "It's to do with R.G."

At seven o'clock all the family except Sydney was present—even Syd Sampson was there—seated in the spacious lounge room around the fire place.

Kate Menzies was sitting next to Mrs Green, and Jim Menzies had in front of him a small table with a pad and pen on it—the head of the house.

"Where's Sydney?" asked Jim Menzies. "Where is Sydney?"

"Why are we here?" asked Mrs Green.

"When Sydney arrives I'll tell you," he said. "I must have you all to get your opinions."

But Sydney didn't arrive for some time and father went ahead and told the story, declaring there had been disloyalty to Bob.

"Now Bob is thinking he should step down. Should he take this action?"

He began to ask each member of the family in turn for an opinion. At this stage Sydney, then a man of about forty, strolled in and Jim Menzies snapped, "Sydney! You're late!"

"What's going on?" asked Sydney.

Jim Menzies said, "it concerns Robert as to whether or not he should step down."

"Of course he should," said Sydney, something of a character. "He's been there long enough. Is that all you asked me here for? In that case I'm going. Cheerio." And off he went, leaving Jim Menzies with a startled expression on his face because of his son's attitude towards this momentous decision.

After getting all the opinions father weighed them up and finally said, "Isabel, go to the telephone and get Robert."

Mrs Green asked the switchgirl to get the Prime Minister in Canberra and waited on for a minute or two. By then Jim Menzies was standing at her shoulder. Impatiently he said, "You haven't told them it's his father wanting to speak to him."

After a minute or so Jim Menzies got through and told the Prime Minister the decision reached by his family, which was that he should resign.

In Cabinet soon afterwards Menzies made a bitter speech and

134

announced his intention to resign. He referred to the disunity that had crept into the Government's ranks, and to persistent attempts made to undermine him since his return from England. Menzies did not mention names, but he dealt scathingly with the U.A.P. rebellion, also attacking Australian newspapers, claiming they had set out to force him from his position.

Some expressions of support were made and the wrangle went on for two hours. Cabinet adjourned and a meeting of the U.A.P. began immediately at 9.30 p.m. with Country Party members being recalled from their hotels to Parliament House.

At this meeting Menzies spoke of his intention of resigning, and Arthur Coles savagely criticized U.A.P. members for what he termed forcing the Prime Minister out. He told them they should be ashamed of themselves and called them "disloyal creatures."

Bill Hutchinson then delivered a scathing blast against Coles, pointing out that his own behaviour since returning from England did not entitle him to call anyone disloyal as he had reflected indirectly on Menzies' ability.

In the argument that followed Coles announced his resignation from the party, walked out, locked himself in his hotel bedroom, and refused to answer the telephone or knocks on his door.

The only other support for Menzies came from Jack Perkins, the New South Wales member, who in turn was criticized by Sir Charles Marr. The meeting broke up and at 10.30 p.m. immediately afterwards, a joint U.A.P.-Country Party meeting began.

Whatever happened to induce the Prime Minister to change his mind is not known, but he made a final effort to cling grimly to the cliff edge of power. After the U.A.P. meeting he remained in the same room for the joint meeting with one last card up his sleeve.

After a few minutes he proposed that if he could be guaranteed 100 per cent support from the Parties to get the Government through the forthcoming war measures Budget he would then offer himself for re-election to the combined Government Parties.

"An adverse vote will mean our Government will have to resign," he told the meeting. "If I can be assured of your support, gentlemen, to get me through the Budget I'll offer myself for re-election to the combined parties and abide by the decision."

A compromise, an appeal to the Australian characteristic of giving a man a fair go, a hard thing to deny a Prime Minister especially in time of war.

The issue was quickly put to the meeting: Could the Prime

Minister be guaranteed complete support until the Budget? There were murmurings of agreement.

Bill Hutchinson, seated towards the back, got up: "Yes, I think that's quite fair, Mr Prime Minister. . . ."

Sir Charles Marr, sitting a little further behind, said he, too, thought it was fair enough, and gave his backing.

The meeting waited for McCall, the last of the rebels. He was seated right at the back. The proposal was thrust on the meeting and the rebels had no opportunity in the tense atmosphere of communicating with one another. After a few seconds McCall stood up. "I am not in agreement," he said. "I am not in agreement."

Looking directly at the Prime Minister he went on: "I've heard clearly what you've said. I wish you to please understand what I'm going to say, and if you don't, I'll repeat it.

"I will take the first opportunity to defeat on the floor of the House *any* Government of which you are the leader. Is that clear?"

Menzies said quietly, "Perfectly clear."

Pale, the Prime Minister eased himself out of his chair and stood up, his ministers seated around him at his long table. This brilliant man with the gift for words was silent for perhaps twenty seconds. He stared at the ceiling.

Finally, the Prime Minister said, as though to himself, "I feel I've lived a hundred years." Then, "Gentlemen, I offer you my resignation."

In the moments that followed the Prime Minister said that as he was unacceptable to large sections of the public and the Press, the only remedy was for the Government Parties to elect another Prime Minister who might have more hope of restoring stability, and he recommended that his successor should be chosen at once by the combined meeting of the Government Parties.

McCall walked across to Fadden, seated near the members' letter boxes, laid his hand on his shoulder and said, "It's up to you now, Artie."

Hutchinson moved that Arthur Fadden be elected Prime Minister Designate. Sir Charles Marr seconded the motion, and since there were no other nominations Fadden was unanimously elected.

Menzies was first to leave the meeting, managing a joke with reporters grouped outside the party room. "You fellows look as if you've been to a funeral," he said. Soon afterwards he issued a written Press statement. Percy Spender was one who also made a statement, saying the circumstances in which the Prime Minister vacated his office could only bring the greatest credit to him personally.

For Bob Menzies it was tragic. He handed in his resignation to the Governor General next day.

A week or so later he and Pattie Menzies took one last look at the Prime Minister's Lodge as they said goodby to a small gathering of friends—only their *true* friends were there to see their departure.

Mrs Menzies wept when she farewelled the servants. Only the previous week she had finished a two-year job in completely redecorating The Lodge.

"Mrs Fadden will find it all nice," she said. And as the train pulled out of Canberra Railway Station for Melbourne there was one sad woman on board.

Bob Menzies was already a joke. He was thought to be defeatist, a Neville Chamberlain, a hopeless leader. A has-been.

13

Why does a man, when faced with a great challenge in his life, resign? Is it because he believes another man can do a better job in the circumstances? Or is it because he himself feels inadequate to meet the crisis?

In the opinion of Arthur Coles—today Sir Arthur Coles, retired, of Toorak, Melbourne—the resignation of the Prime Minister at that time was not an act of courage.

"He threw the towel in," he says, "but what a time to throw it in!"

Sir Arthur thought then, and still does, that the Prime Minister should have stood up to his critics. He himself was solidly behind the Prime Minister at the time and believed he was the only man who could lead Australia. Menzies had the knowledge and ability, and the Australian people were scared and looking for leadership.

In Sir Arthur's opinion Australians were willing to forego some of their easy-going pleasures and happy-go-lucky life, and get cracking in the war effort. He is satisfied about that.

"That Bob Menzies was unpopular at the time there is no doubt," he says. "He'd been unpopular previously, but this was his opportunity to tell Australians in no uncertain terms what their duty was. The country was at his feet waiting to be led.

"Armed with the knowledge he had, and faced with the great challenge before him, it is beyond my comprehension why he resigned instead of standing firm. One can be quite wrong in trying to interpret it but to me it was almost a disaster.

138

"Why should he have had to argue at all? He was the Prime Minister at the critical stage, the only informed man. If I'd been in his position I'd have said, 'All right boys, fight me in the Party room.'

"At that stage he was no different to a soldier in the trenches—if a soldier walks home, who fights the war? I am uncompromising on this point, and to me that was the most vital blow I have ever received.

"I was very disappointed with him at that time. I had thought that here was a man who would stand to his colours, but he didn't—he resigned.

"It was disappointing and frustrating to see Bob go. Here was I making speech after speech and doing everything I could to get Australia conditioned for war, and I had pledged myself in writing to support this man. Suddenly he's gone and I'm left with two feet off the ground. It's amazing the feeling you get, the whole world is cut away from you.

"My first reaction was: I will resign, I'm not going to support the rabble that has done this thing. I thought to a certain extent he had been forced out, but not entirely, and that is why I announced I had witnessed a lynching. I think that phrase did a lot to save Bob Menzies' political future.

"I think he should have stayed and fought. I don't think it was a case of disloyalty to him. Dissatisfaction or dislike is more like it. Members were against him on personal grounds and, I think, Sydney on political grounds. But if he'd stood up to them they could not have forced him out. It is difficult to define what this portrayed of the man.

"I have no doubt the Prime Minister was not doing enough at the beginning of the war. I can remember going to a U.A.P. meeting and hearing the Prime Minister say that after the first World War Australia had enormous quantities of waste material, and this time the war effort must be organized in such a way that there was no waste, no beating of the air.

"To me this was anathema. If you have an enemy with a certain amount of equipment, men and materials and fire power and so on, you've got to build yours up so much you fall on him and overwhelm him. When that happens you've got an enormous amount of stuff left over. But if you don't, you're the one who will go under.

"That got under my skin and I did not think we should approach a war that way with our whole life at stake. I was fearful of what the results could be and information from reliable Government sources told us before the war broke out that Germany, Italy, and Japan would all come in together.

"I believed Bob Menzies realized all this, but too late. At that point they got him out."

Sir Arthur Coles believes Menzies missed his great moment of history in his decision to resign as Prime Minister when Australia's greatest crisis came.

His view is that it was futile of the Prime Minister to talk of returning to Britain when Churchill obviously could do so little to defend Australia—but, of course, that was while Australia still flew the Union Jack, before the American alliance began.

Bill McCall, the man who technically put Menzies in limbo, is also of the opinion that the Prime Minister folded up.

He claims the Prime Minister missed an important qualification in his statement to him at the time of his resignation when he said he would take "the first opportunity" to defeat any Government of which he was the leader.

McCall today declares: "If he had asked me what I meant by 'the first opportunity' I would have told him I did not intend to defeat him on the Budget. You would not have to be a Rhodes Scholar to know that I wouldn't have liked it tagged on me that I was the one who had sacked the Prime Minister two-thirds of the way through his Budget in the middle of a war.

"I think the fact that I have not been blamed for this proves it was not my intention to put the Government out at once. I would have given my support until after the Budget and he could have gone on a little longer. If he had called my bluff by saying, 'all right, you do it,' I would not have done a thing.

"Let's be frank. I wanted him out. I pulled a bluff and it succeeded. He was too emotionally upset to see the qualification."

This writer asked one of Menzies' chief wartime Ministers his considered opinion of the performance of Menzies and his Government up to the time of their defeat: "We deserved to go out," he says. "That Government deserved to be thrown out because we did not mobilize the country for war.

"In my view the Prime Minister had created the impression that his hand was not on the tiller. His 'business as usual' attitude was a shock to us when France was over-run.

"It should not be forgotten that this crisis when it fell upon us, was one for which we were totally unprepared—a result, in my view, of the complete unreality of the defence position prior to the outbreak of war."

140

Menzies was a lonely man after his downfall. So much so that apparently he saw an only friend in Arthur Coles when Coles walked out of the U.A.P. meeting at which Menzies indicated he would resign. Although Coles told the hotel switch operator not to put any telephone calls through to his room, the operator that night connected the retiring Prime Minister.

Menzies asked Coles if he would not say anything to the Press or anybody else until he had had a talk with him. Next morning he called around but had nothing particular to say, except perhaps to call the Government Parties a rabble, and he gave the impression that he only wanted someone to talk to.

Everyone thought Menzies was finished. But he was a far-seeing political fellow. When he stepped down he made no attempt to see that his successor should come from his own Party, knowing that the Country Party and a few in his own Party were building up Fadden's popularity—as though popularity were the best quality for leadership—and he felt Fadden might not last.

When he resigned the U.A.P. leadership he threw his weight behind Billy Hughes, which some people regarded as a move to play for a card of re-entry. Hughes obviously could not have long to go—the Little Digger was then seventy-seven. That astute move was the key to subsequent history.

After declaring his loyalty to Fadden, Menzies retained the portfolio of Minister for Defence Co-ordination and resumed his law practice in Melbourne. And each week he broadcast through Radio 2UE in Sydney over an Australian-wide hookup on overseas and Australian topics.

He told a member of his family in his legal chambers: "You know, I find this a most satisfactory experience. I'm back at the law where I've got to do some exact thinking and I'm giving this weekly talk which has become a bit of a chore, but I find there's a political philosophy in it."

Menzies was not wasting his time but opening his mind, and doing some creative political thinking.

Somewhat ironically, Doc Page was chosen as special envoy to the British War Cabinet—an idea he had proposed to Menzies.

Menzies blamed not only the disruptions in his own Party but the Press campaign, particularly by the *Sydney Morning Herald*, for having engineered his political downfall. He believed that some reporters in certain quarters had abused his confidence—but apparently it did not occur to him that his increasing inaccessibility had been responsible for his unpopularity with many Pressmen.

The only indication Menzies gave of being hurt, that he might find revenge to be sweet, was in the dining room of the Hotel Canberra one day.

At breakfast he approached Arthur Coles, sitting with Mrs Coles, and placing his arm around his shoulder, said, "You know Arthur, what would do these fellows a lot of good?"

"What's that, Bob?"

"A long period in the Opposition."

"Don't worry, Bob," replied Coles, "they're going to get it."

Fadden's Government, which drifted for forty days and forty nights, got it. Fadden has always claimed in Parliamentary circles that he was undermined, and while it is true that such an attempt was made, this had little to do directly with the defeat of his Government.

The undermining attempt occurred in this way: A person who became associated with Fadden was disloyal to him. The person had an assignment to bring Fadden down.

From his association with Fadden he compiled a damaging report containing allegations about a "slush fund," with references also to Fadden's private life.

This man then took a copy of the allegations to Curtin who, being a man of great integrity, did the decent thing and took the file to Fadden, telling him where it came from.

But what Curtin did not know was that copies had also been supplied to two of his lieutenants, Dr Evatt and J. Beasley, who had already disseminated the information.

The background was that the Menzies Government had established a fund to counter subversive activities with propaganda. The Attorney General, Billy Hughes, had the responsibility of operating it, and during Menzies' absence Fadden gave Hughes approval to assist in a campaign to curb industrial unrest.

When the informant handed his damaging report on Fadden to Curtin, he also provided copies of confidential and official documents in an effort to substantiate the allegations against the new Prime Minister.

From public statements made later it was shown that the official documents referred mainly to (1) certain confidential messages between Fadden and Menzies while Menzies was in London; (2) the "secret fund" and payments made from it; (3) allegations that telephone calls from Menzies' Ministerial office in Canberra had disclosed distorted accounts of a discussion on finance problems between the Advisory War Council and Commonwealth Bank Board officials.

Curtin declared in a public statement: "My opinion is that the documents were given to me because, in view of what happened in recent political discussions, it was believed that by giving the information to me, it would enable an attack to be made on Mr Fadden."

A Royal Commission eventually set up with limited terms found that a total of £4,995 was paid into a special account, £4,942 of it going into a campaign carried out under the name of the Australian Democratic Front; in spite of previous union denials the Commission found that £300 of this had gone to Charles Nelson, the Miners' Federation president in accordance with Fadden's instructions.

The Commission also found there had not been any disclosures of Government financial proposals in telephone calls from the office of Menzies.

Fadden was very bitter after his downfall. He used to refer to Menzies repeatedly as "that big bag of ———."

The reasons for Fadden's fall were something quite separate from this little bit of political chicanery, although the controversy arising from the act of treachery certainly did not improve Fadden's standing.

Fadden disliked Coles intensely. And when Coles had returned from England he had sought an interview with Fadden, then Acting Prime Minister in Menzies' absence.

Fadden kept him waiting for a considerable time, deliberately, but eventually gave him a hearing.

Coles, who had made a close study of the war effort in Britain, was seized with the vision of what he thought Australia should be doing, but Fadden could not agree with him. Thinking of the appeasement of strikers in Australia at that time, Coles felt there was no firm hand on the wheel. He was disappointed with Fadden's performance as stand-in Prime Minister.

Undeterred by Fadden's rebuff, he outlined twenty-three major points on what Australia should be doing and saw this published in the Australian Press. He also had printed and published a booklet called *England At War* which he sent to every member of Parliament and to other interested people.

It has always been claimed privately that Coles voted the Fadden Government out because he was refused a position in Cabinet. That is not so. Coles made it clear he would not give his support to Fadden until a definite war policy had been stated and a Cabinet appointed to carry it out. He did not ask directly for a Cabinet post, but naturally would not have refused one if it had been offered him.

The fall of Fadden came early in October, when Coles reached the conclusion that too little was being done about increasing the war production. He had been in politics long enough to realize that the justice of your cause does not matter if you've got the numbers.

Although only one hostile vote was needed, he looked around for support. The obvious choice was Alex Wilson, the Independent, a wheatgrower from Wimmera in the Mallee.

Wilson had suffered from the drought and was disgruntled, wanting a better deal for the farmer. He was a Douglas creditor, a believer in the scheme from Alberta, Canada, that money loses its value once you get it so it must be spent quickly—an automatic method of equalizing spending power.

A more dissimilar political pair you could not imagine, though both being Independents they shared a room. But they had in common their conviction that the Government should go. Coles never quite knew why Wilson was disgruntled and Wilson never understood Coles, who was very much a loner in politics.

"Let's go for a walk," Coles said to Wilson one day. "The walls have ears in Canberra."

So they went for a stroll in the Australian section of the gardens near Parliament House, walking slowly up and down among the gum trees. Coles said he was considering voting against the Government on the Budget. They talked for a while and Wilson said his views were much the same.

Coles felt that his fellow conspirator was a strange character. He could not reason out Wilson's theories, and he did not seem to want any particular advantage for his own district. But these things mattered not—they would merge anyway.

Wilson agreed Coles could speak first, and he was anxious that it should not be known they were acting in collusion. As they had both thought independently of voting against the Government it really didn't seem like collusion to get together like this, but it was imperative that their move should come as a complete surprise.

And so, during what was outwardly nothing more than a leisurely stroll in the spring sunshine among the gum trees, the vote was organized to throw out a wartime Government—a move by Coles that required a great deal of courage. This was the same Coles who at Gallipoli often went out through the barbed wire each morning at the first flush of dawn to revet machine guns under Turkish fire.

144

Wilson said he knew Chifley well and would make contact with him. Next day Ben Chifley came to Coles in the Parliamentary billiards room. "John would like to come and have a talk with you," he said, without elaboration.

Curtin came to Coles' office and after a brief hushed conversation said, "You know, our Party has not agreed to many of the things you are standing for?"

"John," said Coles, "all I want is a stable Government that will face the realities of this situation and when the crisis comes, we will be in a position to meet it. I don't know whether you'll be called to Government or not, or whether there will be an election, but all I want is a promise from you that you will have all your people in the House when the vote is taken. That's the only promise I want."

It had often been said that Labor did not want to govern in the war, but even if that had been true at one time, it certainly was not now. Curtin was so happy his eyes sparkled behind his glasses.

He began to talk . . . Coles could have had almost anything he wanted in the way of political appointment. "John," said Coles, "don't say it. Just have your fellows in the House."

Menzies did not know of the move. No discussion whatever had taken place with him, except his intimation in the dining room that he would like to see the U.A.P. in Opposition. As far as Coles was concerned the only people who knew were Wilson, Chifley, and Curtin. And Errol Knox, the boss of *The Argus* whom he rang late at night so *The Argus* could get a good cover.

In the debate soon afterwards, Curtin moved that the Budget be reduced by £1; the regulation British Parliamentary way of objecting to a Budget. Coles and then Wilson supported this amendment and when the vote was taken they had only to walk a few feet to cross to the other side of the House. Fadden, conceding defeat, handed his resignation to the Governor General, and Labor took office.

What followed is history. The immediate transformation was that the Japanese struck at Pearl Harbor on 7 December, frightening the daylights out of Australia and the United States, which promptly entered the war. And the Australian Parliament under John Curtin was united.

Under Labor, Australia was utilized to its maximum war output. Uniform taxation was brought in with those earning over £5,000 a year paying 18/6 in the pound; conscription of industry, call-up of manpower and womanpower, a breakdown of the wages

145

awards, training schemes for process workers to work on ammunition lines; union rules for skills broken down.

Rationing of food and other essential items was introduced under the control of Arthur Coles who showed his business ability and organizing capacity by introducing an Australia-wide scheme in six weeks from a standing start. There were no premises and Coles and his team began with thirteen desks in the head office of G. J. Coles in Melbourne, employing the office girls and copying machines there to provide a rationing scale drawn up in the board room.

Without any records of consumption figures but with the help of a Coles' statistical accountant named Jim Galbraith, a complete scale of consumption for Australia and requirements for Britain was introduced. Later in London the Board of Trade expressed amazement and delight that Australia was the only country which could announce its own cotton requirements eighteen months in advance and live within the scale.

Curtin, an intensely patriotic Australian, did not like the British idea that the Far East and Australia were expendable and could be recovered later. This led to his rows with Churchill and his famous appeal to the United States for help "free of any pangs as to our traditional links with the United Kingdom."

The result was massive American aid with General MacArthur having a free hand in military planning; the eventual winning of the Pacific War, the establishment of a firm friendship with the United States, and a gradual drawing away from the British flag.

Curtin's disputes with Churchill, which dragged in President Roosevelt, evidently caused the British Prime Minister to decide that he would never visit Australia, and he never did. Curtin had the strength to stand up for what he believed was right for Australia, and he saw through what Labor considered to be a lie by Churchill. This was the diversion of the Australian Seventh Division to Burma, before the Australian Government had given its consent to Churchill's proposal that the homeward-bound troops should be diverted.

One view of history is that Churchill was right, and that the addition of the Australians at that time in Burma could have prevented a Japanese victory there. But the major Australian viewpoint is that Curtin was right. The Seventh Division arrived in Australia in March, 1942, and was the only fully-trained formation available when troops were required for the New Guinea campaign. Sent there in September, they stopped the Japanese advance—the first time this enemy had been defeated since Pearl Harbor.

When the pressure of the war lessened, Curtin paid a tribute to the work done by Menzies for Australia early in the war. If it is accepted that Menzies did not do enough to mobilize the war effort, it must be accepted that he laid down the blueprints. The Labor Party did not alter any of these, or change any of the key appointments he made—Sir Thomas Blamey, Commander of the Army, being perhaps the classic one.

Curtin was a great Australian, but not in the way that Menzies and Casey achieved their distinction. He put Australia first, even before the Empire—Casey had intervened on behalf of England in 1931 when Prime Minister Scullin appointed the first native-born Governor General in Sir Isaac Isaacs.

Curtin had none of the outward gifts of Menzies. He came up through the Labor movement and the unions and, as a young man, practised his oratory in an empty office after everyone had gone home. He was a reformed heavy drinker who slept little during the war, feeling a terrible sense of responsibility in all his decisions and doubting his own ability. All through this period his wife was seriously ill.

Curtin died in office at the Prime Minister's Lodge in Canberra on 5 July 1945, without seeing the end of the war.

He was brought up a Catholic but in adult life was an agnostic. Just before he died John Scullin, a devout Catholic, went to him and said: "I know you don't believe much in God, Jack, but don't you think it's time you made peace with your Maker?"

"I've seen it through like this so far," replied Curtin, "and I'm not going to change now."

No Australian Prime Minister had greater integrity.

14

When a man has the rug pulled from under him it makes him think.

If he is intelligent, and sensitive, he will examine himself to find the reasons for his fall. When he learns why, his strength will grow out of those weaknesses.

Menzies had plenty of time to think while in the wilderness. He had such phrases as Billy Hughes' to ruminate on: "Menzies couldn't lead a flock of homing pigeons."

He sat on the back benches, in the doldrums. When Prime Minister Curtin, trying to make a point, declared in a debate that members of the Opposition had prevented the Right Honourable Member for Kooyong from continuing as Prime Minister, Menzies told the House quietly: "I wish honourable members would leave me alone. It is a most unpleasant experience to be exhumed."

Menzies had always been a walker but now he took to going for long walks, four and five miles at a time, alone. He had never been disciplined before, he'd had a clear uninterrupted run of academic successes, and been in the position to more or less control his own future.

As one man who has known him for more than fifty years remarked: "It's a pity he hadn't gone into the Army for a couple of years. A great leveller, you know. It would have done him a lot of good."

From the back benches he could see the ruins of the coalition and his own Party around him. Menzies even held back on interjections and clever remarks as he took stock. But Menzies is, if nothing, a realist and as he looked around he told himself he was far from finished.

Early in 1942 while strolling through Kings Hall, Parliament House, the journalist who met him in Melbourne in 1932 when he doubted his chances of ever becoming Prime Minister, bumped into him again for the first time in several years.

"I've just been for a walk," said Menzies. "I'm keeping myself extraordinarily fit because I believe I've still got a job of work to do for this country."

The journalist didn't believe it, and nobody else in Canberra did at the time, but Menzies apparently thought he could make a comeback.

This chastening period out of office was the making of Menzies.

Bill McCall takes credit for having been the one man who put Menzies in purgatory. He believes Menzies would not have survived later without experiencing the ashes-in-the-mouth lessons of defeat.

"I did Menzies the greatest service any man ever did him," he said in analysing the events since 1941.

"Menzies learnt not to be so superior, and to take a little more notice of those around him. He tried to get the better of me by being superior, not in fact but merely in manner, by setting himself above me. That was hopeless.

"He used to stride through Kings Hall in the most aloof manner. Not that I mind a bit of arrogance, I can be arrogant myself at times, but like most of the others at the time I was frustrated by the Prime Minister's superior air. You couldn't talk to him, and that was a complaint most members had.

"I don't think Bob had the ability to handle a large number of people and get the best out of them. I'm not saying Bob was not enthusiastic himself, but you have to show people you *are* enthusiastic so they can be impelled and carried on by your own attitude.

"Bob resented any questioning or criticism and the only way you could get any reaction was to shock him. This I did.

"I genuinely believed he was not doing the job required of him as leader, but I do admit that when it became a strong personal issue between us, I did feel something like a pirate out on the high seas—it was a case of shoot first or be sunk yourself.

"Now, Menzies could have easily corrected this. All he had to do was call Charlie Marr, Bill Hutchinson, and me to his office and talk it over, and been big enough to admit that he might not have taken enough notice of us when we sought information. We were only trying to do our jobs, and if he'd listened to our side a little we would have been right behind him. We would have called it a day and he would have stayed on as Prime Minister, and history might have been different.

"It was not a matter of compromising on his part. All he had to do was follow the example set by Joe Lyons, and encourage people to work with and for him.

"Take Joe for instance. Often on a Thursday afternoon in Canberra before Parliament rose he would send for me and say, 'Bill, what's on at the week-end?' I'd say I was addressing certain meetings, or that certain conferences were on, and he would probably ask me to get somebody's opinion on some matter.

"I would come back bursting with enthusiasm to tell the Prime Minister what I had learnt. Joe did this with other members, acknowledging that they were part of the team.

"It didn't matter to me that the information when I passed it on might be useless because he explained once, "Bill, don't ever get upset if you've worked hard, and have your opinions on how I should act, and I happen to do something completely unexpected. It will only be that other information has come to me as Prime Minister and you will know nothing about it. It won't be personal.'

"Joe Lyons knew how to handle men. I can't ever remember Bob Menzies asking anyone in the Party room what they thought because he was so goddamned superior he believed he knew everything.

"I can only think that Bob Menzies in later years became more amenable—and that's being very fair to him."

McCall's revelations after nearly thirty years prove that Menzies was not thrown out by the powerful interests, by newspapers like the *Sydney Morning Herald* and *Melbourne Herald,* and by the Collins Street graziers of Melbourne, however much their campaigns may have helped create the climate.

Menzies' downfall was due to his own personality and lack of personal contact with his fellow members as much as anything. He might well have stayed in power if he had understood men, because in spite of what has been said and written over the years, only three had the courage and conviction to stand out against him and in the end, only one.

Hughes, Page, and a few others wanted desperately to see him out but their organizing died on the vine of Party pressure— McCall was the architect of Menzies' downfall and he acted independently of these members, staying in the fight with Marr and Hutchinson after all other supporters had dropped out.

150

Menzies made no attempt to come to terms with these men although he had a majority of only one. He tried instead to beat them down simply by acting The Boss.

Menzies had gained his goals through life by being clever. It finally dawned on him that his opponents did not sit on the opposite side of the House—they sat with him on his own benches.

And before setting out to beat his opponents on the opposite side of the House he had to come to terms with his own partners first. Menzies had invited the warfare that went on and he knew it.

Indeed, a slightly humbled Menzies began noticing people around him for the first time. But he continued to preserve his great self respect. For instance, he made no attempt to conceal his contempt for the "average" politician. To him the "average" was not good enough. His view was that democracy depended not on the leadership of the average but on the leadership of what Confucius called "superior man." There were few who thought Menzies concealed tactfully enough, even after defeat, his conviction that he was such a man.

But in contrast to his previously expressed defence for the rights of the top dogs Menzies now had something to say on behalf of the middle class.

Some of his other statements at this time were far from popular, such as an article in the *Manchester Guardian* stating that it was better to beat Hitler first and let the Japs wait, an attitude directly opposed to the Australian Government policy.

Nobody minded when he condemned anti-British feeling, but a great many Australians were glad he was in defeat when he described the Australian anthem, "Advance Australia Fair," as a revolting melody.

"There has been too much of this talk of our independence and our rights," he said in the same speech. "We must concentrate on the fact that we are a great world power because we are subjects of a common King."

Menzies was in almost total eclipse. Frustrated, he formed what was known as the National Service Group, made up of the more conservative members of the Party he once led.

Early in 1943 Menzies began his bid for control of the U.A.P. again. But the first hurdle was Billy Hughes, who believed the measure of a Party leader's success lay in his ability to avoid calling a Party meeting. A leader could not be beaten if his Party never met.

In order to pull off something spectacular, Menzies in the middle of 1943 went in to the Labor stronghold of East Sydney,

151

where Eddie Ward reigned supreme, and addressed a wild meeting. Nuts and bolts and pieces of pig iron were hurled onto the stage; some grazed him on the leg and a mob tried to attack him and were held back by police.

He was hooted unmercifully, counted out, and howled down almost every second sentence. Groups stood up and gave the Nazi salute, women screamed "Fascist!" and "Send him to the Bastille." One man dumped a lump of pig iron on the stage and yelled, "Pig-Iron Bob!"

When another man in the front row sprang up and shouted, "Listen comrades, this is the bloke who jailed Maxie Thomas," police had to wrestle to hold several men back from the stage.

Menzies had opened his address with, "Ladies and gentlemen. I did not know there were so many aliens in Sydney until I came here. It is one of the great proofs of the freedom of this country that there are more Fascist salutes being given in this hall tonight than in the whole of Italy."

When the meeting broke up a yelling, milling mob of about 300 waited outside for Menzies. Despite his police escort he was punched several times, and a sergeant commandeered a private car to take him to safety.

In spite of remarks by most of his colleagues that "we would never win with Menzies," he worked extremely hard to re-establish himself. Feeling that some support was lacking in Melbourne, he went to Sydney and picked up a good deal of support from business leaders there, finally got his way and was elected U.A.P. leader again. His old friend the *Sydney Morning Herald* recorded: "With a candour which is necessary in discussing a public man with claims to greatness, one must record that Mr Menzies is an unbelievably self-centred person. From this fact spring the faults which have led him to most of his worst mistakes.

"His personal vanity, his reluctance to give unstinted praise to, or express confidence in, anyone else in the world from Roosevelt and Churchill downwards, his unwillingness to have close to him men whose ability remotely approaches his own, his general judgment of men which is far from good, are all reflections of this.

"It was depressing to see him taking advice from those far beneath him in ability and judgment, and his choice of associates was often really deplorable.

"These are hard words to say of any man, but there is every indication that had he been continually successful these faults would have grown worse. Only his fall, which he took with such intense and bitter vindictiveness, could possibly have given him a hope of overcoming them.

"From that fall has already emerged a Mr Menzies less jaunty and self-assertive, more wary and better able to dissemble, but with an absolute determination that this shall not be the last of Mr Menzies. It is inevitable that he should have gone through the purgatory of being disillusioned, first about political life, and secondly about himself. If he can purge his system of the bitterness which that disillusionment brings he will most assuredly emerge a greater man."

True.

Menzies fought the 1943 elections as Leader of the Opposition, having replaced Fadden, and suffered a landslide defeat. Opposition members were walking around saying if only they could get rid of Menzies they'd win. Menzies had few friends.

And to overcome his humiliation he accentuated his air of arrogance. When Labor members interjected he would show he was deeply hurt but would not answer them back. Yet all the time an observant member could sense that here was a man asking himself, "Is this the end of the road for me? I've just got to do something."

Out of this humiliation there emerged a toughness and ruthlessness that were to achieve for him a measure of greatness. And the way through the ashes for this man of firm conviction, of intolerance, was a genius for persuasion.

The mask he wore, deliberately created, was to become impenetrable to all but the closest friends, who were few and far between.

Menzies saw that his opportunity might lie in the unification of all the non-Labor political organizations in Australia. And there were plenty of them. So many Parties in the various States had used the title "United" that the word had become sinister. When the National Party had become the United Australia Party and the Country Party the United Country Party, the question of unity reared its head almost at once.

The U.A.P. had met a definite need in its early years but now had lost its inspiration. It had come to be identified, in the public mind, with a passive defensive policy which was out of keeping with the new era that would emerge at war's end. Many people were looking for a Party that would give them a real rallying ground.

But Menzies did not originate the move which resulted in the unity of non-Labor political organizations, although generally credited with having done so. A mark of the good politician is to take a sound idea—it matters not whether the idea is someone else's—sit on it for a while if necessary, then turn it to your advantage by using it as your own.

Menzies was to become a master of this technique.

Today even Liberal Party literature credits Menzies with the idea of creating the Liberal Party of Australia, when in fact, the idea for such a Federal party had its genesis in a little café in Sydney, which was the rendezvous of seven or eight U.A.P. men.

These men, among them Lyall Scott, Harold Venn-Brown, John (later Sir John) Cramer, and Harry McCourt, met every Thursday for lunch in the Blue Room Café in Rowe Street, in the heart of the city, to discuss the Australian political scene.

They determined in 1943 that a new Federal political organization was needed. It would have to be less conservative than the U.A.P., whose stocks were at an extremely low ebb.

One of the main principles for such a body, they decided, was that it should not accept money from any organization for political purposes in a way that would enable such an organization to dictate policy—as had happened through Collins House or the Consultative Council in New South Wales.

It was agreed to wind up the U.A.P., and John Cramer was delegated as spokesman for the group to approach Alec Mair, Leader of the Opposition in New South Wales. As a result, the U.A.P. in that State was washed up at a meeting of the U.A.P. Council and a new party, the Democratic Party, formed with a view to making it Australia-wide.

Many small Parties cropped up, died and resurrected themselves in New South Wales with often bewildering speed, but the Democratic Party formed branches throughout the State and contested the 1944 elections, which it lost.

Federal members of the Party were embarrassed by the change because it robbed the U.A.P. of Federal unity. Menzies himself was upset, so was his loyal supporter in New South Wales, Eric Harrison, who had lobbied strongly against the change in political allegiance.

At the conference which formed the Democratic Party, members asked Menzies as U.A.P. leader if they could form a Federal body. Arising from this, Menzies succeeded in calling together in Canberra and Albury in November, 1944, eighty delegates representing non-Labor organizations from all States to discuss unity. He had finally embraced the plan, adding his own philosophy.

While it is true that Menzies became the driving force behind this move, the idea began elsewhere.

The unity meeting showed changes in the political thought and intentions which Menzies developed while relegated to the back benches. He emerged as something of a political evangelist and reformer with an objective, a plan of organization, and a nucleus of a policy which though not entirely new, met the needs of changing times.

It was unchanged in its abhorrence to socialism in Australia, and adherence to the profit motive and private enterprise which he declared to be the dynamic force of social progress.

But he no longer appealed only to the middle class as the mainstay of the new Party, which he clearly hoped to lead back to power in Canberra in 1946. He appealed also to about 80 per cent of wage and salary earners who, he declared, still depended upon private enterprise for employment and progress in the period of post-war reconstruction. He appealed to young men and possibly young women for the Party and in Parliament.

He talked frankly of Party finance, his speech amounting almost to a declaration of independence from the individual donors of large sums to Party funds. While large individual subscriptions would be always welcome the money should come from members in small amounts, so that supporters would know that the political fight was based upon the work, policy, and money of hundreds of thousands of individuals.

This idea, taken from the Democratic Party, reflected Menzies' own integrity and his desire to be free from pressure by monied groups or individuals. The financial structure of the Party was based on a refusal to take money from trade groups or associations. While the Party was the poorer financially for this, it would be freer from outside pressure.

Menzies did not hesitate to use the word propaganda, demanding a central bureau of research and public relations. Melbourne and Canberra journalist Charles Meeking was appointed his Press Secretary. He used the term "liberal party" so often it was clear this was his choice although he did not say so, skilfully leaving it to the rank and file to decide.

That was the beginning of the Liberal Party, a party name which, in the early days of the Federation of the six Australian States in 1901, stood for a progressive individualism. The name was used by anti-Labor forces until 1917, when the National Labor Party led by Billy Hughes, who had broken with the Labor Party over conscription, joined with the Liberal Party under Sir Joseph Cook to form the Nationalist Party and Government.

For the first time Australia had a conservative party that was not just anti-Labor or anti-anything. And as it became uniform in every State, the ordinary Australian found that he could identify himself with it. Menzies was on the long comeback trail.

Menzies had a contempt for people who had money and nothing else. He himself had so little money at this stage that when he wanted to go abroad he had to give a series of legal consultations to raise the money.

In 1945 Menzies' father died, aged eighty-three. Kate Menzies followed a year after, aged eighty. The night before he died Jim Menzies asked for some papers to be placed on a table but he wasn't well enough to look at them. Next morning Kate Menzies rang Isabel and told her to come at once.

He thanked his daughter for her affection, told her that her life had been a hard one, and talked briefly about that. Then he said, "Now, I want you to do this, you must go on giving public service. Don't ever get away from giving public service as long as you can do it." Those were his last words before he went to sleep.

Mrs Isabel Green, now seventy-five and a woman of charm and sincerity, keeps a small portrait of her late father in the main living room of her Melbourne home. When she needs guidance or strength, she gazes upon it to regain the benefit of his influence.

The Menzies parents had every reason to be proud of all their children. Les Menzies, the eldest son who was to die in 1953 of cancer, did well in the public service. He became Secretary to the Commonwealth Trade Commissioner in New York for four years and later Commonwealth Assistant Trade Commissioner in New Zealand for several years.

Mrs Green married a settler and lived on a Victorian farm until her husband's death in 1938, when she moved to Melbourne. She became associated with several leading business firms, and was later appointed secretary to the Melbourne Exhibition Building Trustees. Mrs Green has given generous service to charitable organizations in Melbourne, who greatly appreciated her executive ability. She gave talks to hundreds of organizations, a chore in which brother Bob gave advice.

Syd Menzies followed a business career, becoming an executive with G. J. Coles. He served with the Department of Munitions and on several wartime committees, then was a director of two companies and finally managing director of a prominent manufacturing firm.

Frank Menzies, the family "stalwart" who inherited much of his father's qualities in helping those who were down-and-out, finished his law course at Melbourne University in 1920 and took a job in the Crown Solicitor's office. He was appointed Victorian Crown Solicitor in 1926 and remained in that post until 1954. He took a Bachelor of Arts degree at Melbourne University in 1951.

Frank Menzies served on two Royal Commissions, the first in 1955 to advise the Southern Rhodesian Government on the siting of their territorial capital, the second in 1960 presided over by Lord Monckton to advise on the constitutional development of the Federation of Rhodesia and Nyasaland. The United Kingdom Government invited him to sit on this Commission because of his association with constitutional developments in Australia over the years.

Since his "retirement" in 1954 he has kept himself busy on the boards of several companies, and has been a member of the Australian Broadcasting Commission Advisory Committee and chairman of the first Freedom From Hunger Campaign for Victoria.

15

Bob Menzies, in his drive to come back from the political dead, and prove to himself and others that he *was* a leader, was helped largely in organizing the Liberal Party by the 1943 elections. These elections saw the defeat of a number of men who opposed him, especially those in the borderline seats.

One of those who lost his seat was Bill McCall.

McCall found that after his 1941 rebellion against Menzies he had to face overwhelming opposition in the next election. In numbers of candidates he was opposed by a virtual cricket team, and lost. McCall continued to serve on the Rationing Commission until it disbanded in 1949.

When John Curtin asked him to go on the Rationing Committee in 1941 after the Fadden Government's fall, McCall ran into trouble with the U.A.P. Curtin had offered the job to John (later Sir John) Spicer but the U.A.P. bulldozed him out of it.

After Curtin made the offer to McCall he suggested he go back and tell the Party before he accepted. "I make my own decisions," said McCall, and accepted.

McCall was summoned to a meeting of the U.A.P. and Bob Menzies was among those who criticized him for taking the job in a Labor administration. They felt this would be to the advantage of Labor.

McCall considered this parish pump politics and believed it was more important to get on with winning the war. He waited till everybody had had their say before speaking: "I've been directed to do what Mr Spicer did. I've already accepted the position and I'll tell you why.

"When Mr Fadden was defeated, he said, and it was pub-

158

lished in every newspaper in Australia, that Mr Curtin could be assured he would do everything in his power to help the Labor Government when it came to war effort. And this went for every member of the Party and when Mr Curtin offered me this job I didn't think I had to come back and ask you." End of meeting.

Following his defeat at the polls McCall was asked by Curtin to continue his work on the Rationing Commission, on the offer of a salary of £1,500 a year. McCall declined the salary and did the job.

McCall, the man who wanted to make a million, was already well established in business with his own private investment company buying and selling shares on the Stock Exchange. He first broke into big money when news of the breakthrough in the Maginot Line reached Australia. Reading the signs that his self improvement methods had taught him, he "divined" that the Germans were further ahead than was realized.

So he sold forward all the shares he thought would be badly affected by a rapid progress of the war; the "cats and dogs," the good shares such as picture shows, the lot. And he made a *coup*.

Arthur Coles was not defeated at the 1943 elections, but it was not for the want of trying on the part of the U.A.P. who wanted him out for defeating the Government. The chairman of his election committee reluctantly stood down because the U.A.P. threatened to boycott his business if he supported Coles.

Coles also went back in 1946 and was made chairman of an Airlines Commission to start a national airways system. The war was over, he had achieved his aims in Parliament, and had done what everybody agreed was a first-class job as Chairman of the Rationing Commission, the War Damages Commission, and the Manpower and Resources Committee, so instead of speaking at pleasant Sunday afternoon meetings and opening dog shows and the like, he resigned from politics to enjoy what was the centre of his life—his home, wife, and six children.

Menzies in the 1946 elections for the first time had a cohesive organization working. Already he had largely overcome the suspicion of himself from within Liberal ranks and won the confidence of *prima donnas* in the Party.

Australians were beginning to listen to him again, in spite of plain talk such as condemning the Australians' "Saturday afternoon" approach to problems. He told electors they must work if they wanted benefits, using the drive and genius of the individual to achieve progress because the old, easy-going order of the past had gone forever.

Some of his statements continued to be far from popular, such as when he called striking watersiders "skunks."

But the insults were by no means one-sided in this Australia stirring to the problems of reconstruction. Eddie Ward scoffed, among other things, that Menzies was a "posturing individual with the scowl of Mussolini, the bombast of Hitler, and the physical proportions of Goering," and Dr Evatt, the Minister for External Affairs, declared that he lacked Australianism.

On that point Menzies replied with the Empire view he always maintained: "Dr Evatt seems to think that true Australianism involves aggressive hostility to other people. The truth is that the best kind of Australianism is that which clearly perceives the place of Australia in the British community of nations and recognizes that we exercise our best influence in the world and evolve a joint British Empire opinion which, as such, would be much more powerful than a set of separate opinions."

Menzies always had the courage to say what he thought. Even before the war ended he had stated that world peace depended on a prosperous Germany and Japan, a statement which, although it might have rankled at the time, was proved right.

In the 1946 elections he indicated the foreign policy he intended following—a system of collective security in which Australia would have to accept the reciprocal duties with "powerful friends and allies." He asserted that Australia, to establish international co-operation, should begin with the British Empire and the United States, two nations which instinctively thought the same about war and peace.

All Menzies' election meetings then were unruly affairs, largely because he could not resist trying to score off interjectors. Those who went along for entertainment value, as many did, were fully rewarded.

A meeting in Launceston (Tasmania) in the final week before the election was fairly typical, but he made an unwise jibe on this occasion at the audience, a section of which had made hostile interjections for fifteen minutes.

"I am not," he said, "directing my speech tonight to the descendants of convicts, but to free Australian citizens."

(Later, when he finished speaking, he immediately sought out reporters and appealed: "You won't use that, will you?" Not much! Every reporter sent it off.)

When the hooting and booing died down, he said he wanted to talk to the sensible members of the audience, not "the wild beasts of Ephesus."

Menzies appealed to the crowd to pay no attention to the "essentially Fascist-minded people" making the noise as "they don't want free speech, no Communists want free speech."

Promising to cut taxation Menzies asked members of the audience who did not want their taxes cut to stand up. One man got up and began to shout. Undeterred at the poor response, Menzies shouted back: "Only one of the vast audience!"

Uproar followed his remark that Labor supporters could not find a flaw in his policy, and he called back: "I knew you were a miserable lot of quitters and could not take the truth. If any of you rabble at the back of the hall think I was ever frightened by rabble like you, forget about it."

One man told Menzies he wouldn't get his vote and got the answer, "I don't want your vote. The day a Commo votes for me I'll go and hang myself on the nearest tree."

There seemed no end to the interjections. A voice: "You've made your money out of politics." Menzies: "I *lost* more money from going into politics than the average Labor politician has *made* from going into politics." Voice: "Pig-Iron Bob. You won't get in." Menzies: "When anyone says pig iron you can tell at a glance he's a Communist."

The audience usually tired of it before Menzies did and towards the end of this meeting it quietened down and gave him a hearing.

In Launceston at that time Menzies passed a turning point in his life. At the Brisbane Hotel after the meeting, he and Mrs Menzies were having a cup of coffee. Menzies was unhappy over his election prospects and they had had a tiff. "Bob," said Mrs Menzies, "I want you to promise me something. I want you to promise that if you don't get in on Saturday, you will give up."

Finally, after some delay, Menzies replied: "All right, darling. I'll give up."

He didn't win—neither did he give up.

Menzies, in fact, had a wonderful opportunity to come back because so many people were scared of socialization, a situation which he exploited to the full.

In the campaign leading up to the 1949 elections Prime Minister Ben Chifley stated quite simply and bluntly his views were unchanged since 1937 when, as a member of the Lyons-appointed Banking Commission, he recommended bank nationalization. Only the constitution had prevented Chifley from bringing in legislation to nationalize all private banks, and in the 1949 election campaign Menzies flayed his nationalization policies with such slogans as: "The abolition of choice is the death of freedom."

The anti-bank socialization campaign was so expensive that funds had to be sought abroad. British investors, with a high volume of capital in Australia and a keen interest in seeing that socialization failed, paid up. At least £100,000 was said to have been raised in Britain for this fight, and members of the Labor Party are generally agreed that R. G. Casey was an emissary in these negotiations.

It was a new Menzies who went before the electors. Some of the best brains in Australia had been busy trying to build him up as a new personality. And he and Country Party leader Artie Fadden had sunk their differences and for the first time announced a joint declaration of policy.

Menzies barnstormed Australia, working at a furious pace and as tirelessly as had President Harry Truman in the United States a year before. This man, whom the Stormy State of New South Wales had considered such a political liability two years previously that they declined his offer to campaign for them in their own elections, inspired his followers with his determination and refusal to acknowledge any defeat as permanent.

In a pre-election build-up Menzies moved away from meetings in halls and held them in the open air in streets and parks, helping to break down the legend of Menzies the Aloof, the Superior, the Unapproachable. And to the surprise of some of the faint hearts in his own Party his personality went over well.

In preaching to the unconverted he put himself before the electors as a personality rather than a disembodied voice, plugging for all he was worth the strangling growth of Communism in the unions and the lag in Australia's production.

The old inclination to score off people with the biting remark was put aside, and for the months of the lead-up he was very affable and friendly with Pressmen, the result being that he had an excellent Press in the campaign.

Newspapermen were surprised during the tour to see him walking the main streets of country towns, having an occasional drink in a pub and arguing with the locals! Surprised, because he regarded beer as "a greasy drink," and while he did not mind having a drink with officials or dignitaries, he had always steered clear of the ordinary man.

In places like Rockhampton in North Queensland the locals see political leaders only at election time, and they had a very sinister idea about Menzies. But when he walked in among them and met them on their own ground they thought very highly of Pig-Iron Bob.

162

Even Artie Fadden, a Queenslander, who still retained his old devilment and who privately and jocularly used to refer to Menzies as the Big Bastard, admired his skill in breaking down the barrier, although he found the large entourage following him a bit hard to swallow.

Menzies had also discarded his careful lawyer-arguing platform technique with its logic, fine presence, and excellent though flat delivery. In its place was a man speaking with conviction and a bit of fire, and using gestures and other tricks of oratory.

Menzies received most applause when he promised to repeal the bank nationalization legislation and to outlaw the Communist Party.

His followers were dismayed at one stage when he broke down through throat strain, causing him to cancel two meetings in Sydney and to rest in Melbourne for two days. It was an exhausting 15,000 mile tour in less than a month, with a heavy schedule of meetings, often two or three a day.

Menzies won with a resounding majority and became Prime Minister again from 19 December 1949.

But it was no easy victory. And there had to be a few pay-offs for the support which helped put the Liberals in.

Perhaps it may have caused the resurrected Prime Minister to toss uneasily at night occasionally, for in his earlier days he showed no regard for anything approaching a compromise and was one of the very few in politics who would stand by a point of principle, even when the consequences of his action threatened to be bleak.

But in his new political wisdom which enabled him to walk the corridors of power again, he no doubt felt convinced that in order to strive towards a goal of major good and succeed, it is often necessary to accept some minor evil.

To win, Menzies needed a big swing in Queensland where a big Catholic population exists. So he co-opted the service of a Canberra politician to work on it. The politician succeeded in persuading Archbishop Duhig of Brisbane to send a circular to Queensland Catholics denouncing Chifley as a socialist and telling them to vote against Labor.

The result was that the Liberals won a big majority of seats in Queensland and were returned to power largely because of it.

The politician, as his pay-off, got a seat in Cabinet.

Some angry members of the Labor Party wanted to bring the matter before Parliament but Evatt, Deputy Opposition Leader, talked them out of it on the ground that it would mean "sectarianism" and would not regain any Catholic votes.

163

Later, Archbishop Duhig ran into trouble when he invested money on behalf of the Church, in Roma (Queensland) oil. The money had been subscribed by Catholics for a new cathedral.

But the old gentleman got his fingers burnt in the deal and lost the money. The subscribing Catholics made a joke of the Archbishop, almost a potentate in his own right.

But the Liberals stuck to him for his election favour. They sent the hat around and collected £30,000 which was given to Archbishop Duhig for the cathedral. Many Catholics still colloquially call it the Church of the Holy Oil, and they are still waiting for it to be built.

Archbishop Duhig was later knighted by the Queen on the Liberals' recommendation.

At the time the "faceless men" in Melbourne supporting the Liberals and known as the "National Council" included Sidney Baillieu Myer, Sir Clive Baillieu, and a top executive of the Shell Oil Company.

Among the first actions of Menzies as Prime Minister was to elevate to Ministerial rank Dame Enid Lyons, widow of Joe Lyons, a move that, although popular, was seen by some people as placatory.

Dame Enid, who decided to take up politics after her husband's death, had become Australia's first woman member of Federal Parliament in 1943. Menzies appointed her vice-president of the Executive Council in 1949, making her the first woman Minister in the Commonwealth Parliament.

Menzies knew that his election victory was his big opportunity, and that he would never get it again if things went wrong this time. He set out to consolidate his position with the Party and the nation. He worked extremely hard.

If ever a man found happiness and satisfaction in a job, he did. After three months as leader of the Government he looked years younger, giving that this-is-where-I-belong impression as he went about his duties.

A smartening of dress on the upper levels of the Public Service became noticeable. These departmental heads, on their own interpretations, did not feel it diplomatic to turn out like a tailor's dummy in a window display when Ben Chifley was in power because Ben dressed plainly, drably in fact. And Dr Evatt as External Affairs Minister with the knot on his tie away from centre and hats that would have been fashionable in 1920, clearly showed he was no sartorial wolf.

Party members soon noticed modifications in the "new" Menzies, that affable, down-to-earth fellow who in the election campaign enjoyed rubbing shoulders with his fellow Australians. He was still easygoing and friendly compared with his reign of the war years, but he was beginning to show a tendency towards remoteness once again.

Parliamentary newcomers were a little disappointed that he did not make the fuss of them now that he did on the hustings. They did not fully appreciate that he was now the busiest man in Australia, that he was determined to get a grip on the job that he did not demonstrate in 1941.

But there was generally very little criticism of the Prime Minister. He had got them back into power and was something of a hero among his men. Labor members went about in the first few months saying, "There are no cracks in the Government forces—yet!"

They were basing their hopes on reports of some Party members that the Prime Minister was not taking rank and filers into his confidence. Frequent Party meetings were held but the Prime Minister gave little away. One complaint was over the Government's Bank Bill on which there was no discussion in the Party room. Members had to be content with the Treasurer reading details of the Bill to them shortly before the measure was placed before Parliament.

Menzies went to unusual lengths to keep Government business secret until he was ready to release it. He constantly warned Ministers not to discuss Cabinet affairs with Pressmen. And they obeyed him, all of them regarding him as The Boss and most of them referring to him as such in conversation.

The new Prime Minister's bi-weekly Press conferences were so much puff and friendly diversions until reporters made it known they wanted newsworthy information. And Question Time in the House of Representatives—traditionally a rich source of information—was becoming, under Menzies' rule, predictably barren.

The Prime Minister dodged thorny Labor questions with the old Parliamentary subterfuge that a reply would involve revealing Government policy and Question Time was not the time for policy statements. But it was noticeable that Menzies did not exactly take fright at some questions asked by his own followers, questions which gave him the chance of scoring a political point at Labor's expense.

Menzies appointed so many sub-committees to deal with specific questions that one Minister found he was a member of four sitting simultaneously. More than a dozen were set up, and like some political generalissimo the Prime Minister kept in touch with every one, checking their reports, suggesting lines of inquiry, and himself remaining an ex-officio member of them all.

The main criticism of the sub-committee system was that it slowed down the work of Government, providing Cabinet with a too-easy method of avoiding decisions which it should make promptly but put off because the sub-committee was dealing with the question. But nobody resented this because the Prime Minister himself set the pace and often worked in his office until midnight, although he took as much time as possible to entertain with dinner parties at The Lodge, which had been closed in Ben Chifley's era.

Business representatives too, found him changed. He had been reasonably accessible to them in the war years but now he was difficult to see. Menzies was determined to show the new Liberal Party did not represent any particular group of the Australian community.

Public servants had to keep on their toes in the new broom atmosphere and were frequently sent bustling to gather information for the man at the top.

Menzies was building up, drawing to him the power that rested in the Prime Minister's royal-blue swivel chair, and getting an iron-clad grip on it.

In the early months of office Menzies went on a forty-five-day tour around the world. He returned with international standing and $150,000,000 from the International Bank for Reconstruction and Development for Australian expansion. Wherever he went he created a good impression, meeting kings, presidents, and statesmen. In Tokyo he saw General MacArthur and tried to get permission to visit the fighting forces in Korea.

His enthusiasm for the British, English-speaking, Western world and United Nations unity seemed to suit everybody and he had a good Press. *The New York Times* editorialized: "Prime Minister Menzies' words of courage, firm resolution, and down-to-earth common sense during his visit here have been an inspiration to the American people." And Australia was praised as a valued partner in any future trouble.

The rest of the world was only beginning to catch up with Australia. The previous picture had been made up of the tough reputation of its second World War fighting forces, the austere personality of Ben Chifley, and the cranky fighting speeches of Dr Evatt at the United Nations as the champion of little nations.

In Menzies they saw a new kind of Australian, appreciating his urbanity, his good sense, polish, and ability to speak wittily and compellingly off the cuff.

Menzies addressed the United States Congress without a note—an unprecedented thing for a visitor, and he received an extraordinary ovation.

Overseas people who thought of Australians as backwoodsmen, if they thought of them at all, regarded Menzies as the representative of some new frontier Down Under.

And in a way they were right.

16

Sarah Bernhardt in her book *The Art of the Theatre* aptly summed up the approach of an actor to his role.

"Whatever I have to impart," she said, "in the way of anguish, passion or of joy comes to me in rehearsal in the very action of the play. There is no need to cast about for an attitude, or a cry, or anything else. You must be able to find what you want on stage in the excitement of collaboration. Everything must come from suggestion."

This was Menzies—from the time he consolidated his role until he left the stage as the record breaker: Sir Robert Menzies, Knight of the Thistle, Privy Councillor, Companion of Honour, Queen's Counsel, Fellow of the Royal Society, Lord Warden of the Cinque Ports, Senior Prime Minister of the Commonwealth of Nations, Chief Commander of the United States Legion of Merit . . . a man with more honours than any other Australian in history.

Menzies used Parliament like a Shakespearean player used the theatre in the round. Here was an Elizabethan from another era.

He spoke to the audience but never directly except on an election platform. He spoke to the Speaker, to his own members, to the Opposition, as an actor speaks on the stage—never square on to the audience but involving it, using the full theatrical trappings.

You knew in the gallery, as one does when attending the theatre, that here was a play being enacted and you were looking in on it. Menzies was not a person standing up and declaiming. He was more an actor than an orator.

Addressing the Speaker, his members, the Opposition, he was

like an actor playing his role on stage with other actors. An actor never really addresses himself to an individual but communicates with the audience by talking to those on stage. This is what Menzies did: he had the gift of being able to speak to the masses by involving them in what he was saying. He knew the common man and could identify himself with his attitude.

Menzies had the great gift of being able to *ad lib,* to sense something, make a play on it and return to his lines never to be thrown off. He was the playwright-actor, always writing his own lines. Menzies, like any good actor, never lost his part; the part of Prime Minister.

Few people knew him as a man. They could know him as a very friendly companion, but not a man. Most saw him only as a Prime Minister. Menzies acted the role of Prime Minister so well it was difficult to know where he began as a man. People would say of Menzies, "Isn't he natural?" in the same way an audience has remarked on a great actor. This was because he was consummate in his work.

In the early days of the Hollywood star system, before the advent of mass media, one did not know what the man or woman was like behind the actor's role. Menzies had this aura; this sense of mystery around him.

Except on ceremonial occasions, Menzies never walked through the front door of Parliament but through a side door. Perhaps this was for convenience, being nearer to his office, but it added to the illusion that here was an actor using a stage door to enter Parliament. And when he reached his office before going into the House one could almost imagine him making himself up to go on stage.

One illustration of Menzies the actor occurred in 1957 after he had slipped in his bath in Perth (Western Australia) and injured himself. When he came to Parliament House, Canberra, he was in pain. To enter the House from the Prime Minister's suite he had to walk along the brown parquet floor of the Government lobby, adjoining Kings Hall to reach a green curtained alcove near the Speaker's chair, whence he entered the chamber.

Obviously thinking nobody was around, and in agony, Menzies shuffled down the hall, bent over and holding his back with his left hand, a sheaf of papers in his right.

Suddenly a secretary shot from his office to cross the lobby and took the Prime Minister by surprise. "How are you, sir?" asked the secretary. Menzies said quietly, "not bad."

Then, before pulling the curtain back to walk on stage, he

drew himself up and assumed the stature of Menzies the Prime Minister.

In the chamber he sat down, turned to his colleagues and waved nonchalantly with the left hand, and stood for prayers when the Speaker came in. And right through Question Time and while walking back to his office he held his pose, nodding politely to several people.

A real actor loves power; the power that flows from conquering the lines, the character he's portraying, the audience. He doesn't always expect sympathy from an audience but he likes to feel he is holding the audience. Menzies always liked to hold *his* audience, to get on top of it.

One wonders whether the lack of Press conferences in later years was because here was an audience he didn't like. They were cynical, critical. And Menzies didn't like criticism—no actor does. Although he rankled at personal criticism he threw it off publicly.

Menzies had the actor's gift of reading lines as if speaking extempore, orating from a script without deviating from it by one word, and you could not easily tell he was reading. Although he felt restrained in having to do this, he could commit several lines to memory, talk to his audience with whatever gestures he felt the part required, and always glance back at the precise place in the script, continuing without the slightest hesitation. You had the impression he looked at his speech only now and then.

Menzies felt awkward when in Opposition in the House because he stood with the table on his right. It meant that when he made a point with his favourite habit of thumping his fist down he had to do it with his right hand instead of his left—as Prime Minister he had been accustomed to thumping the table with his left hand.

Whenever he had to face up to a situation in the House some Ministers would say: "We'll get some pretty good ham from Bob tonight." And yet, any idea that he was just a ham actor is wrong. He was tremendously apprehensive and was always worried that he would make a poor speech. Before any major speech he liked to spend an hour or so alone, usually walking up and down, to marshal his thoughts.

His audiences saw him as a man of immense assurance, of swaggering confidence, but if they could have seen him before he went on stage, usually nervous and fearful that he would not make the best impression, they would probably have felt sorry for him.

Menzies always prided himself on never preparing his speeches, although he liked to make a few headings and study his subject beforehand. He detested being asked to stand up and "say a few words"—a phrase he would repeat with heavy distaste, telling his friends he would never stand up unless he had been able to think about it beforehand and prepare himself in his own mind.

That, of course, was the barrister's training. But his speeches were off the cuff in that they were seldom written down and he amazed people, particularly in the United States, with his ability to speak this way. And he could talk with equal ease to any audience.

In playing the role of Prime Minister, Menzies always had a strong sense of the right appearance. He would never walk straight in to anyone's office, he never just arrived anywhere: he always made an entrance.

For instance, when entering the Parliamentary office of Harold Holt whom he was grooming as his successor, he would knock lightly on the door, then open it slowly so that the occupant saw his whole bearing. On the threshold had arrived the Prime Minister! Then, graciously, "good morning." And, if he wanted to speak to Holt, "Is the young master in?"

Menzies had an immaculate sense of timing and propriety. At the Guildhall, London, for a social gathering of Commonwealth Prime Ministers, the Mountbattens, and other important people always arrived before Menzies. And as the party began to die slightly, after the notables had been met and the lesser lights were engaged in cocktail chat, Menzies had gone. He was on his way back to the Savoy.

He did this in Parliament, appearing for the time he wanted to and sending messengers running to and from his office if things weren't going right. On one occasion when a Minister had been drinking and was making a fool of himself in the House, Menzies could have gone into the House himself but he sent a messenger to sit him down—it was not an appropriate time for the Prime Minister to be seen with one of his Ministers.

Menzies always established himself before speaking by a quick glance, then a slight pause as though to say, *this is the Prime Minister*. It was so much a part of his technique that probably he did it unconsciously.

A great simplifier, Menzies made a case rather than delivered a speech. But even his critics admitted they knew no other man with the same ability to express himself cogently, clearly, or for such a long period without becoming boring.

On the question of speaking he gave some advice to a group of young Liberals on one occasion as to how they should comport themselves to win the election. "Whenever I go to a public meeting," said Menzies, "I think on the way there of two or three points I want to make, no more, because people will not carry away from the meeting more than three points.

"I make those points then I go on and develop a different approach to them but come back always to those points, and if possible I do that again another way, repeating the process. And I make those points believing the people will at least carry them away.

"And when question time comes I try to ignore them until something comes up that I want to hear. Then I say, 'My friend at the back has asked me such and such,' and I repeat it because no one will have heard it, and I say 'My friend at the back has asked me this. Now this brings me to the point I was trying to make. . . .' "

Menzies did the same thing with interjections: he heard only those he could score off and disregarded the others.

Menzies was a master in the use of English. All his speeches in their entirety were grammatically perfect. His was probably the best educated Australian voice in public life in his time. His voice had English inflections but he could never be mistaken for an Englishman. The Americans particularly picked him as an Australian, noting a marked difference between his speech and typical English speech. Somebody once, accurately enough, likened him to a product of Trinity College, Dublin—an international cosmopolitan style of English.

And yet, for all his persuasions and lucidity, Menzies was not an orator, in the strict sense. He had the bright ring of words, but his brilliance was the diamond brilliance, not the glow of a ruby.

An orator has something of the demagogue about him, appealing to the senses. Menzies appealed more to the intellect. And his oratory never swayed Parliament.

The Australian Parliament has had few orators. In the memory of men long connected with politics only four can be named—Billy Hughes, Curtin, Scullin, and Bert Anstey, also a Labor man. All could bring a tear to the eye, a lump to the throat.

But in debate Menzies was often brilliant, and had few equals. In moving an important motion, his speeches as a trained barrister were at times highly impressive. He stood in front of many a brief he detested, but as the great Shakespearean actor with the face, the good looks, the carriage, it was up to him as a perfectionist to make it good. And in this way he dragged many a weary debate out of the dumps.

But in debate it depended on Menzies' study of the subject and the mood he was in. Sometimes Curtin would maul him rather badly. And perhaps because he did not make a close study of a contentious subject the plain-talking, down-to-earth Chifley could sometimes make his arguments look silly.

When running short of arguments he would often encourage interjections to which he could make a smart reply. But the Opposition sometimes sensed he was relying on interjections and remained silent, and he had to work hard to complete his speech.

Menzies' habit of deliberately provoking interjectors at election meetings often had the reverse effect to what he intended. In dealing with members of the audience he did not have time to get his message over. And in trying to turn on wit like a tap running water he did not always produce a good performance.

His gift of repartee was dangerous because the more brilliant it was, the more cutting its effect on the victim, and the more likely to cause an emotional and personal, rather than an intellectual reaction. Some of his attempts at ridicule were little short of custard pie standard such as the éclair of genius he directed to an interjector at Canterbury Hall in Melbourne: "If you had twice as many brains you'd be a half wit."

But he could always be relied upon as a public performer who would react, such as when an egg narrowly missed him at one meeting in Brisbane and he remarked, "With eggs at fourpence ha'penny each I call that gross extravagance."

His humour was basically the lawyer's type, rather heavy and at someone else's expense in the George Reid, Birkenhead style. One of the better and more memorable ones concerns a remark he passed about the then Chief Justice of Victoria, Sir Charles Low.

Sir Charles had a remarkably craggy face, as though it had been hewn out of quartzite, but with character written on it as deeply as in the face of Abraham Lincoln. Menzies turned to one of his colleagues at a Melbourne dinner after thoughtfully studying Sir Charles and said, "You know, I doubt if anyone could really be as wise as Charlie Low looks."

Because of Menzies' desire to wrap himself in an icicle of isolation, particularly after his comeback, his treatment of people often left them with an enduring resentment.

In 1946 a young journalist went to meet Menzies, then leader of the Opposition, as he left a train in Melbourne. Employed in the Melbourne news bureau of Australian Consolidated Press he had an envelope from the managing director, Frank Packer, marked personal which he was to hand to Menzies.

The youngster made his way through the Opposition leader's entourage and apologetically explained his mission. Menzies looked him up and down with a cold grey eye and said, "Didn't your master tell you that I don't give kerbside interviews?"

He refused to accept the letter and told the lad to deliver it to his hotel. Of course, Menzies had no liking for Press barons and Frank Packer's Australian Consolidated Press publication, the *Daily Telegraph*, had severely criticized his wartime administration in a booklet compiled by a team of first-class journalists.

Menzies did nothing to dispel the opinion which this reporter held of him when next they met almost twenty years later, in the Prime Minister's office in Canberra. He was then in public relations, and had occasion to visit Menzies on behalf of a client. Menzies showed him his Cabinet room and dispensed a drink. Holding a brandy in his right hand he said, "Now that you're no longer in journalism I feel I can ask you this question without any inhibitions. Is the *Sydney Sun* still being edited by fourteen-year-olds?"

It has been said of Menzies that almost without exception his friends were intellectually inferior, that he preferred to be patronizing than among equals.

While this may have been partly true, the more likely explanation is that Menzies, who had little enough time for mental and physical relaxation, liked in his leisure moments to be with people whose motives were clear cut and among whom he felt he did not have to be on guard or defend himself. For that reason it is natural that he should have preferred people who were uncomplicated and apparently extroverts.

Perhaps the best example of this was his choice of Hugh Dash as Press officer. In Dash's company he found great delight. Dash came from Sydney and Menzies commented soon after appointing him: "Why did I have to wait so long to get a PR man from under the shadow of the Bridge," implying that it should have happened to him sooner.

Dash was completely unlike anyone Menzies had ever been associated with: racy, a raconteur of blue stories, a hearty drinker, and full of irreverence and zest for life. Menzies was always fascinated by such a character.

Picture Dash in London once going out to Windsor Castle, his squat familiar figure noticed by a fellow Australian in a shady lane outside a pub taking in a pint or two in case it was a long time between drinks in the Royal establishment—that was Hugh.

Menzies once remarked he did not know how Dash managed to

do his job. "He's got nothing to tell them," he said, "but he keeps them at bay."

Of course, that was what the Prime Minister really wanted, someone who could keep the Press away and tell them nothing.

Sometimes on Sunday afternoons Menzies would go to his office for a yarn and a few drinks with Hugh Dash. He seemed to enjoy Dash's colloquial sayings, such as "to come the raw prawn," an expression that had little meaning outside Sydney. These sojourns enabled Menzies to keep in touch with the views and feelings of the common man, as observed through the eyes and ears of Dash.

Menzies, never really gregarious, was even less so after his come-back. He had a group of friends, not many in number, whom he retained throughout, mainly members of the Bench and a few selected friends of the social set of S.E.2, the established gentry of Melbourne's silvertail district, or "Cliveden group."

In Melbourne, the Lord Mayoral office is a plum social job, for which the requirements are wealth and standing. It is, in effect, a millionaire's club, with the Lord Mayor ultimately becoming a knight. No Labor man has ever held the post for at least thirty years, and the council itself is largely constituted along similar lines of social position rather than political appointment. The Johnny-come-latelys of this, and other influential classes,—those who made their money and gained their status in more recent times and are therefore generally held to be not quite as respectable as those whose prestige goes back further, never really appealed to Menzies. One exception, of course, is Reg Ansett, the airline operator.

Menzies was not a glad-hander and at home was not a prolific entertainer. He was a devoted family man, his daughter Heather being the apple of his eye.

The eldest son Ken is more like his mother in make-up and Ian, a farmer and something of a law unto himself, is different again.

It keenly disappointed Menzies that neither of his sons gradua-ted in law. He wanted Ken to do law and he went to university for a year but wasn't a student and his father said, "If you're not a student it's a waste of time going on. If you do law you must be a student all your life."

To his sister he has been a perfect brother, thoughtful, generous, affectionate, and kind. While travelling to the United States by ship with his wife and sister once he invited Mrs Green to his suite for a pre-dinner drink as they approached Honolulu and said, "I've just been looking at the timetable and you've arranged all this very nicely. You can reach Honolulu on your birthday. I'm going to give you the best birthday party you've ever had."

At the Royal Hawaiian Hotel he arranged a birthday party for Mrs Green with eighteen guests present, an orchestra playing Happy Birthday, the Prime Minister making a speech, and it was a never-to-be-forgotten night.

When abroad he never fails to buy gifts for the female members of his family. In New York he always goes to a particular store and buys frocks for his daughter. On only one occasion has the frock not fitted her perfectly. He has a keen eye for clothes and rarely fails to comment on women's hats.

In London in 1956 he found on Sunday afternoon that he was leaving early next morning without having done any shopping. He told his Scotland Yard bodyguard who arranged for a merchant to open his store. When he walked into the store he saw a length of red and gold brocade.

Turning to the Scotland Yard man who knew Mrs Green, he asked, "Do you think that sort of material looks like my sister?" The bodyguard thought so, and when Menzies gave it to his sister on his return he reminded her, "I'll have you know this was the most expensive piece of material in the shop."

Menzies always liked the women in his circle to look gay. He did not spend much money on himself but when it came to buying presents for his wife and family the price didn't matter.

He always dined and wined well as Prime Minister, but in private his tastes in food were simple. He mixed probably the world's most potent martini, the strength of which was notorious. On one occasion an Australian public servant walking in a London street, after downing two of the Prime Minister's martinis at the Savoy, had to be physically restrained by a companion from popping banana skins down the dresses of passing ladies.

Menzies was fond of Irish stew, perhaps not the most appropriate dish for his waistline. In country hotels he always inquired if it was on the menu.

Once in Scotland he travelled to Aberfeldy to visit Castle Menzies. He was interested in seeing the castle restored but up till now it has been too big a task. He was not happy about the derelict appearance of the castle, nor the sign hanging on a side gate, "fresh fruit and vegetable for sale here."

At the hotel his host had prepared a menu of a wide array of Scottish food especially for his visit—Bonnie Prince Charlie this and that—and handing it to the Prime Minister asked if it met with his approval. Menzies, who had been dining well at the Savoy and felt like simple fare, replied, "No, it doesn't really. I'd like an Irish stew."

Menzies liked his drop of Scotch and Buchanan's was his favourite brand. He was not a drinker in the sense of being a "grog artist" but he liked to use social alcohol and casual conversation as a form of relaxation. He could hold his liquor well, though—once on a back-to-Jeparit week-end he sat up all night with some of the locals, and although socially it was a very wet occasion, he finished the night sober as a judge.

Menzies liked to see a party in full swing and on these occasions was always in benign mood. Those who believed him aloof and arrogant would perhaps have been surprised if they'd seen him within the family circle, while his niece Judy Menzies played the guitar, singing "Tie Me Kangaroo Down Sport", or leading the chorus of "One Black Bottle Came Sailing Home to Me".

Occasionally Menzies stepped out from behind the mask he created for himself and let his guard down, but not often. He had a habit of walking home to Kew and in doing so passed the Richmond Town Hall in Melbourne. One night a Labor Party conference was being held there and all the lights were on as he passed by. On the spur of the moment Menzies decided to pop in.

He stood around for a moment or two until somebody nudged the mayor, who was taking part in the conference, to let him know the Prime Minister was in their midst. The mayor promptly adjourned the meeting and retired to the mayoral room where he broke out the Scotch. They sat there and chatted to the Prime Minister until a reasonably late hour.

When he left after an unexpectedly pleasant evening he said to his hosts, "Well, you chaps, I'll tell you something. It's no good asking me for anything because whether I give it to you or not I know I'm wasting my time—I won't get your votes." They all laughed and told him he was quite right.

The mask of Ming showed out in odd ways. An Australian-born woman journalist, Michele Dearing, while working as a personality writer on the London *Evening News* was sent to interview Menzies at the Savoy. Miss Dearing, who had lived and worked in Paris, Casablanca, and Tangier, has an international accent and could easily be mistaken as English.

She had an English photographer with her and the interview went along smoothly, so much so that the Australian Prime Minister hardly drew breath in his expressions of admiration for things English and Miss Dearing, far from having to worry about the right questions to ask, could hardly get a word in. Then she happened to casually remark that she herself was Australian and, in fact, had been born in the Sydney suburb of Drummoyne.

End of interview!

Menzies reproached her for not having told him immediately she was not English, that he had talked more freely to her because he thought she was English and after asking her how old she was and how much journalistic experience she had had, he showed her out of the suite.

The next day Miss Dearing was in the Savoy again to interview another personality and running late for her appointment, dashed around a corner into another corridor and ran smack into the stomach of the Australian Prime Minister, almost winding him!

He glared for a moment, then his sense of humour came to the rescue. Graciously doffing his homburg he drew himself up and said in a slow deliberate voice, "I do believe this is our second encounter," and moved off at a stately waddle, trailed at a respectable distance by two or three distinguished looking gentlemen who tried to look as though they were not really present.

Menzies was, of course, a vain man. One sign of his vanity was his big bushy black eyebrows. He would not let barbers touch them, explaining, "What will the cartoonists do without my eyebrows?"

In Sydney he always had his hair cut in the barber's shop of the Hotel Australia, not an exclusive place at all although a leading hotel. He tipped generously and the barbers there thought highly of him because he always asked them their opinions and engaged them in lively conversations. But it was well known that he was touchy over his big black eyebrows.

Eddie Ward used to get under his skin in Parliament while the Prime Minister was talking by saying just loud enough for him to hear, "just a Melbourne snob," and then sometimes when interjecting or speaking himself, declaring, "it's as false as the dye on the Prime Minister's eyebrows."

The Prime Minister was very conscious of his double-breasted suits. The Australian Wool Board had some trouble with him over these. A new type of worsted had been produced which, once pressed, was supposed to retain its creases and the Wool Board people thought it would be a good idea to have the Prime Minister promote it. Arrangements were made to make him a suit and the material was sent to his tailor.

An appearance was arranged for the Prime Minister, then the Wool Board promoters learnt he was to appear in a double-breaster. "No, no," they said, "it's got to be a single-breaster."

Reluctantly, he agreed to pose once only in a single-breaster and his tailor worked right through the week-end to produce it in time. He was very self-conscious about this promotion, in Melbourne, and wore the suit only that once, later making various quips about its narrow lapels and other features.

Menzies rarely relaxed when talking with a group of people, and he always put up a defence barrier, playing one against the other. It was only when he talked to one individual that he was seen in his true nature.

He could not bear to be ignored by any member of a group to which he was chatting: any smart person wanting to get his attention would move slightly away from him, perhaps towards a corner, taking no notice of him and Menzies would soon come across and bring into play his considerable personality.

In his political life Menzies bore all the signs of a man who was afraid of life, and who over-compensated as a result. The compensation theme runs throughout his life—the boyish reverence for cricket, the devotion to Royalty, the acquisition of honours.

He had a fear of ridicule, yet he ridiculed others. His barbs in the House were numerous. Once he replied to a member, "The conducted tour of the honourable member's mind would have been more instructive if it had not taken place in gathering darkness," and, another time, when told he had a superiority complex, replied, "Considering the company I keep in this place it is hardly surprising."

Les Haylen, then a Labor M.P. from Sydney, had a reputation in the House of having a sharp tongue. On one occasion he called Menzies "an intellectual hill-billy," and the shaft went right home.

Menzies rarely went in to the Members' lavatory but on this occasion he followed Haylen in, washed his hands and said, "That was a bit hot just because I play you at your own game." For Menzies to admit he was hurt, was a revelation.

Another time Haylen pulled a corny but effective one on the Prime Minister. Pointing to him in the House he said, "There he stands, like jesting Pilate." Menzies again took umbrage, followed him into the lavatory, and with a touch of humour said, "I'm washing my hands again, you'll notice."

Menzies, publicly, never really got out of the acting role he had created for himself. Perhaps it was not an entirely conscious creation, because some of the things about which he was most sensitive kept cropping up throughout his life, and this caused him to withdraw into himself and hide his true feelings.

To protect himself from the hurt of interjectors jeering that he had not gone to the war, he co-opted a chairman, a big man and returned soldier, who for years went to his meetings and ordered down the interjectors. He always felt he had to be on guard. When asked at a meeting in 1951 why his two sons had not gone to Korea, he twice asked the interjector to repeat his question, then shouted, "I have been waiting for this dirty lie. . . ."

Such was the coat of chain mail that Menzies developed around himself so that even when members of his family—for whom he had a deep and abiding affection—called in to see him while he was at the Prime Minister's desk, he did not like displaying his feelings. He would look up, with what seemed like a dazed look in his eyes, then slowly put down his pen.

Menzies was an intensely nervous man, but he hid it well, so well, in fact, that only a few of his Ministers suspected it, and none was sure of it. The Opposition never found him so.

At times he did not think he could face up to things, so apprehensive and nervous was he about some of the challenges of office. Only members of his family and perhaps one or two intimate friends knew this.

To a certain extent Menzies can be likened to T. P. O'Connor, who, early this century was regarded as the father of the House of Commons. One writer has said O'Connor had a fearful inferiority complex, was incredibly shy, and setting out to overcome these difficulties had become one of the really great orators of the Commons.

Menzies was self-critical but he never admitted to any faults. Occasionally he defended himself as, "I'm accused of *not* suffering fools gladly, but on the other hand I am accused of *suffering* fools." But as a rule he kept any self-criticism to himself and, in fact, convinced even his intimate acquaintances that if he had criticized himself he then told himself what a good critic he was!

Once or twice he admitted (like any other realistic man) that his greatest debunker was his wife, who in 1954 became Dame Pattie. She frequently "took him apart" and where he did not take kindly to any criticism from other quarters, he took considerable notice of her.

In this respect Dame Pattie was the typical wife, and Menzies was fortunate to have had such an incredibly good partner who devoted her life to his interests. Through all his political battles Dame Pattie never altered her attitude towards his opponents, always remaining pleasant and charming, except perhaps in the case of Sir Earle Page following his attack on her husband.

Although he could not generally be regarded as a magnanimous man Menzies had many generous impulses. In the Middle East in 1956 Hugh Dash had only one suit, a thick worsted affair and in the heat he was perspiring copiously.

Menzies sent his secretary, Hazel Craig, out with money from his own pocket to buy Dash a lightweight suit. "I can't bear to see him suffering in the heat," he remarked.

He showed great personal loyalty to his junior officers in the Public Service and this contributed to his success. One of these officers was a heavy drinker, and he several times let the Prime Minister down at the wrong moment.

But Menzies' loyalty to him was such that, although he could not retain him, he saw him through a variety of hospitals because of his alcoholism and paid the bills himself.

One of the things frequently remarked about Menzies in private conversation is that his enthusiasm for cricket and Australian Rules football has been nothing more than a pose—a pose to associate him with popular sports in order to improve his public image.

He is no true lover of cricket, it is said, and far from understanding the finer points of the game, is the type who goes to bed with a copy of Wisden and has a mere statistical knowledge.

This writer does not subscribe to that view, at least as far as cricket is concerned. He will concede that perhaps it was somewhat of a dramatization for the Australian Prime Minister to have had a television set installed in his Daimler so he could watch the Test cricket while travelling between the Savoy and 10 Downing Street.

But every man must have his moments of relaxation. Cricket was one of Menzies' greatest ways of relaxing. His love of cricket went back to his schooldays.

He didn't play much, firstly because he was not good at it, secondly because it was more important to concentrate on his lessons and win his way through life.

If his regard for the game was a pose, then he must have fooled many a Test cricketer because he impressed many of them with his knowledge of the bowler's plan of campaign and other aspects that only a true adherent can discuss intelligently in detail with experts. He genuinely appreciated the concentration that went into bowling and, as far as possible, sat by himself or with a chosen friend. He looked for the reason behind every move on the field.

At Melbourne Cricket Ground where he sat in the committee box, he became very testy if anyone talked to him about politics or law. Whenever his brother Frank accompanied him to the cricket he would sit Frank on the end of the seat and tell him, "You're there to keep the earbashers away."

There was never any suggestion of ceremony in his arrivals at Melbourne Cricket Ground. They were never by arrangement and he always took his seat without formality.

Certainly at Lords and elsewhere he tried to fit his arrangements in so he could see an hour or so of play, but how many thousands of others do the same?

Menzies loved being among cricketers, for whom he had a kind of hero worship. He was always relaxed with them, giving the impression it was his privilege to be with them.

He gave dinner parties for former players not only in London but in Melbourne, Sydney, Canberra, or indeed anywhere. And anyone who heard Menzies describe to cricketers some of the favourite innings he had seen, as he described one of Stan McCabe's, would feel sure he had a genuine love and appreciation for the game.

Menzies had a good range of cricket stories. His favourite one involved an old boy in the Long Room at Lords in 1939 who, seeing an attendant come along and begin wrapping up the pictures and busts to take away, turned to his equally anxious companion and said, *"This is war!"*

Cricketers have been able to practically get away with blue murder with Menzies. This has been particularly true of Lindsay Hassett and Sam Loxton, former Australian Test players. Loxton is a member of the Victorian Parliament and Menzies used to speak at all his meetings.

These players over the years have said things to Menzies in the company of others that perhaps no one else would dream of. Menzies seemed to like the straightforward brash approach of Sam who always called him Boss. There was always a good deal of backchat between them.

At a dinner at the Melbourne Cricket Ground Menzies rose to speak at about 11 p.m. and said, "Well, I'm sure that at this hour no one is interested in hearing me make a long speech," and before he could say anything more Hassett called out, "You're dead right for the first time."

Parties for cricketers were held now and then at the Prime Minister's Lodge in Canberra. One such gathering was fairly lively and the Chief, as Hassett called him, was a little late arriving down to breakfast. Hassett was sitting at the breakfast table busily putting drops in his eyes when the Prime Minister sat down.

"You look bloody awful, Chief," said Hassett. "You can't see an important fellow like Subandrio today looking like that."

"Why, what's wrong?" asked the Chief.

"Your eyes look terrible. Christ, we'll have to fix that," and he went round the table, pulled the Prime Minister's head back, told him to open his eyes, and popped some drops in.

In a way Menzies envied the Hugh Dashes, the Lindsay Hassetts, Sam Loxtons, and other extroverts of this world.

17

A man can be a leader by earning the affection of those around him and taking them into his confidence, or he can set himself up as The Boss and rule in a dictatorial way.

Menzies was not a loved leader: he was feared. He was a one-man band, wanting to control everything that went on around him. He didn't mind strong men in his team, provided they played the same tune.

As a political figure his capacity to express himself and his mental stature were such that they were enough to completely dominate all around him except the foolhardy or the courageous. Invest in him the authority of a Prime Minister and here clearly was a father figure.

It has been freely claimed by many M.P.s that Menzies preferred to be surrounded by minnows, that he did not like tritons near him. That is overstating the position a little.

But most of his Ministers believed he liked men of firm and independent minds around him only if their firmness and independence supported him!

There is a touch of the dictator about that, but it has a measure of truth. Certainly he did not seem to mind sycophants around him.

Menzies was a triumph of personality over intelligence, ability, and knowledge—as a human being he towered in his powers of persuasion, in his sense of overriding authority, over people who were less aggressive, articulate, and lacked strength in the presentation of their views.

If Menzies ran up against a person of great ability or force of mind he would not take a negative attitude so much as a persuasive one. If a strong person was not inclined to follow his line of thinking he would use persuasive rather than overpowering or intimidatory powers. If this did not succeed he would not forget; he was not a forgiving man, although he did forgive Harold Holt for having stood out against him during the war.

No doubt the well-to-do ladies of the Australian National Guild, who used to entertain him to luncheons in Kew, felt the fate of the nation could not have been in safer hands with a gentleman who, to quote their phrases, "used the Queen's English and represented Australia so well in London."

With his magnificent elder statesman appearance and cultivated personality he was the sort of man most middle-aged ladies would have trusted with their fortunes without question.

But in Cabinet he was a man to be feared unless you followed him faithfully. You knew that if you stood up to him or argued too much, it would not be forgotten.

Perhaps the real problem was that Menzies was head and shoulders above everyone around him in gifts and ability—an awkward situation to be in.

Ministers, trying to argue their case with him, found they could not get past or around his mental stand, and felt intimidated in trying to influence his decision. And some, the lesser minds, saw him as an intellectual bully.

Most people in Parliament believed he was—to quote the word most often used against him—arrogant, but some put his attitude down to mental superiority. Perhaps it depended on the intelligence of the person making the observation and his personal experiences with Menzies.

Certainly Menzies did not appear to be arrogant with other men of outstanding mental stature in his team, like Percy Spender and Garfield Barwick. Few stood up to him and it would be true to say there were not enough people offering him good ideas or prepared to go before him to reason out or argue their proposals.

Although Menzies did tolerate lesser minds—a lesson he learnt from his earlier defeat, that you cannot ride roughshod over all those around you—the general impression was that he was intolerant. His attitude very largely depended on the loyalty of the Minister or Party member concerned.

Most members of his Party understood that it was composed of "goodies" and "baddies." The goodies were those who followed him blindly, and the baddies who were a menace to his control or who challenged his authority to the point where they became irritating, were either disposed of or at least they realized their future was behind them.

One of the independent minds who retired from sheer frustration was Joe Gullett. A number of other men of independent thought remained in frustration on the back benches.

Menzies, as any leader must, demanded complete loyalty. Ministers who followed him faithfully were of the opinion that the Prime Minister did not mind them expressing their views though they differed from his, provided they were genuine. He would then explain his stand in a way that did not offend.

But most Ministers were frightened because of his habit of challenging their views and devastating them by a logical process. Many felt they earned a black mark by arguing with the Prime Minister, and also fearing they would be exposed or criticized for weaknesses in their arguments, frequently held back their real views.

Any Minister, of course, who went before Menzies with a shoddy case was asking for trouble. A Minister who posed, who pretended he knew something he didn't, would most likely be ruthlessly exposed and held up to ridicule before his fellows. Commendable, perhaps, in the interests of efficiency but hardly the way to win friends. More and more, therefore, Ministers tended to defer to him—and he achieved loyalty by power.

But not even those who were completely loyal, either because they believed him to be right or because they were afraid of his superior capacity, could escape his often overbearing attitude. The Prime Minister was inclined to be moody at times and on these occasions even the goodies could run into trouble.

An example was when he "took apart" Senator George McLeay, a pleasant and inoffensive Minister who was among the more faithful of his followers. McLeay presented some papers in Cabinet and Menzies asked him for the main points. McLeay said he'd like to read them and Menzies, a little testy on this occasion replied, "Oh, come on, just let's have the main points."

McLeay said he could not abbreviate the details and insisted on reading them out. Menzies finally agreed and McLeay began reading. After a while McLeay stopped and said, "Oh, this can't be right. No, I don't agree with this. . . ."

Menzies held up his copy of the document and asked, "Am I to understand that this is your signature at the end here?"

"Yes," answered McLeay, "but I didn't know this was in it."

"Well," said Menzies, "haven't you read it? What is the meaning of coming here without knowing what your proposal is?"

Menzies became angry, made McLeay look foolish by the condescending lecture he gave him, then attacked other Ministers who might feel they could come before Cabinet without preparing their cases properly. Some Ministers thought the Prime Minister had carried on unnecessarily.

Menzies was not averse to flattery, provided it wasn't overdone. He was quick to recognize flattery but would allow it to continue if it were not laid on too thickly. Nevertheless, the flattery that took place in Cabinet over cups of tea was enough to nauseate a handful of his Ministers, although none had the audacity to say so in his presence.

Gough Whitlam, the Australian Labor Party leader, got close to Menzies on only one occasion—when he passed a complimentary remark to him.

Menzies was an impressionable man in that he was inclined to be moved too easily at times by people who told him things.

In the clubs of Canberra some public servants used to tell the story of one aspiring colleague who had the acumen to write many of his minutes to the Prime Minister in cricketing terms. He would use such phrases as "I feel, sir, we are on a sticky wicket," or "here's one you can hit for six, sir," or "I think, sir, this one should be allowed to pass through to the keeper." Other public servants talked jealously about their colleague because they claimed he achieved promotion faster than they.

One of the enigmas about Menzies is that in politics the greater the belief a man has in himself the greater his chance of getting to the top. How does one equate this with Menzies being sensitive, shy, and easily hurt?

Just because a man has great abilities it doesn't follow that he does not also have great defects. Menzies overcame his political defects of sensitivity and shyness by immense egotism and vanity.

These qualities enabled him, when acting the role of Prime Minister, to show no humility or modesty. In public life, in contrast to his private life, he lacked humility, except in the presence of British royalty, and even then that is doubtful in one or two cases.

Those away from politics who knew him privately, as a friend, saw a different side of his character. They knew him as a humble man.

There is every reason to suspect that Menzies resented ability in his contemporaries. For instance, in conversation he always referred to Sir John Latham as "that crashing bore Latham." Latham was a scholar, a great jurist, and respected by every

Parliamentarian who knew him. Menzies' disdain for people he did not like always seemed to come to the surface.

The Prime Minister had an inclination to malevolence on occasion. Once when a distinguished Army officer made a Press statement that amounted to criticism of the Government, Army Minister John Cramer knew instinctively the soldier was headed for trouble.

Cramer immediately took action to have the officer posted to get him out of the way for the time being. Soon afterwards Menzies demanded to the have the officer's "head chopped off"—and it was probably only the Army Minister's prompt action that saved the day.

On another occasion several Army men were killed during an exercise in heavy waves in Port Phillip Bay, Melbourne. Without hearing any evidence Menzies demanded that the Army men responsible for holding the exercise be dealt with—"make an example of them."

John Cramer finally told the Prime Minister that as Minister responsible, he refused to take any action against the men concerned, after weighing up all the facts. After that, Cramer was accorded the celebrated Menzies' coolness!

Departmental heads, though, could penetrate the Mask of Ming if they were prepared to stand up to him and show unusual courage.

Menzies had been giving Patrick McGovern, head of the Taxation Department, a rather torrid time at one stage on a departmental matter and McGovern finally decided he had had enough, and told Menzies in no uncertain terms he was not prepared to take it any longer.

The Prime Minister's attitude changed at once, he relaxed and smiled and made a truce with the words: "I only do that with my friends, Pat."

Menzies succeeded in being urbanely dictatorial in the Party room and getting away with it. Seldom was a vote taken. Menzies' attitude usually was, "well gentlemen, I have listened carefully to all your views and they will be given consideration."

An Australian Prime Minister always has the power of appointment, but Menzies held out preferments in the Party room subtly, plausibly, and deliberately, thereby exploiting his strong position to the full.

That was made possible to a large extent by the spinelessness and weakness of those in the Party room. Others who did have the

strength to stand up and criticize were disgusted by the pusillani-
mous attitude of their colleagues.

These critics did not get on. One eloquent case is that of W. C.
Wentworth, of Sydney. Much of his work, such as the standardiza-
tion of railway gauges, has been of great value to Australia, and
here was a man you would expect to merit a Cabinet portfolio.
But Wentworth spent his years under Menzies in the cold climes
of the back benches.

Wentworth is certainly something of a radical with extreme
views, but he is also a man of high intelligence, broad knowledge,
and great energy with the drive to succeed in anything he takes
an interest in. It could be argued by Party theorists that Wentworth, something of a hobbyist by sentiment, therefore had defects
which did not qualify him for the Menzies Ministry.

But the simple truth is that, in a political sense, Menzies hated
Wentworth because he criticized him so often both in the Party
room and, to a lesser but very real extent, in Parliament.

At one stage when Wentworth was spurring Menzies hard, he
censured him in the House. He was also in the ascendancy in that
he was making good speeches. Menzies went to a fellow Victorian,
an Opposition member, and said—again while washing his hands
—"When are you fellows going to get serious and do something
about Wentworth instead of just threatening? When are you going
to help me get rid of him?"

It was the first time Menzies let down his guard and indicated
that Wentworth was upsetting him.

Another illustration of Menzies' dislike of Wentworth occurred
when Les Haylen did a bit of repertory theatre work in the House.
Against the run of the debate Wentworth was using the forms and
orders of the House to attack the Labor Party on Communism.
Haylen donned a white coat to look like a doctor and called for
the "green cart" to "take Wentworth to the lunatic asylum."

For this diversion Haylen was temporarily expelled from the
House. After being expelled, Haylen, as chairman of the Parliamentary Library Committee, had to go to Menzies' office to receive
the Queen's present to the library, some original records of
Captain Cook.

Menzies stood at the door of his office smiling broadly when
Haylen approached him. "You know, sir," said Haylen, "I'm not
supposed to be here. I am denied the precincts of the House."

"The Prime Minister's quarters," said Menzies, "are *not* precincts of the House. Sit down and have a whisky!"

Menzies was most charming, delighted that Wentworth had been humiliated.

With State interests to consider Menzies had some problems in selecting his Ministers, but a general consensus was that he did not always choose the best men for his Ministry. He picked them carefully, watched their behaviour in the Party room and it was generally accepted that anyone who showed a rebellious spirit had no future in the Menzies administration. You waited for the bright member to be promoted but saw him passed over.

Professor Francis Bland could be regarded as one such individual: A man of great talent and energy, he was a member for ten years from 1951 but did not reach Cabinet rank. He spent his energies as chairman of the Public Accounts Committee, waging war against Government wastage and the powers of bureaucracy.

The Menzies Ministry was something like a Greek Taurus, with the Prime Minister being the one big star in the constellation; Bob cracked the whip, the lesser lights went to their corners and echoed what he said. Nobody resigned from Cabinet because they disagreed with him, though many a disgruntled and frustrated Minister vowed privately that he "couldn't take it any longer."

And yet Menzies often showed pride in the quality of his Cabinet—on one occasion after the Press had been critical he remarked to friends that he would not exchange his Ministry for that of Harold MacMillan. He claimed that man for man they were better than the British Cabinet.

In this respect Menzies was a loyal colleague and, perhaps unsuspectingly, very sentimental about the people he liked.

But from the time he became an established factor of Australian life as Prime Minister—five or six years after his Phoenix-like return—he was an autocrat.

His path from that point on was reasonably smooth, his only real crisis being an almost disastrous credit squeeze on the Australian economy in 1960. This had been caused by the Government's policy of allowing too many unnecessary goods into the country and inflationary tendencies had to be curbed.

The Government, by a blanket lifting of import restrictions, caused the country to be flooded with goods it could easily have survived without, such as chocolate-coated ants. The obvious solution to the chocolate and lollies policy was to admit that a mistake had been made and reintroduce limited import restrictions.

But the political leader who admits to mistakes is probably leaving himself too open to reaction from the voting public. Instead, Menzies listened to a Treasury officer who had the reputation of being able to write the best reports in the Public Service. He was fascinated by his report and allowed himself to be swayed by the officer, accepting the idea of a severe credit squeeze. The result cast serious doubts on Menzies' ability as a financial brain.

A capital restrictive budget was brought down causing mass unemployment, the closure of a number of industries that sent hundreds of people, even thousands, bankrupt. The majority of Australians, including the financial experts, considered the measure unnecessarily harsh.

The Liberal Government had no real solution of its own in the immediate aftermath, because in the 1961 election soon afterwards they lifted the main points from the previously-announced Labor Party platform, using them as their own in the election. Cabinet had considered much the same ideas as Labor put forward, but Menzies dallied and did not make up his mind until he saw what Labor intended doing.

Menzies scraped back into power by only one seat, and then only by 500 Communist preferences for Jim Killen's Queensland seat of Moreton (but he did not hang himself from the nearest tree, as he once said he would, at having to depend on Communist votes!).

This meant that Menzies, as in the war, again governed by only one vote. But he had learnt the lessons of his defeat and in any case was so much in control by now that he had earned the nicknames among many of his followers of Great White Father and King of Canberra, tributes to his standing.

Menzies was more sure of himself because of the backing of big interests such as British shipping companies, the private banks, the Catholic Church, and the oil companies, particularly the Shell Oil Company.

He could even afford to be distant and imperious with the men in the Press gallery because, whereas in the 1930s and up till his fall he had shown liking for them, but more or less contempt for the Press barons, he was now getting the barons on his side, although in general he hated newspapers. In 1958 he recommended a knighthood for Jack Williams, managing director of the *Melbourne Herald* group, and in the following year a knighthood for Frank Packer, managing director of the Sydney *Daily Telegraph* group. And a little later he approved the bestowal of a knighthood in the Melbourne *Age* organization. But the *Sydney Morning Herald*, because of his longstanding feud with Warwick Fairfax, missed out.

Menzies' Press conferences became fewer and fewer and so

tightly did he control his Ministers and departments that news was reduced to the handout form, with the public being told what Menzies wanted to tell them.

No longer could reporters bump into a Minister and get a story. In pre-1949 days a reporter could casually meet Ben Chifley in Kings Hall, and the Prime Minister might easily give him a two-column story.

The Menzies' clamp-down reduced journalists to panting and often cursing futility.

Even the occasional news break by an enterprising reporter was resented. Harry Mills, reporting for a Melbourne paper, got a scoop in 1958 on the forthcoming appointment of a new Minister. The Prime Minister's Press secretary told Mills the story was wrong and that Menzies wanted a retraction. Mills refused and a week or so later the name he had published was announced.

Menzies once held journalism in the highest esteem but came to regard it, in many cases, as low in its motives. Certainly he may not always have had the best of luck with the Press but his haughty attitude did not help.

He resented criticism, even legitimate criticism. And when a luckless journalist had to go to him with a tough or perhaps unkind question from his boss, Menzies would often spare him the point of his barb by giving a rejoinder along these lines, "Give so and so (mentioning the proprietor's name) my regards and tell him to go back to his trough."

But in contrast to earlier years, he often seized on the opportunity of taking a rise out of Pressmen, as on the occasion when a Sydney journalist, Jim North, approached him at Sydney Airport and introduced himself by saying, "My name's North, I'm from the *Daily Mirror*, Mr Menzies." Menzies bowed slightly and said, "You have my deepest sympathy."

The story is widely told in Canberra of the Press secretary newly appointed to Menzies who, trying to do his job for the baying members of the Press corps, went to the Prime Minister with a series of questions on tariff policy and said they demanded an answer. Without a word or even looking up from his desk Menzies picked up the questionnaire, ripped it in two and dropped it nonchalantly into the waste paper basket.

"What am I going to tell them?" asked the perplexed Press officer.

"Tell them a funny story," replied the Prime Minister.

There are two ways of looking at that: either the Prime Minister was showing he was not going to be bustled by the Press or he was showing his contempt. Probably a little of both.

Menzies was rather pampered in the years after he became unassailable as the Elder Statesman of the British Commonwealth. The ladies sweet and kind were particularly influenced, and others who flocked to the fold all made a great fuss of him. Perhaps he was permitted to have his own way too much—legitimate but unfortunate, although it was not necessarily unfortunate except for Pressmen and the Parliament.

Menzies adored the higher echelons of wealth and position in Australia, not for their own sake, but because at first they had trampled him. The Mornington Peninsula group and other members of the Melbourne moneybags set took a long time to accept him. But he became so important to them for their own preservation that they eventually made a fuss of him.

Menzies did not go out of his way to court them nor did he change very much; but The Establishment, for whom he became the spokesman, did, in that it had to shift ground to embrace him.

That in itself is a great tribute to the poor boy from Jeparit. Menzies had a great deal of self respect and moral reserve, a great deal of principle in his attitude to things. As a politician he would not set out with the intention of using anyone—he would never do that.

Menzies so established himself as a figure of power, as an actor, that he was able eventually to refrain from repartee and turn this to his advantage. He had only to hint he was going to do something to bring a spontaneous response from people, both inside and outside Parliament.

Someone, for instance, would interject. In earlier days the political animal that was Bob Menzies would slay him with a scornful rejoinder. But it reached a point where Menzies would merely have to glance with surprise and raise those eyebrows or give a slight scoff as sufficient effort on his part for the audience to applaud.

But not so with people like Eddie Ward. Menzies underestimated Ward and knew he had, but condoned his error and would not admit it. For years he treated Ward as a larrikin, thinking perhaps he was doing his Party a good turn. But while Ward, a tough and active opponent, was acting up to the role of larrikin in which Menzies cast him, he got in some heavy sling shots at the Prime Minister.

In later years Menzies did tell a close associate that he knew he could not beat Ward at in-fighting, and tried to tow him out on to the broad ocean where he could deal with him. They insulted each other for many years, the honours being about even.

Menzies was inclined to be complacent with some of the Ministers he retained. It can only be assumed they were kept on out of loyalty. One of his favourite Ministers was a man who used to humour him, but who knew how far to go.

Menzies remained The Boss at all times, even to the extent of doing the Ministers' own thinking for them in many cases where they sought his advice. Thus he took power away from lesser mortals around him, as well as those who disagreed with him, and in exercising power this way he ruled and enjoyed it.

One example of how he ruled by fear can be seen in his appointment of Ministers. Just after the 1958 election he called various people to his office in the process of a Cabinet reshuffle and spoke to them. Some Ministers did not get the call. One was Fred Osborne, the Minister for Air. Like some of the others he did not know whether he was in or out.

Assuming he was out he went to members of his staff, tears in his eyes, and thanked them for all they had done. Then he went to see Harold Holt who that year was taking over as Deputy Prime Minister on the retirement of Artie Fadden.

It was not until he was aboard a Royal Australian Air Force Convair on the way to Sydney that night that Senator Bill Spooner and Holt told him he was still a Minister.

And it wasn't till that night that a Press secretary, who had travelled on the same plane, rang his Minister in Sydney, at the Royal Motor Yacht Club where he was dining with his wife, to tell him he was still the Minister for Social Services. He, too, hadn't heard a word from The Boss.

Whether Menzies the thespian did this to extract the last ounce of drama can only be guessed at. But it showed he obviously enjoyed the use of power.

Although not normally repressive, Menzies could certainly be so when determined about something; the great example of this was the jailing of journalist, Frank Browne, and businessman and newspaper proprietor, Ray Fitzpatrick, for an alleged breach of Parliamentary privilege.

They were brought before the Bar of the House on an ancient House of Commons principle, and jailed without what the Australian citizen regards as the normal processes of the law—that is without a definite charge, without a chance to prepare a defence, without legal representation (which was refused), without a public hearing, and without a judicial atmosphere. The Parliamentary Privileges Committee reported there had been a breach of privilege by *intimidation* of a member, Mr C. Morgan. The Committee had already been advised in writing by the Clerk of the House, Mr Frank Green, that no question of privilege was involved, that under House of Commons rulings "intimidation" to be a matter of privilege, would have to be *physical* intimidation, and would not include an article in a free advertising sheet. Mr Green's submission was ignored. Sir John Latham, former Chief Justice, was critical of the manner in which Parliament handled the matter, and his comments were reported in the Press.

Following a public outcry Menzies promised in an announcement in Parliament on 13 June 1955, that in the next session legislation would be introduced declaring Parliament's privileges and the procedures to be adopted, but it was never tabled.

Menzies and Browne were quite well known to each other personally. In 1945, as president of the Bondi branch of the Liberal Party, Browne moved a vote of no confidence in Menzies after he addressed a meeting of the State Council of the Party, and it was carried by ten votes. The next day Menzies sent a note to Browne congratulating him on a fine speech, and invited him to join him at lunch. The motion of no confidence was rescinded at a subsequent meeting. Some time before the Parliamentary privileges incident, Browne condemned the Prime Minister in his news sheet, *Things I Hear*. The whole incident resulted from the falling out of friends, Fitzpatrick and Morgan, who as a solicitor had acted for Fitzpatrick's interests. When they fell out, it developed into a feud.

Generally since 1949 if there were rumours of likely censure at a Party meeting or in Parliament, Menzies would invite the rebel or rebels into his office and after a drink would talk them out of uttering any discordant note. An ante-room lay between his office and the Cabinet room, and drinks and friendly words were dispensed there.

Some repressive measures which his Government introduced, such as telephone tapping for security reasons, were very much against his grain and he acted reluctantly here.

He skilfully avoided trouble with the Country Party, having learnt to live with a minority Party in a coalition government. He knew that such a Party sometimes attacked to show it was different in order to justify its existence, and he set out to deny the Country Party any opportunity of attacking him, and by integrity and knowing when to give way, he gained Country Party support.

Menzies usually submitted to McEwen in Cabinet when McEwen indicated the Country Party would not support any issue, but it is doubtful whether he ever conceded anything of imperative importance to Country Party pressure.

Whenever Menzies wanted to get his own way in Cabinet on a contentious matter, he would speak first, saying, "Well, I have studied this matter and this is my opinion. . . ." After that, only a brave man or one with a powerful intellect could oppose him. McEwen, when Acting Prime Minister, worked differently and usually sought a consensus of opinion from his colleagues.

Menzies definitely liked to get his own way, and sometimes dragged Cabinet meetings out to inordinate lengths, in order to get it, gradually wearing his colleagues down. But he was not inflexible, and often did change his views when he found his colleagues did not agree with him.

An example was when he told Cabinet he was going to submit to them that the Australian pound should be appreciated and brought closer to parity with sterling. He researched the subject and made a submission with his usual clarity and skill, but was surprised when his Ministers opposed it.

A majority of Ministers felt that in a time of falling commodity prices this would not help the Australian exporters or the economy generally, and he dropped the idea immediately.

Menzies was definitely better at saying "no" than "yes" because, as an able barrister, he preferred to argue against a proposal than accept it off-hand. But for that very reason he promoted full and detailed discussion in Cabinet, except on those occasions when determined to have his way. Often a man will start out being for or against something but when he hears other points of view he will sometimes change his mind—truth is arrived at by these dialectics.

Menzies was a good presider, and usually a patient one. An eminent Australian who has sat at conference tables around the world for many years, legal and political as well as business, says he has encountered Menzies' equal as a chairman only two or three times.

18

Menzies was often ruthless. He did not easily forgive anyone who he felt had been disloyal to him or who was a doubtful supporter.

But you can be ruthless in a genteel manner. Menzies was not vicious, he would not cut your throat, but if you had to go, he would prefer to ease you out by promotion—a fine old British tradition.

The cynicism is agreed, but few people got hurt in the process; some potential rivals or critics of the Great White Father did very well for themselves around the world with knighthoods, diplomatic posts, and big salaries.

The truth is that Menzies had no real rival for the Prime Ministership from the time he made his successful comeback. But he took no chances and did not take kindly to censure, even at times to suggestions, because he was apt to feel that he knew more than the person making the proposals. And he did have a considerable grasp of a number of subjects.

T. W. (Tommy) White, a son-in-law of Alfred Deakin, one of Australia's earliest and greatest Prime Ministers, was a difficult Minister in that he argued with The Boss. He was knighted and sent to London in 1951 as High Commissioner.

The announcement by the Prime Minister said the London post would provide Mr White with "another opportunity to advance the interests of the nation which he had already served so faithfully and well."

White replaced Eric Harrison, a loyal Menzies' man who during his year in London had retained his position as Deputy Leader of the Liberal Party—thus, no up-and-comer was promoted.

Howard Beale was another Minister whom Menzies was not regretful to see go. Beale had New South Wales backing and worked very hard on Ministerial duties. It could have appeared that he was ambitious.

He used to irritate Menzies by arguing with him in Cabinet, one barrister to another. Menzies disliked him accordingly and used to call him "Oliver" to annoy him. Beale's names were Oliver Howard but he had dropped the Oliver which he hated.

Beale was sent to Washington as Australian Ambassador in 1958, knighted and stayed there until 1964.

A classic case is that of Richard Gardiner Casey, who from being Minister for Supply and Development in 1939 was sent by Menzies in 1940 as the first Australian Minister to the United States.

He departed with the greatest goodwill and a cheerful farewell from the Prime Minister.

Casey had no reason to believe he was, in effect, being eased out. There was not the slightest hint of this and after all, he was going to an important post.

The Casey sequence of successes had taken him from Gallipoli and France in the first World War with D.S.O. and M.C. to Canberra, then in second World War to Washington, Whitehall, and Cairo. Casey had always gone to the right places and done the right thing with one sensational exception—when he stood out against Menzies as leader.

Casey's grandfather was a pioneer doctor, his father a company goldminer sufficiently successful to start young Dick Casey off on the blue-ribboned road that Stanley Melbourne Bruce had trodden. From the ancestral Casey home at Werribee between Geelong and Melbourne, he went to Melbourne Grammar School, Melbourne University, Trinity College, then Cambridge in the Bruce tradition.

He began public life as a Bruce protégé in diplomacy, dropped his mining and business interests to act as Australian liaison officer at the British Foreign Office, and for six years (1924-30) happily made the grand tour between Australia House, Whitehall, and Geneva; immaculately groomed, impeccably mannered, absorbing atmosphere, knowledge, and tradition in the cold shadows of the Swiss Alps.

Still true to tradition, he was unhappy with a Labor Prime Minister, reached Canberra by way of the Corio electorate, and entered Cabinet in the Bruce way too, via the Treasury. He settled in to a big house in Canberra which later became the headquarters of the Canadian High Commissioner, played tennis and squash, found relaxation in manual labour, was "like Churchill, an expert bricklayer," and was fond of pottering around with carpentering tools.

Casey was a big success in Washington where he and his wife flew their own plane. But he told Churchill in 1942, in response to a question during a railway journey, that he was not working happily with the new Labor Cabinet in Australia and felt they did not completely trust him nor fully inform him. There was the hint he might do better in some other job and months later he was offered, and accepted, a place in the British Cabinet as Minister to the Middle East and moved to Cairo. Casey went over equally as well in Whitehall as he had at the White House.

Then in 1944, on the suggestion of Lord Louis Mountbatten, he became His Excellency the Governor of Bengal, a £12,000 a year post. Thus Casey, who had never been Prime Minister of Australia had become a British Minister, a big-shot Governor while mentor Bruce had to be content with a High Commissionership, and Menzies with the Opposition leadership.

Casey retained a strong love of his own country and was content to become a Companion of Honour though he could obviously have had a baronetcy at least.

Those close to Joe Lyons had believed that if he'd been able to speak when Governor General Lord Gowrie visited him on his deathbed, he would have advised that Casey be called on to succeed him. The significance of this is that had the blue-eyed, guards-moustached Richard Casey become Prime Minister, Menzies might well have gone to Washington, perhaps got the Middle East job, and become the Bengal Tiger.

Casey, Australia's best-dressed man, had remarked in the early months of the war: "I will consider myself lucky if the end of the war leaves me with no more than the suit I am standing up in."

When Casey returned to Australia in 1946 it was a toss up as to whether he or Menzies was the best-known Australian abroad. On trying to re-enter Federal politics Casey soon learnt there was no enthusiasm from leading Liberals to have him in the team. Casey might well have pondered the words of the Prime Minister early in 1940, "The departure of Mr Casey means a great loss to the Cabinet and to me personally. . . ."

Casey was so upset at the lack of encouragement in finding him a seat that he even considered opposing Menzies, then Opposition Leader, in his own seat of Kooyong in the 1946 election.

Casey's letters to his friends overseas were sad and full of frustration. He was in 1948 made Federal President of the Liberal Party of Australia, a gesture regarded by many as a sop while this very active and distinguished man was kept out of politics.

Casey in private conversation was reported as saying he now realized Menzies had wanted to ease him out when he sent him to Washington.

Menzies, when asked by a Parliamentary associate what type of chap Casey was, replied, "He has a woolly mind."

Eventually in 1949 Casey gained preselection for the Victorian seat of Latrobe and re-entered Federal Parliament. A long list of appointments followed, among them Minister for External Affairs. In this field Casey was an extremely popular figure in Asia where his name was warm and alive, showing he understood and liked Asians, and the Americans in particular thought him a first-class man in this job.

Casey had many disagreements with Menzies over Foreign Policy and strongly disapproved of Menzies' intervention in the Suez Canal crisis of 1956. Finally in 1960 after receiving a baronetcy Casey left politics because, as he intimated to his close friends, he "couldn't take" his leader any longer.

Menzies seemed to go out of his way to ridicule Casey around the Cabinet table, making a fool of him in the presence of other Ministers.

In 1965 came the surprise announcement that Casey had been appointed Governor General of Australia. This was on the initiative and suggestion of Menzies, who gained credit for making perhaps the most popular appointment ever made in Australian history.

Casey himself was astonished. After Menzies had approached him and before the announcement was made he took friends aside and murmured, "What an extraordinary thing!"

In a sense Casey may not have become the great man he intended to be but as an influential Governor General of Australia, he became the great man he *didn't* intend to be.

There is another school of thought on that subject, which time may resolve. Some people see the appointment of Casey as the end of a long succession of Englishmen in this position, that an Australian will be Governor General again next time and the far-seeing Robert Menzies could be that man!

However, in the generally believed reasons for some appointments involving departed rivals, some injustice has been done to Menzies and other prominent Australians.

Percy Spender was said to have been thrown out by Ming the Merciless in 1951 when he became a threat to the throne.

Spender, in fact, was not kicked upstairs. But there was a coolness between the Prime Minister and his Minister for External Affairs, and Spender's political future was somewhat clouded.

This had developed in 1950 because of Menzies' lack of interest in New South Wales. It was said of him that he was interested only in Victoria and the Savage Club in Melbourne.

Menzies was Melbourne-ocentric all his life. He felt most at home in Victoria in a geographic sense and that feeling also manifested itself in the people he asked to serve on committees to advise the Government. They were very largely from Melbourne.

University, medical, and business people in Sydney all felt that was so, and it was a cause of great resentment. On statistics, by the counting of heads, the number of people he appointed from Melbourne was much greater than Sydney and any advice be obtained on the purchase of paintings for public purchase or collection usually came from Melbourne.

Clearly Menzies did not like New South Wales, and at this time he did not like Canberra much either.

Powerful interests in New South Wales, believing to some extent that Menzies was showing the same old characteristics as in the 1940 period, decided that the Prime Minister should best come from their own State.

These groups thought Spender would make a Prime Minister. The groups, together with some others from Queensland including some Federal Parliamentarians, felt there should be a change of Prime Minister because, in their opinion, Menzies was not showing the required capacity for action.

It would be idle to suggest that Spender, with the support he had, could not have become Prime Minister. Murmurings about this went on behind the scenes and Menzies got to hear of it. Although Spender himself was not plotting, Menzies came to the conclusion that Spender was part of this movement of disaffection, and had an eye on the Prime Ministership.

Spender and Menzies had never had any differences except on policy and these were never more than perfectly pleasant exchanges between two men of outstanding intellect. But Menzies, seeing Spender in the robes of a Caesar, began to show signs of a distinct withdrawal from the relationship.

Spender was working extremely hard. He had been on the negotiating committee in Washington for the South East Asia Treaty Organization and had developed the Colombo Plan, giving form and life to the ideal of Australian aid for underprivileged people in South East Asia. He was also developing the idea of the ANZUS Treaty with the United States.

Just after the middle of 1950 Spender suffered a bad gastric ulcer and had to rest. He went to Moss Vale, a town with an English setting in the Southern Tablelands of New South Wales, for a few weeks, and did his departmental work from there. He told Menzies that if he continued to work at the same intensity his condition would worsen and he would not be able to carry on, and would have to seriously consider resigning if his health did not improve.

Menzies visited the United States and returned early in 1951. He mentioned to Spender that the term of Norman Makin, the first Australian Ambassador to the United States, was just about to end in Washington and if he was still intending to resign from politics, why not take that post?

"You must not get out of public life with all your experience," said Menzies.

When Spender finally decided to accept the post in Washington, Menzies told Mrs Spender: "I'm losing my right hand with Percy going." And when Spender went to Washington he received a cable from the Prime Minister written in generous terms thanking him for all his help and co-operation and the important part he had played in the scheme of things.

Menzies may have been glad to see the end of a potential rival but he certainly did not push Percy Spender out, however clearly Spender could see storm clouds up ahead.

Spender himself was deeply hurt at rumours that he had been exiled, rumours that were not denied and which he himself felt he could do nothing to prevent.

Spender was knighted and as Sir Percy went on to greater eminence—a Member of the International Court of Justice at The Hague from 1958 to 1964 and President of the International Court of Justice until his retirement to Sydney at the end of 1966.

The departure of two of Menzies' most prominent Ministers, Sir Garfield Barwick and Sir Wilfrid Kent Hughes, caused keen comment and speculation. Barwick, as both Minister for External Affairs and Attorney General was generally believed to have been politically assassinated for disagreeing with The Boss on foreign policy and restrictive trade practices.

No reason has ever been advanced for the sacking in 1956 of Kent Hughes, who was knighted the following year. But in general terms political commentators have said this eminent Australian was dismissed from the Ministry because he dared to disagree with Menzies on foreign policy.

Barwick, it was said, had been told he could become Chief Justice of Australia—or else.

The real reason for the discarding of Sir Wilfrid was that as Minister for the Interior, while on a tour of South East Asia in late 1954 and early 1955, he strongly supported the Americans against the views of the Prime Minister over the signing of the Sino-American treaty when they were feeling lonely and uncertain in that part of the world, and he criticized Churchill while Menzies was in London.

Kent Hughes was never given any reasons for his dismissal. He was simply called in during a Cabinet reshuffle and given the chop.

The whole incident sprang from Menzies' lack of interest in Asia. He could not treat an Asian as an equal, and did not like his Ministers travelling through South East Asia except on specific missions.

For instance, Defence Minister Athol Townley attended a Defence Conference in Singapore then returned home immediately, while the New Zealand Minister went on to Bangkok, Saigon, and other parts.

Menzies had little regard for Chiang Kai-shek and underestimated the importance of the American attitude on Taiwan. He was not in favour of the Sino-American Treaty, the mutual security pact signed on 1 December 1954 to protect Taiwan and the Pescadores — the following month the United States Congress authorized the President to include the off-shore islands in the protected area.

Kent Hughes was only one of about three Australian Parliamentarians who believed that Australia's future security depended on what happened in South East Asia, particularly after the Korean War. He made so many speeches in Parliament on this that Members looked bored each time he stood up.

Menzies' lack of interest in South East Asia was evident before the Korean War. Percy Spender was one Minister who subscribed to the view that if major trouble broke out in the future it would not be in Europe but somewhere in South East Asia.

He put forward the view in Cabinet that, in effect, the centre of gravity in the world power struggle had shifted from Europe to Asia.

The Prime Minister at this time mostly held brief only for what came out of Whitehall. Nothing else was accorded much significance. Before a friendly exchange along these lines with

Spender in Cabinet one day in 1950 the Prime Minister said to him, "Come on Percy, trot out your old hobbyhorse." Two months later the Korean War broke out.

At the beginning of the Korean armistice in 1953 Kent Hughes put forward the view in Cabinet that mainland China would now transfer her attention to the rest of South East Asia.

Kent Hughes had obtained a copy of Mao Tse-tung's blueprint for conquest of South East Asia, which was read into the U.S. Congressional record by Senator Knowlands in April 1954. Later, on 3 September 1965 it was to be published by the *Peking Review* and, in September the following year, broadcast in seven instalments by Peking Radio, which has made it somewhat official.

Hardly anyone in Australia in 1954 took much notice of Mao's blueprint for world domination. Nobody took much notice of Hitler's *Mein Kampf* either—and a considerable weight of opinion believed that we drifted into the second World War because Hitler thought England would not fight again in Europe.

According to Mao's blueprint he intended to "conquer" South East Asia by 1966. Diplomats now agree that whatever Mao's real intentions were, he completely miscalculated the American resistance.

It is only a theory, of course, but many people today believe that if Australia had stood firmly with America earlier than she did, the war in Vietnam might have been avoided, and that China would not have thrown her support in behind the Liberation Front.

The Americans, rather reluctant to go it alone, as are most nations, almost certainly would have been quicker to move in Vietnam if she had been assured of Australian support.

By inference this means that if the Prime Minister, who directs Australian foreign policy as much as the Minister for External Affairs, had shown an awareness of events in Asia, the history of Vietnam today might have been different.

The danger of Chinese militancy in South East Asia was pointed out to the Prime Minister in Cabinet by Kent Hughes in 1953 when the Korean armistice began. But there was little discussion on his belief. It dropped into a bottomless well, without a splash.

The Prime Minister showed no reaction at all. He just did not believe it. In this respect Menzies and his Ministers showed no foresight or anticipation, probably because of their own lack of interest in South East Asia.

The extraordinary thing is that in this period Australia had no real defences of her own and had covered herself with the ANZUS and SEATO treaties.

Menzies did not show his Ministers that he was concerned about aggression in South East Asia until Sukarno's confrontation of Malaysia in 1963. Feelings on Asia, that Australia's future could be tied to it, did not stir in the Federal Parliament until the Liberation Front began in Vietnam in 1961.

Australia's involvement in Vietnam was slow. The first team of thirty instructors to help train the Vietnamese in jungle fighting left Australia on 25 May 1962. The number was increased to 100 two years later, a year after the South Vietnamese Government had asked for it and Kent Hughes had recommended it, after a tour of Vietnam.

Australia had been making a small but useful contribution in general aid to South East Asia through the Colombo Plan. It proved a successful innovation after early mistakes were ironed out —for instance, bulldozers were sent to Nepal via Calcutta and because they could only reach their destination through narrow bridges they never left Calcutta. But the Plan did not create a great deal of interest among the Australian public—there was little enthusiasm or inspiration from the top.

One of Australia's best features in aid to South East Asia was the sending of a road-building team to Central Thailand. The all-weather roads it built have done more than anything else to bring Thailand together as a nation. But in 1954 that kind of thinking was futuristic except for perhaps three or four politicians who foresaw that Australia must integrate itself with the Asian region.

Part of the reason for which Kent Hughes was subsequently sacked was of great moral value to the Americans in South East Asia early in 1955, but Menzies apparently did not consider this.

Menzies did not give Kent Hughes a chance to explain. Even if he had fully appreciated Kent Hughes's help to the Americans, it is doubtful if this would have made any difference because the Prime Minister was more concerned with the fact that Kent Hughes's statements and actions had been an embarrassment with the British.

The Kent Hughes Affair happened this way. As Minister for the Interior, Kent Hughes grew rather weary of signing copious documents and decided he would like to inspect the Australian war graves in South East Asia. He was chairman of the Anzac Division of the Imperial War Graves Commission.

Nobody had ever inspected the graves and a new graves section was being completed in the China Coast region.

So Kent Hughes went to Menzies and proposed that he visit the war graves, taking with him Brigadier Athol Brown, the Secretary-General of the War Graves Commission. Menzies agreed and asked how long they would be away. When Kent Hughes said seven or eight weeks the Prime Minister asked if it could be shortened to five. Kent Hughes offered to pay his own way if necessary, but the Prime Minister said there was no need to do that and allowed him £1,000 expenses plus air fares.

When Kent Hughes remarked that he would be going up the China Coast and visiting Taipeh the Prime Minister wanted to know why. Kent Hughes replied that Taiwan was a free country, that he had been a prisoner of war there for two years, and was interested in having another look at the place.

Before the second World War Kent Hughes had not known where Kuala Lumpur was. But his interest was aroused by spending nearly five years of the war in Asia, three and a half of them as a prisoner of war in Singapore, Taiwan, and Manchuria.

Kent Hughes went to Singapore, then to Djakarta where the Ambassador for Ceylon begged him to ask the Australian Prime Minister to attend the forthcoming Afro-Asian conference. The smaller Asian nations feared they would be railroaded at the conference by Nehru and Chou En-lai. They wanted a strong man to stand up to these two.

The Minister wrote a seven-page foolscap letter to Menzies giving reasons why he felt Australia, as somebody living in the Asian region, should be invited to the conference and pointing out that if Afro-Asian leaders turned down the request they, and not Australia, were drawing the colour line. The letter was delivered to Menzies as he passed through Singapore on his way to a London conference. There was no reply and Australia did not seek admission to the Afro-Asian conference.

The further Kent Hughes went the more his journey became a goodwill mission. In South East Asian countries the Minister for the Interior controls the police forces and is the right-hand man of the Prime Minister. Kent Hughes, therefore, was automatically regarded as a powerful figure.

In Hong Kong he learnt from a friend that diesel engines for landing craft were coming into Hong Kong from British ships and were going on up the China Coast in British ships. They were being imported on the manifest for Hong Kong, described as diesel engines for replacements for the Kowloon ferries.

Kent Hughes went to the Colonial Secretary, Mr Black, whom he'd known in Singapore, and told him of his suspicions. Mr Black was reportedly furious and demanded to know what authority Kent Hughes had for making such a statement.

"I just thought you'd be interested," said Kent Hughes. "I'd like to take a bet that the British Government never applies for compensation for the ship that was sunk by Nationalist planes recently."

Then Kent Hughes went to the American Consul General and told him of his suspicions. A week later he read in the Hong Kong *Standard* that American and Japanese police had raided a ship loading in Yokohama for Hong Kong and had taken possession of 193 cases of spare parts for landing craft engines, uncovering a smuggling ring.

He cut out the item and posted it to Mr Black—a gesture which did not add to his popularity with the British authorities.

When Kent Hughes landed in Taipeh he found he was the first British Minister to visit there, and received the full ceremonial treatment. He was given a five-star-General guard of honour and a nineteen-gun salute. The Nationalist leader and his chief Ministers were on hand to meet him, so were sixty international war correspondents.

Menzies by now was in London and reports of his Minister's triumphant military welcome reached him through Canberra.

The correspondents insisted on a Press conference and Kent Hughes's remarks were widely published in the Western world. He said, among other things, that Australia was interested in Asia "because we live here, just as Sir Winston Churchill has said he is interested in Europe because he lives there."

What really upset the applecart was a remark he made when having a casual drink later with some of the correspondents. One of them asked, "What do you think of Winston?"

"I think he's a grand old man of British history but his trouble is that he's never been able to see east of Suez," replied Kent Hughes.

The remark was made in a club and was "off the record"—and not intended for publication or broadcasting. However, one correspondent apparently failed to appreciate this and cabled the remark, which was broadcast while Menzies was having discussions with Churchill.

The explosive effect of that comment can only be imagined, for Churchill, a man of super ego, was completely intolerant of criticism. Whatever happened, Menzies was embarrassed as a result.

Kent Hughes, in his distinctive Australian way, continued to ruffle the iron-clad diplomacy of the British in his efforts to get at the truth. He searched about trying to find out who was advising Britain on her China policy.

In Tokyo, apart from meeting a Japanese doctor who had befriended him whilst a prisoner of war, he had called on the British Ambassador, Sir Esler Dening, and threw out some bait on the China policy.

The ambassador lost his temper and it was several minutes before he regained his calm, uttering such undiplomatic words as "upstarts," and pointing out he had been on the China Coast for twenty years or so.

Kent Hughes left His Excellency with the thought that they would have to agree to disagree on the subject. Details of that encounter were obviously dispatched to London.

In Tokyo, Kent Hughes conferred with General Hull and gained the impression that the Americans felt isolated over their policy in that part of the world, particularly over the newly signed Sino-American Treaty, which had been criticized strongly by Britain and some other countries.

He went to the Australian Ambassador to see if the Prime Minister had made a statement on the Treaty, and at that stage he hadn't. But the Minister for External Affairs Dick Casey had, and Kent Hughes studied his statement which the Ambassador said he fully supported.

Because he thought it would help the American allies Kent Hughes issued a strong statement on the off-shore islands, which hit the headlines. But at almost the same time Menzies issued a statement in London—one far less enthusiastic over the Treaty, and this was buried in the back pages.

Kent Hughes condemned criticism, especially in the British Press, of a speech on the Formosan Straits by Foster Dulles as playing into the hands of Red China. The Australian Minister for the Interior said: "All the way up the East Asian Coast from Djakarta to Tokyo I have been confronted with the Communist tactics of 'divide and conquer,' aimed in particular at America and Britain and internally in every country in South East Asia. The Reds are the imperialists of the present age, employing the strategy and tactics of the Old Roman Empire.

"The United States has had to carry major burdens on behalf of the Free World in this region and has not been receiving the support which should have been given. A cease fire armistice in the Formosan Straits would not bring peace to the Far East. It would merely relieve the Reds of a threat to their exposed flank, and enable them to continue their predatory programme in South East Asia and Tibet, as was the case in Indo-China after the Korean armistice.

"By open threats, continuous subtle propaganda, and judicious probing for weak spots, the Communists have caused much confused thinking on the problems of the Far East. They have cleverly used the ardent desire for peace among the free nations of the world as the chief weapon in their propaganda armory.

"Fearing a hot war as much an anyone, and in China more than most, they are endeavouring to create a 'bomb happy' state of mind in certain quarters in order to win the cold war. Such a state of mind is easy money for cunning gamblers and expert bargainers in an international poker game. There are no 'trigger happy' top brass in this part of the world but there are many realists who are able to appreciate the situation far better than their detractors.

"It would appear that Red China has much to lose and little to gain from a head-on collision in the Formosan Straits but she will continue to bluff, bluster, and probe, as long as uninformed criticism is aimed at the United States.

"Australia has announced her support of the Sino-American Treaty because she knows full well that the island is the keystone of the arch of the Western Pacific defence against aggression, and it is also the northern gatepost of Australia. Mr Dulles and his Government should be congratulated on having made firm decisions, where firm decisions have been badly needed for some time.

"Another armistice on the same basis as Korea, or another Geneva settlement will purchase peace for only a very short space of time at an undisclosed heavy price, which will later have to be paid. The Free World wants peace, but surely not at any price. You cannot treat Formosa, or the islands off the China Coast of which Hong Kong is one, or Indo-China, or Korea as separate problems. They are all separate portions of the one picture.

"If a cease fire in the Formosan Straits is discussed apart from the march of events in Tibet, South East Asia, and Korea, and the question of reduction of armaments, the free nations of the world will make a colossal blunder.

"Permanent peace, not a temporary makeshift peace, must be the objective, or the last state of the world will be far worse than the present state of tension. If anyone thinks he can buy time in this part of the world he has another think coming. Time in Asia is not on our side. Calculated risks will have to be taken, but they are minor risks compared to those involved in allowing indecision and drift to continue."

Kent Hughes then went up the Imjin River, spent a night with Australian troops, but when he returned to Seoul the Australian Representative on the United Nations there was waiting for him. He had a cable from the Prime Minister in London.

Menzies told Kent Hughes in the cable he would be glad if he would desist from making statements on foreign policy as he in fact had already made a statement on the off-shore islands and he was embarrassed by Kent Hughes's statements.

Kent Hughes knew from that moment that he was for it. Returning to Australia later he found a whispering campaign in progress against him in the Parliamentary corridors. With only a few exceptions the other Ministers avoided him as though he had the plague.

The Prime Minister did not carpet Kent Hughes and did not mention the matter to him at all. On one occasion Kent Hughes approached Menzies in the lobby and said he'd like to have a chat with him, but he never got the call.

Not until almost a year later, early in 1956, when a Cabinet re-shuffle was taking place, did Kent Hughes get called to the Prime Minister's office. The Prime Minister's remarks were along these lines, "Bill, I've got to reconstruct Cabinet. Some have got to go out and some have got to stay in. I'm very sorry but you're one of those who have to go out."

"Why, Bob, after all these years?" asked Kent Hughes. "You're not going to dismiss me with that, are you? What have I done wrong?"

"Oh," said Menzies, "that would be unpleasant."

In the discussion that followed, Kent Hughes pointed out that he had not made one mistake in his duty as Minister for Public Works and the Interior, but the Prime Minister would not give him any reasons for the change.

Kent Hughes then heatedly told Menzies he could not work with anyone who did not deal with him openly, and who did not have him on the mat when it was considered he had done something wrong. Hughes accused the Prime Minister of starting the whispering campaign against him.

Finally Kent Hughes said: "As far as I'm concerned I understand the position fully and I never want to work with you again under any circumstances." And he walked out.

Kent Hughes was then appointed by his colleagues as chairman of the Foreign Affairs Committee.

A little later, as chairman of the organizing committee of the Melbourne Olympic Games, Kent Hughes was quoted on the Games in the *New York Times*. He received a letter from General Hull, then retired as United Nations Commander in the Far East.

Wishing him luck with the Games, General Hull said he would like him to know that his statement on the off-shore islands a year or so before had been welcomed at the Pershing Heights headquarters of the Expeditionary forces in Korea. The General said he did not know what effect this statement had had on his political colleagues but it had been of great assistance to him at the time.

Until now, the American appreciation of Kent Hughes's statement, although it conflicted with the attitude of the Australian Prime Minister, has not been made known. Kent Hughes has never tried to justify himself by disclosing any details, although history has proved him right.

It shows classically the manner in which Menzies ruled, by remaining apart and not taking those around him into his confidence. No doubt the Prime Minister felt justified in dropping Kent Hughes and was exercising the right he was entitled to.

But the manner of the dismissal, while adding to the aura of power around the Prime Minister, caused unnecessary resentment. The speculation that followed also had the effect of demolishing, to some extent, the reputation of a distinguished man who had given splendid service to his country.

Menzies later told a Ministerial associate that dropping Kent Hughes was the most disagreeable thing he had ever had to do.

19

Sir Garfield Barwick was not sacked but he went out under a cloud of political speculation. Barwick, as Minister for External Affairs, had diverged from Menzies' policy on Asia, and although an admirer of the British, was not so "British to the bootheels" as his boss.

In April, 1964, after making highly contentious statements in Manila, he had returned to Australia and had his bags packed for a world tour to promote Australia, including a meeting with Khrushchev. But late on the night before his departure while in Sydney, he was appointed Chief Justice of Australia by a snap meeting of the Federal Cabinet in Canberra, and his overseas tour was cancelled.

Barwick, the brilliant Sydney barrister, entered Federal politics in 1958 and became Attorney General within ten months. His entry to politics was preceded by what must have been one of the most deflating experiences in Menzies' life. The Prime Minister went to Barwick's chambers to meet him just before he was chosen as the Liberal candidate to succeed Sir Howard Beale, and the female clerk in the office demanded to know who he was before letting him in to see Barwick—she didn't recognize the distinguished visitor.

In the broad, Barwick after 1961 was the first Minister for External Affairs to press for an independent Australian foreign policy. Casey had seen the need for a widening of relations with Asia but this had not led to the logical conclusion—that Australia had to choose between continuing its association with the Dutch and their colonial activities, or going out to deliberately make friends with Indonesia.

In earlier times Australia had frustrated Indonesia in her claims to West New Guinea, with Menzies and his Ministers following the purely legalistic argument that this was a question of sovereignty which was entirely for the colonial power, the Dutch, to decide.

In 1945 the Australian Labor Government was one of the first to recognize Indonesian independence, and for the next few years Menzies and the Liberals in Opposition opposed both Indonesian independence and the action of Communist groups on the water-front trying to prevent arms being shipped to the Dutch.

Few politicians like to reverse their actions, even though their consciences may tell them that they should, and Menzies was no exception. When he came to power in 1949 he was reluctant to change his stand on Indonesian claims to West New Guinea, and he prevented Indonesia from gaining the necessary two-thirds majority of votes in the United Nations to have its dispute with the Netherlands debated in that forum. It cannot be said Australia was supported by the United States because America abstained from voting on all these occasions.

Australia could have greatly helped to put the new nation on her feet, but instead she strongly attacked her in the United Nations. There is little doubt that this attitude by a White Australia encouraged the Communist Party in Indonesia, the PKI, to jump on the West New Guinea bandwaggon; to ingratiate themselves with Sukarno, who had not liked them in the past, and thus to gain in power and prestige to a degree that, in the 1960s, endangered Australia's own security.

Menzies was invited to Indonesia several times but made no effort to take up the invitation. Finally he went there in 1959.

The attitude of Australia in the United Nations, plus the fact that as the nearest European nation it did not even deign to allow its representatives to call, generated a great deal of feeling in Indonesia against Australia.

In the higher strata of Indonesian life, people felt they had lost face. And Sukarno welcomed any help he could get in the campaign to obtain West Irian. Eventually, as is well known, his tolerance of the Communists meant that they almost succeeded in taking over Indonesia in a bloody *coup*.

Barwick was the first Foreign Minister to stand up to Menzies on the Indonesian issue; the first to make appropriate gestures towards becoming friends with Australia's nearest neighbour, having a population about ten times as great.

It was a turning point in Australian foreign policy when the young nation, fairly immature in international thinking and attitudes, suddenly favoured the Indonesians and appeared to walk away from European friends.

Although Barwick was not obstructed in Cabinet, many of his fellow Ministers believed he was too enthusiastic for the new paths. By the time Barwick began his New Deal with the Indonesians the Prime Minister understood perfectly well that there was no possibility of any armed intervention in favour of the Dutch.

And although a large section of Cabinet did not agree with Barwick's theory that there was really no idea of territorial expansion in the minds of the Indonesians, he was allowed to have his way and the situation has now been retrieved largely in Australia's favour.

What has not been known outside of Cabinet is that early in 1961, when he was still only Attorney General, Barwick sounded out South East Asian leaders on West Irian without their knowing it. Barwick did this when returning from a Privy Council case in London. He had suggested to Menzies that, acting merely as Attorney General, he could probably find out the views of Asian leaders without raising suspicions, and Menzies agreed.

Barwick called on Nehru, Tunku Abdul Rahman, Lee Kuan Yew, and Ayub Khan, in an unofficial and unobtrusive way.

He learnt that except perhaps for Ayub Khan they were not in favour of Sukarno personally, but they were all of a mind that he was perfectly right to recover West Irian; so that if Australia intervened she would do so in diametric opposition to the Asian countries with whom she hoped to be more closely associated. These unofficial soundings helped a great deal to convince the Prime Minister that it was right to go along with Barwick's trends.

Menzies was slow to diverge from the belief that Whitehall was the centre of the Commonwealth and should remain so. But he did not stand in Barwick's way when he set out to get the Commonwealth away from the centre of London and make it a more bilateral relationship between Australia and England.

Although he never got down to a precise discussion with Barwick on this point, it was generally felt that he would not have agreed with Barwick's views. He was too much of an Anglophile, having lived a long life in close association with the British.

Menzies gave no positive lead to the shaping of opinion towards a feeling of independence for Australia. It was left to others to look for means of asserting Australia's independence; to consciously take independent steps.

214

Australia, of course, with no revolutionary movement behind her, had laboured under the disability of never having to struggle for independence. She has no real national day or event of that kind which nationalism tends to feed on.

But with the crumbling of the Commonwealth and events in Asia, Barwick was one who realized that Australia must have her own foreign policy. A strong believer in the Commonwealth himself, he felt its only chance of continued success with the new nations which were breaking away and becoming republics, would be to establish a great number of bilateral contacts. Australia therefore needed a policy with regard to Africa, to try to make Africa understand this.

In the United Nations, at the weekly Commonwealth meetings, Barwick favoured Britain being removed as permanent chairman and rotating the Chair among the various Commonwealth countries. The British opposed this strongly, but eventually Barwick supported the Africans and Asians in their wish to alternate each nation in the Chair week by week, as a means of trying to orient the Commonwealth around the perimeter instead of concentrating it in the centre.

Barwick even broke away from the Menzies policy of keeping his cards so close to his chest that the Press received no information at all. Although he was, at one time, suspicious of and even hostile towards the Press, Barwick became extremely affable, appointing a senior officer to inform the Press on Foreign Affairs, and encouraging his staff to give as much information as possible.

Some Pressmen interpreted the new approach as a bid by Barwick to get the Press on his side in order to make a successful run for the Prime Ministership, but that was hardly fair.

Barwick realized that in Australia, where no entrenched caste views existed, Government must respond very promptly to popular pressures—perhaps even faster than in other democracies; that foreign policy must be based on a critical opinion, and that it must have domestic support. The Australian electorate is intelligent, and capable of understanding the information which is given to it. Barwick set out to inform the public to an extent that Menzies himself would not have done. The pity of it is that more Ministers did not get up off their knees and do the same.

Barwick did run into disagreement with Menzies over his legislation on restrictive trade practices, but that was not the sole cause of his going out of office, however disappointed he was at not being able to finish the restrictive trade work he began.

Monopolies are a tremendous problem in Australia, and before the 1961 election Barwick had in mind a scheme to counter them. But after the Government just scraped into office following the credit squeeze, it was felt that a highly controversial measure could not be pressed on the public immediately. So Barwick and the Cabinet waited, and did not for some time publicly produce the restricted practices scheme which had been drawn up previously, and entirely with Menzies' concurrence.

Barwick's view was that when you have a Customs ring around a country, as Australia has through its tariff policy, the more powerful countries of the world don't fight your protective policy, they come inside the Customs barrier and profit by it.

They set up their subsidiaries within the protected area, operating legitimately but knowing how to get control of the market if that is possible. That is how human nature works.

And when they do get control of the market, your Government finds it cannot establish what these outside countries have agreed to do. The policies of these combines are following not the policies for your country, but those of their own.

The skilled public servants who drew up the Treaty of Rome for the European Common Market, knew they would need a strong restrictive practices law as soon as they put a Customs ring around Europe, and they made it so.

And here was Australia, developing rapidly, wanting to attract the subsidiaries of the great companies, but with no means of handling them.

The crucial point of Barwick's legislation was that it placed the onus on the company concerned to state in its documents of registration how it intended to restrict competition. The Government was saying to these companies, in effect: if you want to distort the competitive pattern by having a practice that is restrictive in any respect, you must tell us in confidence what it is you are going to do and we'll give you an exchange immunity. You won't have to worry about it until we decide whether what is being done is against the public interest, and then we will challenge you.

The smart business operators impressed on Menzies that this would involve the Government in a tremendous amount of paper work and although he did not issue directives to stopper Barwick down in any way, his attitude was quite plain and was largely responsible for the legislation being watered down under a new Minister.

One aspect on which the legislation was weakened was that traders now are not called upon to declare whether they are carrying on retail price maintenance. It boils down to the fact that the

Commonwealth now has to take action against a trader for monopolistic practices without the trader making any real declaration —a process that might well be more top heavy and unwieldy than the original scheme.

In bending to the wishes of big business, the behind-the-scenes support of Government, Menzies did what may prove to be a disservice to the public of Australia.

When Menzies asked Barwick, in 1961, to take the External Affairs portfolio, Barwick refused to give up the Attorney Generalship as he had done when previously asked. In the period prior to 1961 Menzies had taken External Affairs because he said Barwick would kill himself if he tried to do both jobs. In 1961 he allowed Barwick to take both portfolios, with an assistant in both departments.

After the 1963 election Menzies told Barwick he would have to give up the appointment of Attorney General and Barwick again declined.

Menzies said: "I can't let you continue the attorneys while you have other responsibilities. You've paved the way for things now being considered. You'll have to give up the attorneys."

Barwick asked to be allowed to finish the Restricted Practices Bill but Menzies would not let him. So Barwick, very reluctantly, gave up the Attorney Generalship and the Restrictive Practices Bill which he had prepared so brilliantly.

When early in 1964 the Chief Justiceship of Australia fell vacant on the illness of Sir Owen Dixon, Barwick was nominated for the post. He accepted the nomination, having come to the conclusion that he did not want to contest the Prime Ministership. He felt that such a step would be futile in any case since he was sixty-one and had obviously made as much impact as he was likely to. While he might stay in politics only a few years longer, he reasoned that he would have ten or fifteen years left in which to serve in Australia's highest judicial office.

When Barwick was nominated, the Prime Minister was far from happy. He wanted Barwick to remain and continue his work as External Affairs Minister.

Menzies was reluctant to agree that Barwick should go and he would not make up his mind. It was Menzies' indecision in many ways which caused the crisis over Barwick.

Barwick had been asked by his department if he would go through Europe to try to sell Australia as something other than a sheepfarming country. An extensive itinerary had been drawn up —he was to stop over in Moscow, London, Paris, Bonn, Madrid, and Berlin, with plans to invite to Australia some of Europe's leading Statesmen.

The sequence of events was as follows: Barwick was to go on to Europe after a SEATO conference in Manila. But while in Manila Barwick decided he should come back to Australia to make a statement in Parliament on SEATO, and he came back for no other reason than that.

While in Manila, Barwick made a statement along the lines that the United States would be involved through ANZUS if Indonesian forces attacked Australian troops in Malaysia or Borneo.

That was widely attacked as being deliberately misleading, severely embarrassing to the United States, and the reason for Sir Garfield being kicked upstairs.

This speculation was entirely wrong. Barwick had deliberately dropped the remark in Manila on behalf of the Australian Government to let Sukarno know where the Americans stood. It did not embarrass the Americans, and it had the full accord of Cabinet.

The day before he was to leave for Europe Barwick saw Menzies, who had still not made up his mind over the Chief Justiceship. Barwick told him he was leaving next morning.

Barwick's Cabinet colleagues had told him that whatever he wanted would be done. Barwick's reply was that he definitely preferred to resign from politics and become Chief Justice.

That evening a snap meeting of Cabinet was called to discuss two questions—whether Barwick's resignation should be accepted to enable him to become Chief Justice, and whether they would leave the office vacant until he returned from his overseas journey.

But Menzies would not agree to the tour taking place if Barwick accepted the post. Menzies made a strong stand on this question, putting forward the view that he would not have Barwick going around Europe as a sort of Chief Justice Elect.

He had his way in Cabinet on this, although there were some who considered the attitude somewhat petty, and not merely one of principle. And while Barwick's nomination was accepted, the tour had to be cancelled.

The Attorney General, Mr Snedden, who had proposed Barwick's nomination in Cabinet, rang Barwick in Sydney late that night and told him of the decision—that his nomination was accepted, but the tour would have to be called off.

Sir Arthur Tange, Secretary of the Department of External Affairs, had to sit up all that night sending cables round the world to cancel the tour arrangements.

Barwick then had the problem of how far he could go in a public statement after the announcement of his appointment was made. But the damage was done the next day in Parliament after Menzies made the announcement.

The appointment was attacked by Opposition Leader Arthur Calwell and others as being unusual and remarkable. Newspapers speculated on the strong possibility that Barwick had been politically assassinated.

Barwick realized it was a bad sequence of events, but believed he could not make up for lost ground by issuing a statement, so he kept quiet. At his swearing-in three days later he said the decision had been his own, but hardly anyone believed it. And in Perth, Menzies indignantly said it was ridiculous to suggest Sir Garfield had been forced out. But few people believed him either.

Menzies was very hurt because he knew the allegation was false and, in fact, he had wanted Barwick to stay in politics and was surprised at his decision to retire.

Sir Garfield Barwick achieved a great deal in his six years in Canberra. His Matrimonial Causes Bill, giving Australia uniform divorce and marriage laws for the first time, was particularly notable. In foreign affairs he was the first to follow a line away from the old order of the past and to recognize the aspirations of the New World.

Menzies was a loyal colleague to Barwick—on one occasion he stayed up with him until 2.30 a.m. to vote on the Matrimonial Causes Bill although his Victorian probity caused him to hate divorce, while John McEwen, whom many would regard as a more loyal colleague than Menzies, said he was tired and went to bed.

Menzies, as had often been the case, was too slow in coming to a decision. In the past he usually escaped repercussions from this habit, but in the case of Barwick he was not so fortunate.

As a result many people in Australia today still believe that Sir Garfield Barwick was eased out of office.

20

To make the Queen blush twice within a few minutes in one speech and to carry it off without even the faintest pause, is quite a feat.

Menzies did just that in a welcoming speech to the Queen and the Duke of Edinburgh at Parliament House, Canberra, early in 1963 at the beginning of their Australian tour.

Many Australians winced to read that at a glittering function the night before the Prime Minister prophesied to the tiara-decked guests that when Australians saw the Queen they would recall the words of the poet, "I did but see her passing by, and yet I love her till I die."

Menzies could be unashamedly misty-eyed over Royalty and this was one occasion when he overacted. This writer was present that evening, saw the Queen blush, and wrote the first report in an Australian newspaper that she was embarrassed by the Prime Minister's rather fulsome sentiments.

The Queen was seated on a dais in Kings Hall, Parliament House, when the Prime Minister, looking perfectly at ease as the elder statesman of the Commonwealth, quoted from a verse of "There Is A Lady," by the English poet Barnabe Googe (1540-1594) —

> There is a lady sweet and kind,
> Was never face so pleased my mind;
> I did but see her passing by,
> And yet I love her till I die.

Australians mostly like to think of themselves as democrats who despise English class habits and can take or leave Royalty, but many of them are really among the biggest dress and Royalty snobs in the world. On this occasion the guests showed they really worshipped Royalty by applauding spontaneously.

The Queen blushed noticeably, then stared at the floor. She blushed again a couple of minutes later when about to begin her reply, because the Prime Minister, having finished his speech, in the most enthusiastic manner called for three cheers for Her Majesty. The Queen faltered as she began her address.

It would have been too much for Lord Altrincham, the English critic of the Crown. Without even seeing such a spectacle as this he declared of Menzies that his attitude was "disgusting and stuffily subservient"; that he simply worshipped the Sovereign as someone above criticism.

Here we had the case of a man capable of deep and genuine emotion, but usually holding it back behind his disciplined public mask. On this occasion he gave vent to his feelings, and got carried away.

Whenever Menzies wanted to stress a point he laid it on thickly. This he did with Royalty as, when earlier in his address of welcome to the Queen on that occasion he said: "You are indeed the head of this House, be it entered by the Queen's Most Excellent Majesty, and therefore Ma'am, you are among your friends, and, in one sense, among your colleagues.

"And we, of course, are also delighted to see His Royal Highness Prince Philip, who has been here a few times—not enough, but a few times. It is a proud thought for us to have you here to remind ourselves that in this great structure of government which has evolved, you, if I may use the expression, are the living and lovely centre of our enduring allegiance."

Add to this his oft-repeated statement that he was British to the bootheels and, during the 1963 Royal tour, "we are the Queen's men," and you have a Royalist so steadfast that even some Englishmen must have wondered at times.

But there is no doubting Menzies' pre-eminent position of popularity as a Commonwealth figure at Buckingham Palace. In the past few years, in particular, he has been a "father figure" to the Queen, and greatly admired by all members of the Royal family.

His popularity with the Royal family can be seen in the easy terms he enjoys with them. This can be summed up in a bit of slang Princess Margaret used when he was trying to coax the Queen Mother to visit Australia. "You'll have to pin her down," the princess said, and he, turning to the Queen Mother, said: "May I pin you down Ma'am?"

Princess Marina, the Duchess of Kent, entertains Menzies extensively when he visits London and so does Princess Alexandra.

Menzies' most really amusing experience with Royalty was one night at Buckingham Palace when, of all things, the soup ran out. It was a Coronation dinner for the Queen in 1953 and, with all the Royal personages about, Prime Ministers were two a penny. A footman came round to Dame Pattie, apologized and said the soup had run out. The Prime Minister's reaction is not known, but he was able to see the funny side of it and later received a letter of apology from a Palace official for the embarrassing culinary *faux pas*.

Was Menzies' unabashed worshipping of Royalty sheer snobbery?

Menzies was a rationalist in almost everything he did and if ever he got down to a precise discussion on Royalty—and there is no record of his ever doing this with any of his colleagues—he would certainly be able to give a logical reason why the monarchy should be preserved. He would be able to explain why an Australian should fervently express love for the monarchy, and why it was nonsense to feel that because the monarchy still maintained ancient traditions it was not equipped for the twentieth century.

Menzies would probably subscribe to the view that apart from the structure of parliamentary government, with the Prime Minister or President running the day-to-day business, there is need for a figure, whether coming from the hereditary bloodstock of monarchy or by appointment, to draw the factions together in national unity.

A strong point in this argument is that a grave weakness in the United States today is that the President is both King and Prime Minister. He is so busy being King that he does not have time properly to be Prime Minister. The President is also Commander-in-Chief of the entire defence forces, the man who personally presses the atomic button, a formidable responsibility in itself without the job of baby kissing and vice-regal ceremonialism.

The Kennedys came nearest to being an American Royal family. The desire of the American people to have a national symbolic figure has been shown in the fact that with the assassination of John Kennedy they have created a myth around the late President. America generally would like to have a national head like the Queen of England; a head divorced from sheer politics.

Menzies never set out to be a popular figure as Prime Minister. He left the baby kissing to Governors and Governors-General and concentrated on being the radical surgeon—and that probably more than anything else is why he was the successful Prime Minister.

This writer does not believe that Menzies was a corny Royalist or that he sedulously clung to the Crown while wooing America simply to get the best of both worlds for Australia.

The more likely explanation is that his love of Royalty welled up from his subconscious. It was perhaps an expression of what he had been taught and what he decided when a child; that if you stayed with the Establishment you could not go wrong. We do not do deliberate things from our subconsciousness; Menzies did not have to consciously think of loyalty to Britain, it was in his make-up.

One can easily imagine the shrewd Englishmen in Whitehall being astonished to learn that even after the second World War Menzies was still of the old order. "This chap still thinks we've got something," one can imagine them saying. And they treated him accordingly; with respect, admiration, and honours. It would hardly be human nature to do otherwise.

Menzies did not disappoint them. "London," he said on a visit there in 1948, "is the centre of the world. If you take the great art of self-government, the highest arts of war and the highest levels of pure and applied science, you cannot go beyond these islands."

His dedication to British dignitaries and institutions was extraordinary. Anthony Eden was "the greatest Prime Minister of the century"; Harold Macmillan, the first British Prime Minister to visit Australia in office, was always "my great friend"; Lord Home was "one of the very great men it has been my privilege to meet"; Lord Wavell "wrote like a master," and Lord Birkett had "a beautiful voice and a flashing wit."

Even Lloyd George, whose reign as Prime Minister went back to the end of the first World War, came into his field of British devotion. He "wrote his speeches, memorized them and delivered them in the high Welsh manner, a faculty to which I have never been able to aspire."

Often compared with Churchill—Harold Wilson was the last person who placed him in the Churchillian mould—no other individual, not even Churchill himself, has received so many marks of distinction, such honours, and perhaps such blessing and praise from England. In Britain he was above criticism and his failures were either unknown or ignored.

Menzies technically has more honours than Churchill. He was for instance a Burgess and Guild Brother of Edinburgh, a liveryman of the Worshipful Company of Goldsmiths, president of the

Lords Taverners, a life member of the East Molesey Cricket Club, a Doctor of Law at Leeds, Birmingham, Oxford, and Cambridge, a Freeman of the cities of Swansea and Oxford.

When London granted him the honour of Freeman he drove in State in an open carriage from the Guildhall to Temple Bar.

Despite Menzies' previous protestations about decorations ("better to be plain Mr Menzies"), he did not hesitate when they were offered to him; although, when offered the Most Ancient and Most Noble Order of the Thistle, he was privately staggered by the idea and did ask for time to think about it. He told at least one member of his family he did not want a knighthood.

Perhaps Menzies was worried about the reaction of his country-men, but he needn't have been because it was well received. When sounded out on whether he would accept the Order, Menzies was aboard the Royal yacht *Britannia* during the Queen's Australian tour in 1963. The Queen's secretary, Michael Adeane, made the suggestion to him.

After a discussion in which Menzies was taken completely by surprise he asked, "If the Queen is going to bestow the Order, where is it?"

"Oh," replied Adeane, "it's in my cabin under the bed."

The Order, of Scottish origin, is second only to the highest honour of chivalry, the Order of the Garter, and is the highest British Order of knighthood to which an Australian has been admitted. It is limited to sixteen persons, excluding members of the Royal family. The award, a personal gift of the Queen, was not based on Ministerial advice but was bestowed in recognition of his services to the Queen and to Australia.

Historians believe the Order of the Thistle was founded in the eighth century, making it the oldest order of chivalry in Britain and probably the world. The Order of the Garter was created in 1348 and the Order of the Bath, the next to be founded, was in 1399.

King James II revived the Order in 1687, but it fell into abey-ance soon afterwards until Queen Anne resuscitated it in 1703.

If Menzies was tentative over accepting the Thistle award he had no such qualms about his installation as Lord Warden and Admiral of the Cinque Ports and Constable of Dover Castle. He saw it as an honour to Australia that for the first time in the 900-year history of the post Britain should go outside her own country to appoint an Australian to assume symbolic responsibility of what, since recorded time, has been the gateway to Britain and her window on the narrow seas.

In the pomp and pageantry that only the English can carry off and wearing a uniform reminiscent of Gilbert & Sullivan complete with cocked hat and epaulettes, Sir Robert, in July, 1966, joined such figures as William Pitt the Younger, the Duke of Wellington, and Sir Winston Churchill in pledging himself to defend Dover and all ports and towns within the jurisdiction of the Lord Warden of the Cinque Ports.

Sir Winston loved dressing up and the Cinque Ports uniform was his favourite. But not so Sir Robert: the irony of his installation was that he hates to dress up in anything even resembling a uniform. And although he looked a truly splendid figure, someone did say he reminded them of the Duke of Plaza-Toro.

The cutaway coat, heavy with epaulettes dripping with gold, and slung about with the green sash of his Thistle knighthood, failed, you might say, to flatter Menzies' silhouette. His chins tended to bulge above the high choking collar and seeming not quite sure what to do with his hands at the installation ceremony, he hooked his thumbs in a most unmartial way into the gold belt that rested on the approach contours of his figure. Sir Robert appeared to relax only when he could remove the slightly absurd cocked hat.

Everywhere at the Grand Court of Shepway (which turned out to be a stifling marquee in the grounds of Dover College with Menzies sitting high on a red plush throne) , was the paraphernalia of authority and tradition—swords, top hats, ermine, and maces. The Queen's patent, read to the Grand Court, gave Sir Robert "all and all manner of wrecks of the seas, jetson, flotsam, and lagan goods whatsoever which at any time or times shall be cast away, wrecked or lost, or which shall be taken up, gotten or recovered by the said Sir Robert Gordon Menzies."

Even wearing his operatic uniform and preceded by an attendant bearing the two-foot silver oar which signifies his admiralty, Menzies is unlikely to try anything of the kind, but if he chose to exercise his legal right he could no doubt lay claim to stranded whales, porpoises, and sturgeon.

Once the Lord Wardenship would have involved Sir Robert in raising ships for the realm's defence but now he merely has ceremonial duties to protect "the franchises, liberties, customs, and usages" of the confederation's seven ports. Sir Robert has the right to live in Walmer Castle, Henry VIII's old fort.

On his installation Sir Robert took delivery of an astonishing array of instant history. Walmer Castle is one of Britain's great ancient fortresses and Dover fairly drips with history. The great central keep of the castle has housed kings and held prisoners of the French wars.

From the castle's rampart above the white cliffs, Sir Robert can command the narrow seas that once served as a defensive moat of the realm, and the coast that earned the name of Hellfire Corner in Hitler's war. The church of Saint-Mary-in-the-Castle where the wardenship was hallowed is believed to date from the reign of King Canute. A lighthouse built by the Romans adjoins it, as does a well King Harold had dug.

Thousands turned out to hear Sir Robert announce his pleasure in assuming the ancient office, his flag was broken from the castle keep and with all the attendant ceremony of the slow-sounding nineteen-gun salute, it was about the nearest thing Australia will ever have to its own coronation.

While the new Prime Minister Harold Holt was going all the way with L.B.J., this Queen's man with his British bootheels went completely over at Dover.

It could have been a Covent Garden costume drama but the English intended the Lord Wardenship of Sir Robert Menzies as a compliment to Australia.

Menzies was delighted, as part of the colourful ceremony of honouring the new Lord Warden, to be enrolled as a member of the Hastings Winkle Club, although most Australians regarded it somewhat whimsically. Installed as a Freeman of Hastings as the town celebrated the 900th anniversary of the Battle of Hastings, Sir Robert was presented with the Winkle Club's badge, a solid gold winkle shell.

He must produce his winkle whenever challenged by another member, or pay a sixpenny fine to charity. After becoming a member Sir Robert had to winkle up by holding his gold winkle shell aloft and shouting, "Winkles up."

Not only the English heaped honours upon him. The Americans, too, were keen to show their admiration. In 1963 he became the first foreigner to deliver the Jefferson Oration at Monticello, in Virginia, the home of the famous American president. His speech then was regarded as one of the most important he had made for years.

Towards the end of 1966 Menzies became Scholar in Residence at the University of Virginia in Charlottesville, enjoying his temporary home among the magnolias and colonial-style homes on the century-old campus. He gave a series of lectures on Australian constitutional law, talked at other universities, and proved himself a lively mind to the students.

226

21

The one thing Menzies wanted more than anything else was the acclaim of his own people. And yet, he never quite had the recognition among Australians that he would have liked. To almost half the Australian population he was not so much a great Australian as perhaps the "greatest Englishman Australia had ever produced."

For those reasons Menzies' resignation on 20 January 1966, came as something of a surprise. At seventy-one he was still enjoying reasonably good health, and was so much in control that he could have stayed in office more or less indefinitely.

Menzies had been Prime Minister for a total of more than eighteen years, sixteen of them unbroken, and for far longer than any previous Prime Minister (on 30 November 1954, he had beaten the previous record of W. M. Hughes by being Prime Minister for seven years and 106 days).

Menzies' own explanation for his retirement from Parliament was, "I am tired; my pace has slowed down." And indeed the man's remarkable energy and iron constitution were beginning to wane ever so slightly; he even committed the—for him—incredible lapse of nodding off to sleep in the House on one occasion, and some of his speeches were lacking their old sparkle.

Privately Menzies told his intimates he wanted to write. "All I want is three years of sanity and health to do some writing, the one thing I've always wanted to do," he said. The grave illness at the time of his close colleague, Sir Shane Paltridge, the Defence Minister, from the beginnings of cancer, was a deep shock to him (Menzies' own brother had died of cancer).

Increased involvement in Vietnam with the possibility of conscription was in the air, as were increased problems of national growth and development, but whatever the variegated reasons which shaped his decision the old campaigner who had successfully sniffed every political breeze in the previous sixteen years, decided it was time to go.

For those who may doubt that Menzies did not like to exercise power, he held on to power to the last minute. His resignation was speculated on in the Press but he himself gave no official hint. At what his colleagues thought would be his last Cabinet meeting, he gave no indication he was to step down but remained The Boss in the normal way until five minutes before Cabinet rose.

By then Harold Holt, who was expected to succeed him, had his head slumped almost on his chest in despair, and W. J. (Billy) McMahon, the likely Deputy Leader, was also looking very glum indeed. Just before Cabinet rose the Prime Minister said to them, "Well, gentlemen, this is the last time I shall be with you . . ." and he ended his long rule with a few simple sentences.

Tributes poured in. President Johnson said he had been trusted by four American Presidents; Harold Wilson described him as a great world figure symbolic of all that was best in the Commonwealth concept, and the *Washington Post* called Menzies "probably the most completely successful public man of his time."

The Times thought he had given Australia's younger generation wealth and a sense of a new Australian frontier.

Menzies' supremacy on the Australian political front was so great that he was impregnable; so much so that some of his colleagues, frustrated by his political stature, looked around for peaceful and practical ways of encouraging his retirement.

A trust was later formed which bought a stately two-storeyed house in Haverbrack Avenue, Malvern (Melbourne), as a permanent home for Sir Robert and Dame Pattie during their lifetime.

The trust, established by anonymous "friends and admirers," was in the name of Dame Pattie "to recognize her services to Australia," but it is improbable that the £45,000-sterling memorial fund would have been inspired unless the intention had been to honour and reward Menzies also. The exact situation was that after his retirement, when a representative of the trust asked Menzies how the deed should be worded, he asked that it be put in Dame Pattie's name, to give her some measure of security.

A certain political colleague, who thought Menzies might be encouraged to make a favourable decision if he had a big house where he could display his various emblems and awards, implanted the idea of a house in the minds of some Melbourne admirers. An idea has to begin somewhere, and having been expressed with care behind the scenes it was readily seized upon by those who wanted to show their appreciation for Menzies' public service.

Harold Holt, the man who stood in Menzies' shadow for so long and who finally succeeded him, knew of this plan, and approved of it.

Holt, who had spent thirty years—more than half his life—in Parliament, had long been a loyal and patient supporter, even though towards the end he was occasionally despondent at the realization that he was an Anthony Eden figure.

A man without a complex, affable and friendly to all, Holt was to die tragically when on 17 December 1967, he went for a swim at Cheviot Beach, not far from his beach home at Portsea, 59 miles from Melbourne.

People in many parts of the world have wondered how such a tragedy could occur, how a Prime Minister could go about so casually and without a security guard to protect him twenty-four hours of the day. Australia is probably the last country in the world where a head of State can relax as Harold Holt did just prior to his death.

Holt always loved surfing and skindiving and on this Sunday morning he gathered up a few friends to go for a swim.

Holt was tired, he had had an exhaustive Cabinet session less than forty-eight hours previously, and he thought a dip would do him good.

Any surfer who takes on the big seas will often admit that on the occasions when he has nearly drowned he has underestimated the strength of the surf, diving in without taking a careful enough look.

Perhaps Harold Holt was a little indiscreet on this occasion, for the tide was at its peak with waves estimated between ten and fifteen feet high, and pieces of wood floated about.

But he chose a flat surface without rocks to dive into in his usual style, and appeared to eyewitnesses to be swimming strongly enough.

The Prime Minister, the man Menzies had nurtured, kept swimming out and finally disappeared.

The most likely explanation is that Holt was caught in a rip and, as is the custom, swum out with it to get clear. Swimmers usually then move to the right or left in order to swim back to the beach, or hold up their arms to signal they are in trouble.

Harold Holt apparently did not raise his arm and kept in the same line. It is possible he underestimated the speed of the rip, thought he could swim back through it, but tired in doing so, and drowned.

The memory of the man who moved Australia nearer to the United States ("all the way with LBJ") and South-East Asia, was commemorated at a church service in Melbourne later attended by President Johnson, Prince Charles, Mr Harold Wilson, and many Asian leaders.

Menzies probably could have had greater acclaim from Australians if he had stayed a little longer, but perhaps he realized it was too late in the day for him to change any further. His status did rise noticeably in the last three or four years, not so much because he had changed, although he did mellow a little, but largely because of television's intimate method of communication.

Viewers saw him as though he were speaking to only one person and far from being the sarcastic and too-clever snob that many supposed, he came across as a perfectly reasonable and sincere human being.

But the 50 per cent or so of Australians who never did vote for Menzies could hardly be blamed for not believing he was an intense Australian. He was, after all, the man who wanted to call Australia's new decimal currency notes "royals," and although in nothing did he ape the English he was obsessed with Britain, Royalty, knights, and ladies of the past.

Never had so many Australian service chiefs, public servants, ambassadors, and so on been knighted as in the Menzies' era. It had the effect of firmly implanting the British flag wherever Australian appointments to overseas posts occurred.

He objected to anything designed to make the commemoration of Australia Day an Australia-wide achievement. He would never give himself to Australian Commonwealth participation to celebrate the day on which Captain Arthur Phillip landed in Sydney Cove (26 January 1788), to unfurl the British flag and found the Australian nation. Sir Robert was reluctant to collaborate in the day—organizers could not get Commonwealth departments to promote Australia Day.

The only possible explanation is that he regarded Australia Day as being something derogatory to his sense of the Empire or the British Commonwealth.

Menzies had a very good grounding in English literature—his

favourite poet was Wordsworth—but he never showed a lively sympathy for the Australian writer. Australian writing wasn't mature, it did not have the requisite dignity. In fact, it had big blucher boots on.

His taste in literature was extremely old fashioned. He endorsed the banning of *Ulysses* by Customs Minister, Eric Harrison, and also the banning of *Lolita*.

If Menzies was not abreast of literary developments, music too, in later years, was pretty much of a closed book, although he was fond of a good tune. When he and Dame Pattie moved out of The Lodge they left behind a radiogram which wasn't working. When repaired it was found the radiogram would play only 78 r.p.m. records, which have been unobtainable since they were replaced by the long-playing type in the early 'fifties, seeming to indicate that during Menzies' long incumbency at The Lodge he played few records.

His small-town beginning clung to him in a curious way, not of course in his demeanour, but sometimes in his approach to a big subject, such as literature. Sir Robert considered Australian verse or Australian writing to be of little importance, although he admitted its development.

He would like to have thought that Australian writing was a career in literature, which it isn't, but he showed no sympathy for its growing pains or its agony to express itself. And as Chairman of the Commonwealth Literary Fund he was a great restriction to the development of Australian writers.

He feared the biographer. Just after 1950 when Commonwealth Literary Fund chairman who made the financial grants, it was suggested to him that a series of biographies of famous Australians be written. He appeared quite frightened of the idea.

"Who's going to write this while we are still alive?" he demanded. "Who is going to do this and what sort of a botch will they make of it? No, I'm not interested in biographies at this stage."

Around this time he collaborated with a writer of his own choice ("there's only one man who can do it"), to produce a biography of himself. Funds were dispensed and Menzies himself put a great deal of effort into the project, often feeding material into a tape recorder at Parliament House in the early hours until the morning magpies heralded the approach of daylight. But, through no fault of Menzies, the work never appeared.

In some respects Menzies used the Literary Fund for political purposes. An effort was made to obtain a grant to save a Mel-

bourne leftist magazine called *Overland,* which was absolutely
Australian in its outlook, from dying. But instead, Menzies gave
a £2,000-a-year subsidy to *Quadrant,* a magazine whose contributors were largely academics and intellectuals. Later it transpired
that *Quadrant* was being nicely looked after with subsidies from
the Central Intelligence Agency—an appalling situation from an
Australian's point of view, even though it was no doubt deliberately done with the intention of giving anti-Communist intellectuals a platform from which to answer their pro-Communist
colleagues who had the advantage of Communist-financed pub-
lications abroad.

It will come as a surprise to the United States, Australia, and
to most of Britain, that Menzies was not at first in favour of the
ANZUS Pact, the Treaty which binds together militarily America,
Australia, and New Zealand in the face of aggression.

In fact, if Menzies' advice and wishes on the subject had been
followed in the early stages there would probably not be any
ANZUS Treaty today.

The pact has become widely regarded as the greatest achievement in Australia's foreign relations since the end of the second
World War.

And Menzies in his valedictory, his final Press conference in
Canberra, declared: "I think that our relations with the United
States have improved enormously. If I was asked which was the
best single step that has been taken in the time of my Government, I think I would say the ANZUS Treaty. The treaty has made
the United States not perhaps technically, but in substance, our
ally. . . ."

The real background is that Sir Robert didn't want the pact
when it was introduced because Britain didn't want it. He never
really believed in the Pacific pact. His idea was for Britain and
the United States to range over vast areas in defence.

Although the idea of a Pacific pact was not new, the idea and
policy to carry it through was that of Sir Percy Spender, the
Minister for External Affairs. Sir Percy when he started out on the
road in 1950, with the suggestion that he would support a Pacific
pact, said officially he hoped the Commonwealth would form the
nucleus, but stressed that the United States must be a founding
member.

He knew Nehru would have nothing to do with it, neither

would the Pakistanis who had enough troubles of their own, nor Ceylon. The British in particular were non-responsive.

Sir Percy went to the United States and discussed the pact publicly in generalities, saying he would welcome any States who wanted to join. But he was really feeling his way and had in mind only a three-State agreement between Australia, the United States, and New Zealand. To have said otherwise would have invited criticism which could have destroyed the atmosphere for success-fully establishing the pact.

The Minister put the proposition to President Truman that Australia had been called upon in two world wars and in Korea and had faced up to her responsibilities. He pointed out that Australia could not understand why a policy should be made by NATO, in which Australia had no say whatever, and which meant that she could be involved in another world war without having the slightest say.

Truman thought there was something in a mutual defence pact for the Pacific area, and spoke with respect for Australia and Australians and of their bravery and contribution in time of war.

In private conversation in Australia Menzies poured cold water on the idea. He referred to it as resting on a chimera, as being based on an unstable foundation. He thought Spender would fail.

The British were saying you could not have a white man's pact. What should be aimed at, they said, was a pact involving all members of the Commonwealth, a multi-racial Commonwealth affair.

That was the objection they raised, but almost certainly the explanation for their opposition was that they did not like Australia negotiating with a foreign power. It was the first treaty ever negotiated by a member of the Commonwealth with a foreign power, therefore it marked a historic point of departure in the relations of Australia and other countries outside the Commonwealth.

They also believed that if Australia entered the pact it could limit Australia's capacity to send troops to Europe and the Middle East as in the past—probably one of the strongest British objections.

That difficulty was overcome by a clause in the treaty saying Australia should not be called upon to send her troops outside the Pacific theatre if her own security were not firm.

Although a British Commissioner in Australia was very annoyed that he was not invited to the actual Treaty negotiations as an observer, the British, through Sir Esler Dening who came to

Australia to represent his Government, were kept fully informed of negotiations throughout.

Menzies went overseas at the end of 1950 on one of his numerous visits to the United States. He sent a message back for Pency Spender that there was no real need for a Pacific pact, that he felt America understood the situation and would come to Australia's aid if ever she were threatened.

Spender, however, after discussions with Foster Dulles who came to Australia about the same time as Menzies returned, went ahead and negotiated the Treaty, dictating the details of his own accord without referring them to Canberra.

That is the truth of the ANZUS Treaty. But Menzies, although he did not go along with it entirely at the time, was the superb political practitioner in that he was quick to counter criticism by Dr Evatt, then the Opposition Leader, in order to present a united front. And as Prime Minister he had to take final responsibility for the Treaty; it is a classic case of how Menzies, although not in full accord himself, did not prevent change by an overt action on his own part.

As a sop to the British, Australia and New Zealand joined Britain in ANZAM for the protection of Malaya.

One can only speculate, of course, but ANZUS may well have been the main reason—or one of them—why the United States has shown interest in South East Asia in such force. Without it, and with Britain scheduled to pull out of the area, where would Australia's defensive strength be today?

What Australians generally do not realize is that Menzies would rather have absorbed criticism himself, and put up with it, than have his country embarrassed. In this sense, he was an enthusiastic Australian; something which is not generally appreciated.

One example of this was in 1961 when Britain, without the slightest warning or discussion with Australia, changed its vote in the United Nations on South Africa, from *for* to *against*, leaving Australia almost out on a limb.

Fortunately, in the previous year, Garfield Barwick when Acting External Affairs Minister had changed Australia's vote from *for* to one of *abstention*. Menzies complained to Macmillan, but without success.

The Prime Minister heard of Britain's switch only at the last minute and although it was personally embarrassing to him he changed Australia's vote so she was not at variance with Britain.

"It's pretty rough on me," Menzies told some of his colleagues, "but I won't have Australia isolated."

22

Sir Robert Menzies was a man of principle but he subscribed to the Emerson theory that consistency is the hobgoblin of little minds. He certainly did not make consistency his god—he was as flexible as any successful politician must be, but not to the extent that he would compromise to any great degree.

One glaring example of inconsistency concerned the appointment in 1947 as Governor-General of Mr. W. J. McKell, the Labor Premier of New South Wales and a one-time boilermaker. "Shocking and humiliating," was the comment of Mr. Menzies, the then Federal Opposition Leader.

"The appointment constitutes," he said, "the most deplorable incident in the Government's growing record of political jobbery. One is forced to the conclusion that it is expressly designed to lower the Governor-Generalship in significance and esteem, and so weaken our vital connection with Great Britain and with the British Crown.

"The appointment exhibits a complete contempt for all Australians who call themselves British, who value the British connection and who really appreciate the great truth that it is the loyalty to a common Crown which marks out the relation between the British Dominions as being different from any other association now to be found in the world."

Australians generally were not convinced that Sir Robert's attitude was based only on a belief that the appointment should be free from any local political bias—many felt he was being anti-Australian.

However, eighteen years later, although admittedly the circumstances were different, he was personally responsible for the appointment as Governor-General of fellow-Australian Lord Casey to probably end for all time a British tradition.

In 1946 and at other times Menzies declared that Australia must be extremely reluctant to put down the Communist Party. The proper way to deal with the Communist Party was to bring it into the open and expose its false arguments. "We must not let it be thought that they are such a force in political philosophy that we cannot meet them," he said.

Yet in 1951 he tried to introduce a Bill to ban the Communist Party, and when this was ruled by the High Court as being beyond Commonwealth powers, he held a referendum to alter the Constitution and give Parliament power to control Communists and Communism.

It proposed to place the onus of proof on the individual that he was not a Communist or connected with Communism. Even Liberal Party supporters disliked the coercive nature of the powers sought and the measure was thrown out.

The Liberal Party's W. C. Wentworth, who is so vehemently anti-Communist that it is sometimes said he sees a Red in every bush, opposed the Bill. He mostly defended it publicly but clashed with Menzies on the issue in the Party room, and tried to have it amended.

He believed it was an ineffectual Bill giving too much power to the bureaucracy and was drafted, in his opinion, not honestly to deal with the Communists but to increase the prestige of the bureaucracy trying to get rid of them. He believed it had technically undesirable features, and was in some cases open to abuse.

Wentworth has always advocated that Communists should be dealt with openly. But this has not been the case in Australia and an aura of authority and mystery has grown up around the security police, possibly because the public believes very largely there is something nefarious about their activities. This atmosphere has served to increase the mystery around those controlling the security police.

Sir Robert was ruthless in his skilful playing of politics. Although his Government failed to outlaw the Communists, by means of a referendum which they had hoped would do so, he was able to play up the Communist infiltration of the Labor Party and exploit it to the full to help him win elections.

The Petrov Affair must now be accepted as being partly a stunt to help the Menzies Government win the 1954 election. The situation certainly existed, but it was "pulled" in Parliament twelve days before the election by Menzies with a dramatic announcement of a spy ring gravely endangering Australia's internal security.

Menzies and his followers hoped it would die but it became sensational, resulting in a Royal Commission on espionage which cost taxpayers £140,000 plus heavy security service expenses and the breaking of diplomatic relations with Russia. But it did not unearth one real spy except Vladimir Petrov and his wife, who defected from the Soviet Embassy in Canberra after being aided by the Australian Security Service and paid £5,000.

The drama of the Petrov Affair was that Dr Evatt knew nothing of the impending announcement and was not in Parliament. It was in April, one of those extraordinary days when Canberra is warm and crystalline clear at that time of year, and Evatt went to the airport to return to Sydney. He walked up and down the tarmac apron in the sunshine with colleague Les Haylen, talking about Australian books and poetry.

"I'm going to the old school (Fort Street) tonight," said Evatt, "to make a speech and I'll be back tomorrow." He was most relaxed.

That night Sir Robert made his announcement. It would be no exaggeration to describe it as a dereliction on Menzies' part not to have told Evatt that he should be sure of attending the House that night as something important could be coming up. As sheer political strategy, it was taking a particularly hard line. He did tell the Deputy Leader of the Opposition, Arthur Calwell, but not until after the tea adjournment and just before the House sat, thus giving him little time.

Menzies capitalized on the split in the Labor Party caused by fanatical anti-Communist members of the Party who wanted to give anti-Communism a higher priority. The split came in 1954 and Dr Evatt, refusing to bow to the Catholic Action groupers in his own Party and realizing he could not keep them away from Menzies and the Liberal Party, denounced them publicly. It led to the formation of the Democratic Labor Party in 1955.

The Movement began among the priests of the Roman Catholic Church in Melbourne. Archbishop Mannix and Mr B. A. Santamaria, Melbourne solicitor and Catholic layman, were the arch planners of it. The movement was so clever, exclusive, and subtle that good Catholics going to church every Sunday would shout with laughter if you warned them there was a political group operating.

The planners, realizing Catholics could not win the race or get as far as they wanted with academic power, decided it could be attained on the level of the bureaucracy. The plan was to capture the Labor Party; to get into the unions, journalism, and the Public Service. And Catholics have been very loyal.

Menzies flogged the Red bogey for years until finally that tiger was so threadbare that its ribs were protruding. He then had the brilliant conception of State aid as an election winner.

Financial aid from the States to church and private schools, although it had always been in the realm of politics, had not been introduced because, as a political issue, it was explosive. Sir Robert pioneered State aid for denominational schools after an almost identical scheme had been rejected by the Federal Labor Party following its endorsement by New South Wales Labor authorities.

Menzies shocked just about everybody by slipping away from being a simple Presbyterian—he reiterated in the House over the years, *ad nauseam,* "I am just a simple Presbyterian"—to give Catholics almost everything they asked for.

Here was not a great man in the sense that he spared a thought for the other fellow's point of view, but a politician determined to press an advantage, to psychologically assess the weakness of Catholics wanting to advance themselves, and then take them away from their traditional allegiance. Instead of State aid coming from their old Labor mates, it was to come from the Protestants, and initially from the dour Protestant leader himself. Petrov and State aid were sharply defined political issues, with a merciless connotation.

Menzies could have had more acceptance from Australians if he had let himself go more often and shown his true self. Churchill, for instance, never hesitated to drop a tear if he felt the need was right, but Menzies maintained a calm front publicly and held his emotions back.

Privately he was a warm and friendly man, even a humble man. But the side he chose to show the world tended to irritate more often than not. That is not to say he was not a completely genuine personality.

He was an actor but not an exhibitionist—former Prime Minister Alfred Deakin once returned from an overseas tour and made a point of declaring that he had not spent all the money allocated to him: Menzies would have hated that, as he would any sign of outward-giving or exhibitionism.

There was not what has been described as "pornography of power" about Menzies that surrounded, say, the late President

Kennedy. To quote Malcolm Muggeridge, Kennedy was so much a product of his public relations team, so synthetically constructed a national hero, that it is difficult to feel about his assassination as one does about Lincoln's even across a century.

"The rugged lineaments of Lincoln," says Muggeridge, "his harsh eloquence, the tremendous sense of a living presence that he still conveys, contrasts with the other's television makeup, speech-writers' felicities, and the impression he always made of belonging to a strip cartoon; thinking in bubbles, speaking in exclamations, and his face set in a thick smile.

"No doubt these characteristics are inseparable from leadership in an age of mass communication media, which impose their own exigencies on whoever makes use of them; requiring, as they do, gags rather than thought, smiles rather than perceptiveness, grease-paint glamour, and auto-cue oratory.

"Someone like Kennedy is so skilfully projected that the man behind the projection is lost to view. No one can say with certainty that any sentence he spoke or joke he made was indubitably his own; his very gestures and mannerisms belong to the screen rather than to life. Packaged, promoted, offered to the multitudes like a detergent. . . ."

In that sense Menzies was a genuine personality. He wrote his own speeches and put across his own philosophies in his own style. And towards the end, with the aid of television, Australians were more inclined to like him. By then he had overcome most of his nervousness and no longer consciously set out to ridicule others.

But the ribbon complex remained with him. All his life he was nervous in the presence of decorated soldiers. When the Governor-General visited Parliament House, for instance, the instruction would come from the Prime Minister's Department, "No decorations."

The advice was the same at the funeral in Canberra of the Governor-General Lord Dunrossil and only four politicians went to the funeral properly dressed by wearing their decorations.

This complex of Menzies was so well known among colleagues that one of the first things the new Prime Minister Harold Holt did was to make an inspection tour of Australian troops in Vietnam. And he made sure he was there on Anzac Day, the day on which Australia honours its war dead.

Whenever Sir Robert did let his guard down and took his colleagues and others into his confidence he created an entirely different impression. A classic and unknown example of that concerns Doctor J. F. Cairns, the radical Victorian left-wing Labor member of Federal Parliament.

A fortnight before he resigned Menzies sought out Dr Cairns who had sharply criticized him for almost ten years and for about an hour chatted in a friendly way, changing many of Dr Cairns' previously held views on him.

Because Dr Cairns saw two sides of Menzies and, as a man who honestly speaks his mind, he was asked to give his considered opinion of Menzies for these pages.

"Sir Robert Menzies," said Dr Cairns, "was one of the most effective politicians in Australia's history. He had a way of identifying the attitudes of the average Australian and appealing very vividly, clearly, and incisively to those attitudes, showing a skill and understanding that I didn't suspect he had.

"He didn't *appear* to have the common touch. I thought he was consciously or naturally aristocratic and it surprised me to find out he had an ability to know what the average man felt. I don't know how he did this, but I would say he had a good deal of natural flair for it.

"The second thing that surprised me is that I thought he liked to exercise power but I am now pretty sure that he did not, that he tried to avoid it and put things off. The two things I have mentioned—his ability to sense the average man and his attitude towards power—I believe were quite different from earlier years. I think his attitude in earlier years explains his failure then, and the changes went a long way towards his success in later years.

"He was, I feel, exercising the role of an actor. I think Menzies was a man who liked the spotlight, who appreciated an audience. I would think that being a thespian in many ways gave him much of his satisfaction.

"I think he would have liked to have been a scholar, to make an impression in the field of learning, but could not because of his involvement in politics. It's my impression from things he has said, that he would like now to have enough time to write something that would be impressive.

"In many ways he has never written or said anything that has really been impressive because he's been talking to the average man in clichés, and has done it very effectively.

"I hardly saw Menzies except at a distance, until the last couple of weeks before his retirement. And I got much closer to him in those last two weeks than in the previous ten years.

"What came out of a discussion I had with him then was that

he cared very much what history was going to say about him, and that he was a bit worried about it.

"It came as a result of a speech I made about Rhodesia in which I criticized him for not having taken a more critical position sooner regarding the Rhodesian Government. The following morning he came around to the Party room looking for me and I wasn't there.

"I returned soon afterwards and went to his office and immediately he invited me in and I sat down and we talked for close to an hour. And he was very concerned to correct my impression that he was a supporter of what Ian Smith was going to do in Rhodesia and he was a bit sore at me for criticizing him. I pointed out he had never said anything in public to prove otherwise, so how could I know?

"Then he went on to talk about his own position, about his impending retirement, as though he had not decided. I thought he had identified me as one of his antagonists, that some of my antagonism was wrongly placed and he wanted to correct it. And he wanted to have my approval.

"He told me about his situation over the first World War, about his experiences in the second, and of his worry over Vietnam. And of the breakup of the Empire and the Commonwealth, and that Vietnam and the Commonwealth were things he would like to stay in politics for in order to do something about.

"He told me he was very worried about what had happened to Winston by staying in politics too long. He thought it was sad to see Winston decline before the public eye. And obviously he didn't want to decline like that, and wanted to go out as an impressive figure, which undoubtedly he was.

"He told me he was anxious that I should have access to the same facts as himself, that if there was any official information I required I could have whatever I wanted. This came as a surprise because it conflicted with his previous attitude.

"The interview changed my mind about him considerably, in the ways I have already indicated. I think he put off decisions, that he allowed things to be delayed too long. I believe he *was* a man of principle, that he valued liberty under the law, the kind of liberty the law has established, but it is a regulated kind of liberty. I think he valued this very highly and was a man of principle in respect of this.

"I think he had some lack of sympathy for colour, the coloured people. I think there was also a lack of sympathy for radicals whose position made them a bit unruly. He wanted his freedom expressed in regulated channels. I am sure he had a lack of respect for those whose positions made them a bit unwashed.

"I think he was a liberal in his own time, but he was a little bit slow to keep up, to bring about the necessary changes, that being a liberal required.

"I think he used a liberal muse for political reasons and I don't think there was any need for the intensity of his anti-Communist campaign. You have to look to England for people whose philosophies were similar and where Communism was as much a threat as in Australia, but they did not misuse anti-Communism for political purposes as he did. His main purpose in playing up anti-Communism was to win.

"I think he wanted, not so much power, but office and everything that went with it—the spotlight, the centre of the stage, and I feel he was prepared to overdo his illiberal campaign in order to get it.

"This affects his standing in my eyes as a great liberal leader.

"One of his greatest examples of political engineering was in 1945 when he called his party the Liberal Party: it really was the conservative party of Australian politics and here we had a man who had a lot of liberalism about him posing as a Liberal in a conservative party.

"Therefore, he was bound to overdo the repressive side of things, allowing the security service to grow too much and helping to create a considerable atmosphere of McCarthyism in Australia.

"This would not have gone nearly so far if the Prime Minister had not given his imprimatur to it and my view is that he was far more autocratic than was necessary for him to rule.

"I think this had a very bad effect on Australia. It made debate on foreign policy very difficult. I don't think in any other country has dissent on foreign policy been so much identified with enemies of the country, and Menzies has to accept some considerable responsibility for this.

"One would expect of a liberal with a university background that he would have been a little more sympathetic to dissenters, particularly educated dissenters.

"For some considerable time there has been a lot of pressure against university students and others from carrying on dissenting activities. It has nothing to do with the rule of law, it is an atmosphere, and in my view it was unnecessary repression. This applies not only to Menzies but to all the other so-called liberals in Australia's intellectual firmament.

"I think that in his forays into international affairs he did something that suited his power relations with Britain and the United States and what he lost with the New World in its various forms, he probably gained with the old one. He would have no difficulty identifying himself with the Old World because that's where I think he actually belongs.

"I think that Sir Robert was British to the bootheels, that he realized it was necessary for Australia to have closer relations with the United States but he didn't want to go all the way with L.B.J., only some of the way.

"Sir Robert weakened the Labor Party by his ruthless use of opportunity and he was never slow to take over Labor's policy, but it's good politics to attack an opponent and if you're wise, use some of his material.

"He was a great builder of straw cases, a great searcher for simplification and simplifier of people's positions and of issues. This enabled the ordinary man to grasp them. For instance, in the election after Petrov, he never referred to Dr Evatt in his speeches as the Leader of the Opposition, but always the 'alternative government.'

"I frankly think Sir Robert had more ability than he demonstrated. I'd like to have seen him prepared to take a few more risks on the side of liberalism because I believe he had the ability to carry it off.

"I'd like to have seen him use more of his time to get to know something thoroughly, but I rather suspect he was a bit lazy. He could have done that and enjoyed as much success as a politician, but probably his attitude was brought about by his desire to remain in the spotlight, as he had the ability to do without very great effort."

23

It is very difficult to estimate the value of a Prime Minister so soon after his departure. Only time enables us to determine what, among all the detritus, is of lasting significance.

Menzies, of course, had his share of failures. On the domestic front he promised in 1949 to put value back in the pound, but the value gradually went lower. And his promise then to develop the empty North of Australia was so unfulfilled that in 1966 he had to make a similar promise.

Australian bankers since 1949 have been far from happy with his financial policy which poured considerably more money to the hire purchase companies than banks, a policy which enabled Australians to buy cars, refrigerators, and television sets at very high rates of interest, but not nearly as many houses as were needed.

Until the last two or three years, the policy followed by Menzies' Government was that bank lending was unduly inflationary, therefore you must restrain it. While denouncing the Socialist policy on banks by Chifley, Menzies retained some of Chifley's measures, such as the establishment of a Reserve Bank and a special deposits section to control the credit level of banks.

Internal development, including housing, was held back because free enterprise banks were restricted from making long-term lending. The Government's policy, which meant business not done by the banks was channelled into hire purchase companies at higher interest rates, resulted in an anomalous situation. At the end of the war, hire purchase companies in Australia had outstanding loans of £6,000,000, but in 1966 the outstanding finance amounted to £500,000,000. In the same period, bank loans rose by only five times as much.

The Menzies policy was a tragedy to the ordinary man in that by preventing banks from lending, you cannot stop people from borrowing, and they paid through the nose for it through hire purchase companies. The Government finally woke up to the fact that its policy had greatly narrowed its field of financial control, and it has only been in the past couple of years that an ordinary member of the Australian public has been able to walk into a bank with reasonable confidence of getting a loan.

During Menzies' long term as Prime Minister, Australians saw the consummation of foreign control of their post-war industries; motor cars, oil refining, chemicals, besides foreign control of the ranches and vast new mineral resources in tropical Australia—a trend which the present Liberal Government is trying to arrest through an Australian-based development corporation.

Admittedly Australia has had to rely heavily on overseas capital, but the extent to which Australia's mineral wealth has been sold to outside interests suggests a short-term policy by the Menzies Government, to make life easy for this generation at the expense of the next while overseas interests have drained off mineral deposits worth fantastic sums of money.

It can be said that Menzies took the view which everyone does who aligns himself with liberals—that development should be left to private enterprise, and if this won't do it, then it is not the job of public enterprise to take the initiative. And in this case, it did not matter if the only private enterprise to show any interest was foreign.

Menzies himself had second thoughts on this situation at times, and it may well prove unfortunate that he did not have an overall policy to control and co-ordinate this type of development.

When Menzies came to power a great period of capital expansion began (and inflation, too, for several years), but the prosperity that was generated was common to the entire Western world. It was a period of reconstruction and Australia shared in it. Under Menzies Australia's post-war prosperity was gradually consolidated, but he would be the first not to try to claim all the credit.

When Menzies came in there were 32,000 students at universities in Australia, the population was 7.9 million, savings bank deposits represented £97 a head, there was one car for every 12.1 persons and one telephone to every 10.7 persons. Full employment was a theoretical aim, new housing was not so much short as non-

245

existent, and about 60 per cent of Australians were either home owners or acquiring their own home.

Menzies claimed in 1963 that 76 per cent of Australians were home owners, and 39 per cent of the 3.3 million dwelling units in Australia when he went out had been built during his term of office to that stage.

When Menzies retired the national income had risen from £1,870,000,000 to £7,677,000,000 and private investment from £333,000,000 to £1,632,000,000.

Expenditure on education grew from £8,000,000 to £55,000,000 and there were more than 80,000 students at Australian universities. Savings bank deposits represented £222 a head and there was one car for every 4.1 persons. Full employment had become an accepted part of Australian life and the new Prime Minister, Mr Holt, said that any government which allowed 2.5 per cent of unemployment to develop, would be thrown out.

People in politics are not remembered for their qualities, only for what they do or prevent from being done. Lincoln freed the slaves, and Churchill rallied the British people behind him in the hours of crisis.

Sir Robert Menzies has no obvious memorial to his name.

Menzies himself likes to believe that education might be his memorial. But that is rather an odd one because for years he was an opponent of Commonwealth aid to education.

However, perhaps due to pressure from Government members, the recommendations of special committees he had working, and his own inclinations, he did in fact rescue the universities from financial ruin by taking over State responsibility for financing them, thus opening the door to greater participation in education generally. His interest in education began as a point of prestige, then became a plank in the electoral platform.

He showed little interest in education at the primary level. He pursued the old British tradition, the one under which he had emerged himself, where the child of great talent can obtain a scholarship, a patronage. There was an élitism about his approach to education, which he limited largely to universities.

Another achievement of his was the development of the national capital, Canberra, from what was little more than a country town. In this he showed personal enthusiasm and vision, and without his belief in Canberra, it would not have grown the way it has. He wanted to be known in his last few years as the man who developed Canberra.

His development of the Liberal Party from an idea that evolved elsewhere is perhaps his greatest achievement, and although that may not be remembered as such overseas, it did mean that as a leading politician he largely dictated the policies of the country, both internal and external, and so this affected Australia's relations with other countries.

Sir Robert may be remembered as a speaker, although nothing he ever said stands out as being of lasting significance, and reputations for eloquence are, in any case, usually written on water.

One thing for which Menzies may be remembered in a 100 years is seemingly unimportant at present, but in the years ahead its importance will stand out. This was his establishment of the Institute of Aboriginal Studies, which sets out to record the customs, languages, and other facets of Aboriginal life.

The Aborigines form the only pre-agricultural society left in the world that is not contaminated in its customs by contact with agricultural people around them.

Academically this is probably the most important thing happening in Australia today, one of the few things of world importance being done by Australia.

As a similar study cannot be done anywhere else in the world, all human sociology in future may be based on the methods now being employed with the Aborigines. The idea for the Institute rested with W. C. Wentworth, who gathered a mountain of support from all over Australia for his written proposal, and then slapped the weighty document on the Prime Minister's desk, giving him little chance to oppose it, even if he had wished to.

But probably the thing that will stand to Menzies' memory is the years of quite good management. It must be agreed that he had what was needed for the post-war years; a flair for good management.

And although he was not an innovator, an originator, he was flexible enough to absorb the effects of change. Many Australians still regard Menzies as a reactionary, but that is too drastic a view. Certainly he was a very cautious reformer and was very slow to make decisions. And he did not give Australians any great challenge (they have, for instance, a certain affluence, but no campaign against poverty).

But it would be true to say there were more changes in foreign policy and social reforms in Menzies' time than in any other period of government.

He was, of course, a pragmatist who dealt with the present and did not believe in looking too far into the future.

As a statesman Menzies made some resounding gaffes, as all

great men have. He would never accept the blame for his failure in 1956 when, as chairman of the London delegation, he made no progress in trying to persuade Colonel Nasser of the error of his ways in seizing the Suez Canal.

Menzies was drawn in and used by the British in this issue but he was a willing lamb. He loved to step out into the international arena and always felt disappointed that he did not receive the recognition he thought he deserved. Even Menzies' most loyal supporters today try to put his failure down to his accepting a bad brief. Menzies was in London at the time and actually in bed when he was telephoned and asked to lead the delegation.

Everybody knew that Nasser was a roaring revolutionary for his own country and was not going to let anyone from Australia or Austria or anywhere else tell him what to do. But Menzies went, and failed to conquer. However, it made no difference in Britain's eyes. He returned from Cairo as if in triumph, and the *Daily Sketch* named him "man of the year."

The Earl of Avon, the former Sir Anthony Eden, who was British Prime Minister at the time of the Suez crisis, was asked by this writer to contribute a personal assessment of Sir Robert, and he kindly did so in these terms:

"Though Robert Menzies is a few years older than I am, we are of the same generation which has lived through two world wars. I first met Menzies in 1935, when he was Attorney General and I was soon to become a young Foreign Secretary. When my disagreement with the policy of appeasement, which Mr Chamberlain's Government was then pursuing, grew to the point when I was forced to resign in the national interest, I received from Mr Menzies a message of encouragement at, what was for me, inevitably, a difficult time. This laid the foundation of our friendship.

"Eighteen months later we were at war. Bob Menzies then shared with us the dark days of decision in 1941, particularly in connection with the Greek campaign. Most critics would now agree that this campaign played its part in delaying by at least six weeks Hitler's attack upon Soviet Russia. This was decisive in that year's campaign and probably had far-reaching consequences for the outcome of the war. The consequences were not so evident at the time, but Mr Menzies' part in all these events was both courageous and far-seeing.

"In more recent years, I continued to work closely with Robert Menzies, whose leadership was always helpful whether at the Commonwealth Prime Ministers' conferences or in more direct exchanges concerning our two countries. I also enjoyed the delightful experience of being his guest in Australia when he was Leader of the Opposition and I was also out of office.

"When the Egyptian Government seized the Suez Canal in the late summer of 1956, Mr Menzies was in the United States and about to pay a visit to Japan and the Far East. Without hesitation, he cancelled his tour and came at once to join us in London and take part in our counsels. As I have written elsewhere 'we could not have had a wiser or more forthright colleague.'

"It was Mr Menzies who led the delegation appointed by the London Conference at the end of August, which was chosen to travel to Cairo to convey the proposals of that Conference to the Egyptian Government. Mr Menzies did everything in human power to bring about an agreement. Then and throughout all the later stages of the complex negotiations and final action, he showed that firm and understanding statesmanship which all who know him and many millions who do not, have come to associate with his name. For my part, my friendship with him and his delightful family will always be a happy and unclouded memory."

Menzies made a disastrous essay into the United Nations in 1960. Pandit Nehru launched a blistering attack on him, denouncing his proposals as "negative, untenable, and verging on absurdity," and as one Australian correspondent concluded, Sir Robert's reputation as a world statesman was left in tatters on the floor of the Assembly.

The diplomatic setback came when Menzies proposed a Big Four summit meeting as an amendment to a neutralist resolution by Indonesia, India, Ghana, Yugoslavia, and the United Arab Republic calling for an immediate meeting between President Eisenhower and Soviet Premier Khrushchev. Many delegates believed Sir Robert's action was a face-saving device to let President Eisenhower out of the embarrassment of a meeting with Khrushchev. In fairness, Menzies again had a bad brief and the most charitable thing that can be said is that he did it out of loyalty to President Eisenhower and Mr Macmillan.

The Prime Minister was furious at the result, and came out of the Chamber telling correspondents: "I can't take this."

Menzies was deeply upset that newspapers in Australia were criticizing him while the rest of the Press in the Western world was acclaiming him. New York newspapers, for instance, gave prominence to his blunt attack on Communism in the same speech.

The *Journal American* in an editorial called his speech "the most powerful counter-attack so far against the Communist propaganda offensive led by Nikita Khrushchev this season." The newspaper added: "Mr Menzies' speech was a beautifully delivered gem in content, manner, firmness, and all the straightforward characteristics we've heard about the good citizens of Down Under."

The Nehru-Menzies clash seemed a petty squabble compared to the main issue of preserving international peace, and almost certainly personal background was involved in it. Nehru apparently waited to get Menzies in his sights.

The dispute had its roots in Menzies' intervention in the Kashmir problem at the request of Churchill. He had negotiated about ten years previously on statements between Nehru and Ali Khan, and before leaving Australia to do this he told colleagues how he intended to drive Mr Nehru into a cul-de-sac from which he would not be able to escape.

He was warned that Mr Nehru was one of the world's most elusive men and told: "If you succeed, you will be the man of the age." But he did not think he could fail. The negotiations lapsed at the time because Nehru said he could not make any decision without referring it to his Cabinet.

Perhaps Menzies did not approach the subject with an entirely open mind, having been influenced by the unfavourable reactions to Nehru by his close friend Sir Owen Dixon, who had served as United Nations mediator in the Kashmir dispute between India and Pakistan in 1950, and for whom Menzies had an astonishing affection.

Personal feelings no doubt also played their part. In 1956, while Menzies and his Party were on their way to London for a Prime Ministers' conference, they called in at Bombay and a dinner was given on board the liner *Arcadia* in their honour. Mr Nehru was one of the hosts.

At one stage, with distinguished guests seated all round, Sir Robert leaned across to Mr Nehru and said, "I am very disappointed, Mr Prime Minister, to learn that you will not be accompanying us to London. Does this mean that that dreadful man . . . " (gesturing with an airy wave of the hand and pausing as though he could not remember the name) "Menon is going to be there?"

"Yes," replied Nehru, flatly and without humour. The impression of at least one important guest at that dinner was that the Indian Prime Minister did not appreciate the remark, that the Australian Prime Minister miscalculated the feelings of his host.

The State papers of Mr Nehru have not yet been made available to authors, scholars, and historians but when they are sorted and transferred to the Indian National Archives and the National Museum to which they have been bequeathed, they are likely to throw light on why Mr Nehru tore strips off Sir Robert Menzies in the United Nations. Menzies enjoyed far better relations with another Asian leader, Ayub Khan, with whom he was extremely friendly.

Perhaps Sir Robert's greatest failure as a Statesman was the opportunity he lost in integrating Australia in its region. When he became Prime Minister in 1949, President Sukarno in the same month became President of Australia's northern neighbour, Indonesia, and Mr Nehru had been Prime Minister of independent India for two years.

Throughout the 1950s Australia, Indonesia, and India—the most significant country in Asia from Australia's viewpoint—each had a dominant leader. And there was scarcely any contact between them. Sir Robert seemed to give the impression that the proper place to discuss matters with Asians was in London.

Only twice did he visit India, Pakistan, and Malaysia, the last time in 1959. He visited New Zealand once (in 1954) and Japan twice; Thailand, the Philippines, and Indonesia once—an Australian official who was present at the interview between Sir Robert and Bung Sukarno later described it as one of the most amusing occasions of his life because, he said, "here were these two men, probably two of the most conceited people in the world, meeting, each trying to gain the ascendancy and not yielding a point to the other."

By comparison he visited London at least once a year. Washington, too, was high on his priority list.

India, the most populous parliamentary democracy in the world, has in common with Australia a parliamentary and judicial system and a good and independent Public Service. Accordingly, it is logical that Australia should at least have understood her point of view or tried to see that India understood Australia's.

But instead Menzies gave the clear impression that India wasn't standing up to its moral obligations; it was neutralist, supine, and letting the side down in the Commonwealth. India's attitude remained as civil as it did towards Britain and Australia probably only because Indian parliamentarians had a great respect on a personal level for members of the British Labor Party, and had sympathy for Australian Labor parliamentarians.

An indication of Menzies' attitude towards Asia was shown in the reason he gave for Australian troops being in Malaysia at the time of Indonesian confrontation—the Australian commitment was "to come to the assistance of Great Britain in Malaysia's defence."

He did not put it on the basis that we should take an interest in a country, particularly a neighbour being attacked, but that it was to help Britain. And, of course, Australia's commitment to Vietnam was not because of an interest in Vietnam but as a kind of insurance policy with the Americans.

Sir Robert's approach to matters in Asia was essentially a reaction to events as they occurred.

For two years he sat on a proposal to build up Australia's Regular Army—the result was that when the war in Vietnam eventually reached such proportions that greater Australian commitments were required, conscription had to be introduced because the Regular Army was so depleted. Menzies, however, was able to retire just before this unpleasant electoral challenge reared its head. Had he taken the advice of his Army Minister and Military advisers two years previously, conscription would not have been necessary.

He was interested in maintaining law and order and repressing turbulence.

But clearly turbulence will be stressed in the region of South East Asia until the gross disparity between Australia and her neighbours is removed; just as disparities in opportunities and living standards have shown up within Australia. Menzies made no approach on this level—he made no approach on the basis that America and Britain and other developed countries of the northern hemisphere, with the capital and skill, should assist the vast mass of humanity living in South East Asia to get proper prices for their products, proper health standards and development to ensure a long and full life.

Until disease is conquered, and people can read and enjoy a reasonable standard of living—hopes that can only be realized in the region with the help of America above all, and other developed countries with which Australia compares herself—belated reactions in a military sense will surely be futile. "Sending in a gunboat" will not stop the spread of these ideals.

It could be said that Australia, a big country with a small population, needs all available capital and technical know-how for its own development. And Sir Robert, the gradualist, the good lawyer, was not one to stir up unnecessary trouble by getting involved with other countries, Vietnam excluded.

But if the attitude had been there at the top, Australia could have done much more to make friends in South East Asia and help the developing countries. For instance, Australia is the one European country in the region with agricultural experience in the tropics.

In Borneo and other Asian countries children suffer from scurvy while their mothers feed pawpaws to pigs, not realizing the vitamin C content of the fruit, or their value in this way. A handful of experts prepared to live in the jungle and teach the Borneans these values would do an immense service—and it would cost so little and yield so much in terms of friendship.

And largely because there has been a lack of inspiration from the top, Australian businessmen have been extremely slow-moving in South East Asia, with the result that Japan, who has no raw materials of her own and is drawing considerably on Australia, is beginning to take over South East Asia economically, while Australia still hopefully looks to Britain not to join the European Common Market.

In fairness to Menzies it should be declared that nobody in Australia knew two or three years ago that Britain was to withdraw from South East Asia—not even the Asian-conscious Sir Wilfred Kent Hughes. Menzies' view of foreign policy was based on the "great and powerful friends" framework of alliances with Britain and America. Some would argue that was a very sound policy—and it was, although history has now shown that Australia held on to Britain rather too long economically as well as militarily and in this respect Menzies retired not a minute too soon; and if his advice on ANZUS had been taken, and Sir Percy Spender had not forced the issue, where would Australia be today in defence? The prospect, pure conjecture though it is, makes Menzies' reputation as a statesman somewhat shaky.

Towards the end of his term Menzies began to realize the significance of Asia but the die was cast as far as his reputation in this region was concerned, and in Africa from Cairo to Capetown he was known as a white supremacist. He was the only Commonwealth Prime Minister in favour of South Africa being admitted afresh to the Commonwealth when it became a republic, while other Commonwealth members thought it was an excellent opportunity to get rid of her.

Some of his statements were easily twisted to show he favoured South Africa's apartheid policy, but in fact, he didn't. He showed he was learning to go along with the New World to some extent

253

by refusing to be drawn in as a mediator in negotiations between Britain and Rhodesia.

Menzies' probity, his Victorian probity (nobody saw him with his coat off) and his too-legalistic conception prevented him from making a greater impact as a world statesman. The expediency and compromises of international affairs were anathema to him.

In a discussion with a colleague about an African leader, Sir Robert could see no good whatever in the man. "Why," he declared, "the man's a murderer."

"You forget Henry Tudor," his colleague replied. "He lopped off people's heads after 600 years of Christianity. People like him are not long down from the trees."

His flaw as a statesman was not due merely to too much regard for the rule of law, for that is paramount and must be obeyed by everybody. But Sir Robert's legalisms tended to cloud his judgment. This can be explained by the theory of sovereignty in international affairs, which can be overemphasized in the modern world.

For instance, it could be said that the Dutch were sovereign in West New Guinea, that their actions in West New Guinea had international consequences, just as you might say that the South African Government is sovereign in its own country but what it does has international consequences. Menzies would say the affairs in these countries were domestic and must not be interfered with. But the temper of the world is moving away from that viewpoint and some nations are tending more to interfere.

Menzies' legalism over the West New Guinea question caused his government to stand flatfooted in support of the Dutch in the New World and, as was proved, the ambitions of the Indonesians just could not be disregarded.

Sir Robert Menzies was a sunset-of-Kipling figure in Asia. He could have been born a couple of hundred years previously and, if he had lived in England, cut an even greater swathe. He was the last of the Queen's Men, the last of the Straight Backs, the last Empire Statesman living out of his time.

He was also the last of the Elizabethans who liked to be sent to places as representing the Queen, and with his great love and respect for Royalty perhaps they did not ask enough of him as they did of the original Elizabethans.

Even eighteen months after his retirement he was still pursuing a familiar theme—recommending to the Ditchley Foundation in Britain that there be a unity of English-speaking peoples, as though the English tongue confers special political qualities on those who use it. That surely makes him the Charles de Gaulle of Australia.

But that is only part of the man. His titles may roll off the tongue like the voice of a herald crying from the 18th century, but this brilliant old charmer, for all his shiny British bootheels, led Australia squarely into the 20th century. He saw the pre-eminence of America in the Pacific and if he acted rather slowly, he did align Australia with her.

Australia's Prime Ministers have never been men of great stature, and Australia, a stable and uncomplicated country, does not stir up trouble and therefore rates little mention in the world Press.

Menzies must be seen essentially as a Commonwealth man because his power and prestige came from his being Prime Minister, and as such he rates extremely high.

But Menzies, because of the weight of his personality and conviction and his personal contact with successive British Prime Ministers and American Presidents, must rate a little higher than a good Commonwealth man.

The post-war world has not thrown up too many dominant figures—the Macmillans, the Attlees, the Eisenhowers did not reign for long, and were not men of outstanding stature. Roosevelt had a vast propaganda machine working for him and Churchill lost his appeal in peace time.

Because of the length of time he stayed in power Menzies must range up close to the political greats of his time, if not in terms of achievement, then in terms of stature.

Menzies' successor, Harold Holt, reversed the policy on Asia immediately he took office, and made quite a few changes on the domestic front—a little more say for backbenchers, for instance—but the pattern which Menzies set is still largely followed.

As an aside, the *Sydney Morning Herald* for the first time in sixteen years has given its full support to the Liberal Party and with Sir Robert gone, the *Herald* chief, Warwick Fairfax, got his knighthood.

And as for other principals in the Menzies story, Arthur Coles got his knighthood in 1960, when Artie Fadden retired.

Bill McCall did not get a knighthood, but no matter, he made his million—and he achieved the object of his desire four years ahead of schedule, in 1956, becoming the owner of more than twenty companies.

He was, in fact, "offered" a knighthood by his old friend, Acting Prime Minister Artie Fadden (while Bob Menzies was overseas, you see), but he declined with the comment, "How can you make a knight out of a bootless millionaire?"—a jovial reference to his occasional habit of walking through the exclusive Sydney suburban shopping area of Double Bay in bare feet!

Australia has been fortunate in never having had a dishonest Prime Minister and Menzies, above all, brought great probity and many austere high principles to the office.

He was not interested in money and all he got from politics was a salary which most leading businessmen would have spurned, and which could only be considered at all attractive in recent years.

Federal politics in Australia have been notably free of corruption and in Sir Robert's time not a hint of financial scandal touched any of his departments. It was probably the most honest administration system in the world, including that of Britain, and perhaps the credit for that should go to Menzies for his example and integrity.

It's a peculiar trait of human nature that most successful men will work harder for the sake of rendering useful service—or gaining recognition—than they will for money alone. Menzies could have made a fortune by staying in law but it was recognition, springing from service, that he wanted.

Menzies left one unfortunate legacy in the Australian Parliament which will take a long time to correct, if ever.

He towered to such an extent that he regarded parliament as a rubber stamp for decisions made secretly in government departments or the Cabinet room.

Apart from his power as Prime Minister, other factors have contributed—a weak and divided Opposition, the quality of members, and the demands on their time imposed by the emergence of the Welfare State—but Menzies has been the prime reason.

In the House, complete explanation was seldom given by him or his Ministers on any measure brought forward, and there was inadequate time for debate.

A Minister's esteem, among his colleagues, came to be assessed, in the magic circle of power, by his ability to hoodwink backbenchers of his Party and his skill in sidetracking Opposition members in the House. Sir Garfield Barwick was the one notable exception to that in the Menzies Ministry.

Important and controversial measures were left until the end of the sessions, then rushed through both Houses. None of the few great issues of foreign or domestic policy was explained to or debated by the House for the information of the Press and the public.

Debate, for instance, was quite inadequate for Australia as a nation to decide whether she should be involved in the war in Vietnam, or whether conscription in these circumstances was just.

Until 1950 the House of Representatives could have been described as a "deliberative assembly" and a strong government balanced by a strong popular control through a representative body was the underlying principle of the parliamentary system.

But a rigid Party system introduced by Menzies upset this balance. The initiative of the private member has gone, all important Bills now emanate from Cabinet and the time for debate is so limited that it is controlled.

This means the House has been transformed into an organ of registration of the will of Cabinet, and Party discipline is so strict that there is little likelihood of a government being defeated in the House.

Party discipline has led to Cabinet dictatorship—Australia under Menzies came to have Government by executive.

And because the Opposition will use every opportunity to discredit the Government, the duty of frank criticism from the Government Party has been abdicated because it must swallow its objection to government policy and support it. Nobody is naïve enough to suggest that the debate will not be on Party lines in the House, but there is a deeper implication—the futility of the modern Party debate in itself.

All previous Prime Ministers accepted Party decisions even when a Cabinet proposal was rejected, but Menzies often fought to have his own way.

Clearly, one of the basic functions of Parliament is the proper organization of debates to focus attention on matters of great principle. Scrappy and discursive statements are not good enough, and if it is felt that these matters can be dealt with by day-to-day administrative decisions, made in secret, then the whole fabric of a nation's national purpose may well collapse. Australia today urgently needs open debate, so that common aims can be clearly achieved through conviction in the hearts and minds of the population.

Thus did Sir Robert Menzies tower, able to exercise undiluted power, in a democracy, a great tribute in itself to his ability and personality. He was *not* a parliamentarian, in the strict sense. Part of the man's enigma and skill was that he controlled parliament while professing to be the great parliamentarian; cleverly using the techniques and trappings of Parliament.

If he were to tell a political lie it was better to do it with the Speaker wearing his wig, the uniformed usher bringing in the mace, the packed Press Gallery looking down, and with almost the perfume of incense floating around the Chamber, rather than to baldly state it in a Press conference.

Sir Robert was an accomplished smearer in a technique generally accepted as legitimate in these surroundings. Many members go too far, but Menzies would never say anything that was technically defamatory; he would go to the brink more often and more successfully than anyone else.

The Menzies' domination of Parliament was aided not only by the reluctance or inability of those around him to challenge him, but also to some extent by a permissive monopoly Press.

In addition to politicians, working Pressmen in Canberra were also frustrated by his tight control, a feeling which manifested itself on his retirement by the Press Gallery with an overwhelming majority declining to give the Prime Minister a farewell function to mark his record term.

Robert Gordon Menzies, the boy from the little Mallee town of Jeparit who dreamed of being Prime Minister, left his mark. And far from waning in public popularity towards the end of his term—a sad experience faced by most leading politicians—the longer he stayed the more he grew in stature. He need not worry that the history books won't give him due recognition. He will be remembered at least as the most effective politician in Australia's first sixty years of Federation.

In Jeparit the townspeople have erected a 60-foot-high memorial to their greatest son, surmounted by a thistle emblem. The memorial has a 6-foot-high base around it, the idea being that no one should try to climb the spire.

The climb of Robert Gordon Menzies, the man who was born in one age, lived through another, then adjusted himself to the management of a strange new world, can never be repeated.

Such a man would be too far out of his time.

Index